READY-TO-USE

HUMAN BIOLOGY & HEALTH ACTIVITIES

FOR GRADES 5-12

Mark J. Handwerker, Ph.D.

**THE CENTER FOR APPLIED
RESEARCH IN EDUCATION**

Library of Congress Cataloging-in-Publication Data

Handwerker, Mark J.
    Ready-to-use human biology & health activities for grades 5–12 / Mark J.
    Handwerker, Ph.D.
        p.   cm.—(Secondary science curriculum activities library)
        ISBN 0-87628-446-2
        1. Human biology—Study and teaching (Secondary)   2. Health—Study
    and teaching (Secondary)   I. Title.   II. Series.
    QP39.H26   1999
    612'.0071'2—dc21   99-14142
                                                            CIP

© 1999 *by* The Center for Applied Research in Education, West Nyack, NY

Printed in the United States of America

10 9 8 7 6 5 4 3 2 1

ISBN 0-87628-446-2 (spiral)   ISBN 0-13-029112-9 (lay-flat pbk)

ATTENTION: CORPORATIONS AND SCHOOLS
The Center for Applied Research in Education books are available at quantity discounts with bulk purchase for educational, business, or sales promotional use. For information, please write to: Prentice Hall Direct Special Sales, 240 Frisch Court, Paramus, NJ 07652. Please supply: title of book, ISBN number, quantity, how the book will be used, date needed.

**THE CENTER FOR APPLIED RESEARCH
IN EDUCATION**
West Nyack, NY 10994

On the World Wide Web at http://www.phdirect.com

About This Resource

Ready-to-Use Human Biology & Health Activities for Grades 5–12 is designed to help you teach basic science concepts to your students while building their appreciation and understanding of the work of generations of curious scientists. Although The Scientific Method remains the most successful strategy for acquiring and advancing the store of human knowledge, science is—for all its accomplishments—still merely a human endeavor. While the benefits of science are apparent in our everyday lives, its resulting technology could endanger the survival of the species if it is carelessly applied. It is therefore essential that our students be made aware of the nature of scientific inquiry with all its strengths and limitations.

A primary goal of science instructors should be to make their students "science literate." After completing a course of study in any one of the many scientific disciplines, students should be able to:

1. appreciate the role played by observation and experimentation in establishing scientific theories and laws,

2. understand cause-and-effect relationships,

3. base their opinions on fact and observable evidence—not superstitions or prejudice, and

4. be willing to change their opinions based on newly acquired evidence.

Scientific theories come and go as new observations are made. During the course of instruction, teachers should emphasize the "process" of science as well as the relevance of pertinent facts.

This volume of science activities was designed to accomplish all of the above, keeping in mind the everyday challenges faced by classroom instructors.

On Your Mark!

Begin by stimulating students' gray matter with basic scientific concepts through brainstorming and open discussion.

Get Set!

Kindle interest by making concepts real through demonstration and/or descriptive analogy.

Go!

Cement concepts into concrete form with exciting hands-on experience.

Each of the 15 teaching units in this volume of *Ready-to-Use Human Biology & Health Activities for Grades 5–12* contains *four* 40–50 minute lessons and follows the same instructional sequence so that your students will always know what is expected of them. Each unit comes complete with the following:

- a **Teacher's Classwork Agenda for the Week** and **Content Notes for Lecture and Discussion,**
- a student **Fact Sheet** with **Homework Directions** on the back,
- four 40–50 minute **Lesson Plans,** each followed by its own **Journal Sheet** to facilitate student notetaking, and
- an end-of-the-unit **Review Quiz.**

Each unit has been tested for success in the classroom and is ready for use with minimal preparation on your part. Simply make as many copies of the Fact Sheet with Homework Directions, Journal Sheets, and Review Quizzes as you need for your class. Also, complete answer keys for the homework assignments and unit quiz are provided at the end of the Teacher's Classwork Agenda for the Unit.

Mark J. Handwerker

ABOUT THE AUTHOR

Mark J. Handwerker (B.S., C.C.N.Y., Ph.D. in Biology, U.C.I.) has taught secondary school science for 15 years in the Los Angeles and Temecula Valley Unified School Districts. As a mentor and instructional support teacher, he has trained scores of new teachers in the "art" of teaching science. He is the author/editor of articles in a number of scientific fields and the coauthor of an earth science textbook (Harcourt Brace Jovanovich, *Earth Science*) currently in use.

Dr. Handwerker teaches his students that the best way to learn basic scientific principles is to become familiar with the men and women who first conceived them. His classroom demonstrations are modeled on those used by the most innovative scientists of the past. He believes that a familiarity with the history of science, and an understanding of the ideas and methods used by the world's most curious people, are the keys to comprehending revolutions in modern technology and human thought.

Suggestions for Using These Science Teaching Units

The following are practical suggestions for using the 15 teaching units in this resource to maximize your students' performance.

Fact Sheet

At the start of each unit, give every student a copy of the **Fact Sheet** for that unit with the **Homework Directions** printed on the back. The Fact Sheet introduces content vocabulary and concepts relevant to the unit. You can check students' homework on a daily basis or require them to manage their own "homework time" by turning in all assignments at the end of the unit. Most of the homework assignments can be completed on a single sheet of standard-sized (8½″ × 11″) looseleaf paper. Urge students to take pride in their accomplishments and do their most legible work at all times.

Journal Sheet

At the start of each lesson, give every student a copy of the appropriate **Journal Sheet** which they will use to record lecture notes, discussion highlights, and laboratory activity data. Make transparencies of Journal Sheets for use on an overhead projector. In this way, you can model neat, legible, notetaking skills.

Current Events

Since science does not take place in a vacuum (and also because it is required by most State Departments of Education), make **Current Events** a regular part of your program. Refer to the brief discussion on "Using Current Events to Integrate Science Instruction Across Content Areas" in the Appendix.

Review Quiz

Remind students to study their Fact and Journal Sheets to prepare for the end-of-the-unit **Review Quiz.** The Review Quiz is a 15-minute review and application of unit vocabulary and scientific principles.

Grading

After completing and collectively grading the end-of-the-unit Review Quiz in class, have students total their own points and give themselves a grade for that unit. For simplicity's sake, point values can be awarded as follows: a neatly completed set of Journal Sheets earns 40 points; a neatly completed Homework Assignment earns 20 points; a neatly completed Current Event earns 10 points; and, a perfect score on the Review Quiz earns 30 points. Students should record their scores and letter grades on their individual copies of the **Grade Roster** provided in the Appendix. Letter grades for each unit can be earned according to the following point totals: A ≥ 90, B ≥ 80, C ≥ 70, D ≥ 60, F < 60. On the reverse side of the Grade Roster, students will find instructions for calculating their "grade point average" or "GPA." If they keep track of their progress, they will never have to ask "How am I doing in this class?" They will know!

Unit Packets

At the end of every unit, have students staple their work into a neat "unit packet" that includes their Review Quiz, Homework, Journal Sheet, Current Event, and Fact Sheet. Collect and examine each student's packet, making comments as necessary. Check to see that students have awarded themselves the points and grades they have earned. You can enter individual grades into your record book or grading software before returning all packets to students the following week.

You will find that holding students accountable for compiling their own work at the end of each unit instills a sense of responsibility and accomplishment. Instruct students to show their packets and Grade Roster to their parents on a regular basis.

Fine Tuning

This volume of *Ready-to-Use Human Biology & Health Activities for Grades 5–12* was created so that teachers would not have to "reinvent the wheel" every week to come up with lessons that work. Instructors are advised and encouraged to fine tune activities to their own personal teaching style in order to satisfy the needs of individual students. You are encouraged to supplement lessons with your district's adopted textbook and any relevant audiovisual materials and computer software. Use any and all facilities at your disposal to satisfy students' varied learning modalities (visual, auditory, kinesthetic, and so forth).

CONTENTS

HB1   CELLS, TISSUES, ORGANS, AND ORGAN SYSTEMS / 1

Teacher's Classwork Agenda and Content Notes

Classwork Agenda for the Week . . . Content Notes for Lecture
and Discussion . . . Answers to the End-of-the-Week Review Quiz

Fact Sheet with Homework Directions

Lesson #1
Students will learn to use a microscope.
Journal Sheet #1

Lesson #2
Students will examine epithelial cells under the microscope.
Journal Sheet #2

Lesson #3
Students will examine muscle and connective tissue under the microscope.
Journal Sheet #3

Lesson #4
Students will list the organ systems of the human body and the organs they contain.
Journal Sheet #4

HB1 Review Quiz

HB2   THE SKELETAL SYSTEM / 15

Teacher's Classwork Agenda and Content Notes

Classwork Agenda for the Week . . . Content Notes for Lecture
and Discussion . . . Answers to the End-of-the-Week Review Quiz

Fact Sheet with Homework Directions

Lesson #1
Students will identify bones of the axial and appendicular skeleton.
Journal Sheet #1

Lesson #2
Students will identify different types of joints.
Journal Sheet #2

Lesson #3
Students will dissect a long bone to examine its internal and external structure.
Journal Sheet #3

Lesson #4
Students will lay out an anatomical chart of the human body beginning with the skeletal system.
Journal Sheet #4

HB2 Review Quiz

HB3 THE MUSCULAR SYSTEM / 29

Teacher's Classwork Agenda and Content Notes

Classwork Agenda for the Week . . . Content Notes for Lecture
and Discussion . . . Answers to the End-of-the-Week Review Quiz

Fact Sheet with Homework Directions

Lesson #1
Students will examine major muscles of the skeleton to identify the movements they control.
Journal Sheet #1

Lesson #2
Students will begin the dissection of a chicken wing to identify tissues associated with muscles.
Journal Sheet #2

Lesson #3
Students will complete the dissection of a chicken wing and compare the muscle bundles present to those in a human arm.
Journal Sheet #3

Lesson #4
Students will illustrate the major muscles of the torso and appendages to be added to the human body chart project.
Journal Sheet #4

HB3 Review Quiz

HB4 NUTRITION AND THE DIGESTIVE SYSTEM / 43

Teacher's Classwork Agenda and Content Notes

Classwork Agenda for the Week . . . Content Notes for Lecture
and Discussion . . . Answers to the End-of-the-Week Review Quiz

Fact Sheet with Homework Directions

Lesson #1
Students will identify major organs of the digestive system and set up a daily chart record of the foods they will eat this week.
Journal Sheet #1

Lesson #2
Students will test food samples for the presence of protein and starch.
Journal Sheet #2

Lesson #3
Students will convert starch to simple sugar.
Journal Sheet #3

Lesson #4
Students will illustrate the major organs of the digestive system to be added to the human body chart project.
Journal Sheet #4

HB4 Review Quiz

HB5   THE SKIN AND EXCRETORY SYSTEM / 57

Teacher's Classwork Agenda and Content Notes

Classwork Agenda for the Week . . . Content Notes for Lecture
and Discussion . . . Answers to the End-of-the-Week Review Quiz

Fact Sheet with Homework Directions

Lesson #1
Students will determine factors that affect the balance of fluids between the inside and the outside of cells.
Journal Sheet #1

Lesson #2
Students will identify the layers of the skin and how it helps to control body temperature.
Journal Sheet #2

Lesson #3
Students will identify the excretory organs of the urinary tract.
Journal Sheet #3

Lesson #4
Students will illustrate the organs of the excretory system to be added to the human body chart project.
Journal Sheet #4

HB5 Review Quiz

HB6   THE CIRCULATORY SYSTEM / 71

Teacher's Classwork Agenda and Content Notes

Classwork Agenda for the Week . . . Content Notes for Lecture
and Discussion . . . Answers to the End-of-the-Week Review Quiz

Fact Sheet with Homework Directions

Lesson #1
Students will identify the organs of the circulatory system and use a pie graph to identify the components of blood.
Journal Sheet #1

Lesson #2
Students will observe blood flow in the tail capillaries of a goldfish.
Journal Sheet #2

Lesson #3
Students will examine the effects of exercise on pulse rate.
Journal Sheet #3

Lesson #4
Students will illustrate the organs of the circulatory system to be added to the human body chart project.
Journal Sheet #4

HB6 Review Quiz

HB7 THE RESPIRATORY SYSTEM / 85

Teacher's Classwork Agenda and Content Notes

Classwork Agenda for the Week . . . Content Notes for Lecture
and Discussion . . . Answers to the End-of-the-Week Review Quiz

Fact Sheet with Homework Directions

Lesson #1
Students will identify the organs of the respiratory system and make a model of the lungs to show how we breathe.
Journal Sheet #1

Lesson #2
Students will demonstrate the presence of carbon dioxide in exhaled air.
Journal Sheet #2

Lesson #3
Students will demonstrate the effect of exercise on the air capacity of the lungs.
Journal Sheet #3

Lesson #4
Students will illustrate the organs of the respiratory system to be added to the human body chart project.
Journal Sheet #4

HB7 Review Quiz

HB8 THE SENSE ORGANS / 99

Teacher's Classwork Agenda and Content Notes

Classwork Agenda for the Week . . . Content Notes for Lecture
and Discussion . . . Answers to the End-of-the-Week Review Quiz

Fact Sheet with Homework Directions

Lesson #1
Students will identify the different types of sensory receptors of the skin.
Journal Sheet #1

Lesson #2
Students will dissect a sheep's eye to identify the parts of the eye.
Journal Sheet #2

Lesson #3
Students will identify the parts of the ear and the organ of balance.
Journal Sheet #3

Lesson #4
Students will test the taste receptors of the tongue.
Journal Sheet #4

HB8 Review Quiz

HB9 THE NERVOUS SYSTEM / 113

Teacher's Classwork Agenda and Content Notes

Classwork Agenda for the Week . . . Content Notes for Lecture
and Discussion . . . Answers to the End-of-the-Week Review Quiz

Fact Sheet with Homework Directions

Lesson #1
Students will create a graphic organizer that helps to identify the major divisions and functions of the parts of the nervous system.
Journal Sheet #1

Lesson #2
Students will explain how nerve cells conduct nerve impulses and distinguish between spinal and autonomic reflexes.
Journal Sheet #2

Lesson #3
Students will test the ability of the brain to process different kinds of sensory stimuli.
Journal Sheet #3

Lesson #4
Students will illustrate the organs of the nervous system to be added to the human body chart project.
Journal Sheet #4

HB9 Review Quiz

HB10 HORMONES AND THE ENDOCRINE SYSTEM / 127

Teacher's Classwork Agenda and Content Notes

Classwork Agenda for the Week . . . Content Notes for Lecture
and Discussion . . . Answers to the End-of-the-Week Review Quiz

Fact Sheet with Homework Directions

Lesson #1
Students will identify the organs of the endocrine system and the hormones secreted by each organ.
Journal Sheet #1

Lesson #2
Students will explain how the brain influences the production of hormones via the pituitary or "master" gland.
Journal Sheet #2

Lesson #3
Students will prepare and present a brief summary of the location and function of a particular endocrine organ.
Journal Sheet #3

Lesson #4
Students will write a paragraph explaining the difference between "mobile" and "fixed-membrane" hormone receptors.
Journal Sheet #4

HB10 Review Quiz

HB13   FROG DISSECTION / 169

Teacher's Classwork Agenda and Content Notes

Classwork Agenda for the Week . . . Content Notes for Lecture
and Discussion . . . Answers to the End-of-the-Week Review Quiz

Fact Sheet with Homework Directions

Lesson #1
   Students will perform an external examination of the frog to identify its physical adaptations.
Journal Sheet #1

Lesson #2
   Students will begin the dissection of a frog to compare the arrangement of internal organs to that of a human being.
Journal Sheet #2

Lesson #3
   Students will continue the dissection of a frog to compare the arrangement of internal organs to that of a human being.
Journal Sheet #3

Lesson #4
   Students will contrast the structure and arrangement of organs in the frog to those of a human being.
Journal Sheet #4

HB13 Review Quiz

HB14   HUMAN ANCESTORS / 183

Teacher's Classwork Agenda and Content Notes

Classwork Agenda for the Week . . . Content Notes for Lecture
and Discussion . . . Answers to the End-of-the-Week Review Quiz

Fact Sheet with Homework Directions

Lesson #1
   Students will compare and contrast the human hand with the hands of other primates.
Journal Sheet #1

Lesson #2
   Students will compare and contrast the pelvis and leg bones of primate bipeds and quadrupeds.
Journal Sheet #2

Lesson #3
   Students will compare and contrast the human skull with the skulls of other primates.
Journal Sheet #3

Lesson #4
   Students will examine the lines of descent that lead to humans and other living primates.
Journal Sheet #4

HB14 Review Quiz

Teacher's Classwork Agenda and Content Notes

Classwork Agenda for the Week . . . Content Notes for Lecture
and Discussion . . . Answers to the End-of-the-Week Review Quiz

Fact Sheet with Homework Directions

Lesson #1
Students will examine how the brain processes different visual stimuli.
Journal Sheet #1

Lesson #2
Students will explain the difference between linear and parallel processing of information.
Journal Sheet #2

Lesson #3
Students will describe techniques that can be used to change behavior and improve memory.
Journal Sheet #3

Lesson #4
Students will list and define medical conditions associated with abnormal behavior.
Journal Sheet #4

HB15 Review Quiz

APPENDIX / 211

Thomas Addison
Alcmaeon of Crotona
Aristotle
William Maddock Bayliss
William Beaumont
Martinus Willem Beijerinck
Claude Bernard
Sir William Bowman
Robert Boyle
Charles Brown-Séquard
Walter Bradford Cannon
Nikolaus Copernicus
Raymond Arthur Dart
Charles Robert Darwin
René Descartes
Marie Eugéne F. T. Dubois
Sir John Carew Eccles
Paul Ehrlich
Willem Einthoven
Erasistratus
Gustav Theodor Fechner
Pierre Jean Marie Flourens
August Forel
Otto Funke
Galen
Franz Joseph Gall
Luigi Galvani
Camillo Golgi
Robert James Graves
Ernst Heinrich Haekel
Albrecht von Haller
William Harvey

Hermann L. F. von Helmholtz
Friedrich Gustav Jacob Henle
Herophilus of Chalcedon
Wilhelm A. O. Hertwig
Hippocrates
William His
Wilhelm His, Jr.
Alan Lloyd Hodgkin
Ernst Felix Hoppe-Seyler
Andrew Fielding Huxley
Ibn Al-Nafis
William James
Edward Jenner
Donald Carl Johanson
Arthur Keith
H. H. Robert Koch
Rudolph Albert von Kölliker
Emil Kraepelin
René T. H. Laënnec
Karl Landsteiner
Antoine Lavosier
Louis Seymour Bazett Leakey
Mary Douglas Leakey
Anton van Leeuwenhoek
Cho Hao Li
Justus von Liebig
Carolus Linnaeus
Joseph Lister
Marcello Malpighi
John Mayow
Elmer Verner McCollum
Gregor Johann Mendel

Julius Lothar Meyer
Sir Isaac Newton
Jean Nollet
George Oliver
Louis Pasteur
Ivan Petrovich Pavlov
Wilhelm F. P. Pfeffer
Plato
Joseph Priestley
William Prout
Santiago Ramón y Cajal
René de Réaumur
Francesco Redi
S. Riva Rocci
Matthias Jakob Schleiden
Theodor Schwann
Edward A. Sharpey-Schafer
Charles Robert Sherrington
B. F. Skinner
John Snow
Johannes Spurzheim
Ernest Henry Starling
Arne W. K. Tiselius
Andreas Vesalius
Leonardo da Vinci
Alfred Russel Wallace
John Broadus Watson
Ernst Heinrich Weber
Wilhelm Wundt
John R. Young
Thomas Young

CELLS, TISSUES, ORGANS, AND ORGAN SYSTEMS

TEACHER'S CLASSWORK AGENDA AND CONTENT NOTES

Classwork Agenda for the Week

1. Students will learn to use a microscope.
2. Students will examine epithelial cells under the microscope.
3. Students will examine muscle and connective tissue under the microscope.
4. Students will list the organ systems of the human body and the organs they contain.

Content Notes for Lecture and Discussion

The "founder of modern medicine" **Hippocrates** (b. 460 B.C.; d. 377 B.C.) emphasized the study of the fluids present in the body which he called the "body humours." He believed that a proper balance of these humours was essential to the maintenance of good health and a happy life. He promoted cleanliness and moderation in eating and drinking habits. And, his *Hippocratic Oath* embodies the modern medical ethic to "do no harm" in the search for a cure. The ideas of the Greek physician **Galen** (b. 129; d. 200)—who adopted the "humourology" of Hippocrates—dominated Western medicine for over 1,500 years throughout the Dark and Middle Ages. The Greek physician **Alcmeaon** (c. 500 B.C.) performed and documented the first animal dissections in which he attempted to discover the "sensory channels" leading to the brain. Even before the intensive study of comparative anatomy—which took place two thousand years later during the Renaissance—Alcmeaon presumed that learning about the anatomy of animals would have relevance for the study of human anatomy. We still follow Alcmeaon's lead by dissecting a frog in biology class to examine the structures and relative positions of the frog's organs in order to learn something about our own internal anatomy.

However, the study of human anatomy and physiology remained hampered by the inability of biologists to examine more closely the structures that served as the basic unit of biology: namely, the cell. The early Romans documented observations of plants and animals made through glass spheres filled with water. Improved techniques for shaping glass developed during the 13th century resulted in the manufacture of cheaper and more powerful lenses. The **science of optics** made its first great strides in the 15th and 16th centuries resulting in a revolution in biology. The Danish inventor **Anton van Leeuwenhoek** (b. 1632; d. 1723) is credited with the invention of the **microscope** which he used to observe and draw bacteria and other microorganisms which he called "animalicules." The observations of van Leeuwenhoek and others culminated in **the cell theory** proposed by German biologists **Theodor Schwann** (b. 1810; d. 1882) and **Matthias Jakob Schleiden** (b. 1804; d. 1881) in 1838. In his book entitled *Microscopical Investigations*, Schwann proposed that all living tissues were made up of cells. Later advances in the art and science of microscopy led to the observation that similar kinds of cells form **tissues** that specialize and combine to form **organs**. **Organ systems** allow large multicellular animals such as human beings (e.g., *homo sapiens*) to accomplish the tasks necessary to support life.

Failure at any level in body organization can have the most drastic consequences. Cancer is essentially a dysfunction at the cellular level. In the middle 1800s, the German anatomist and histologist **Jacob Henle** (b. 1809; d. 1885) examined the effects of diseases on a variety of plant and animal tissues and argued that living organisms were most likely responsible for diseases in man. He reasoned that living things alone were capable of reproduction; therefore, progressively morbid

1

infectious diseases must have an organic cause. The German bacteriologist **Heinrich Hermann Koch** (b. 1843; d. 1910) developed "filtration methods" to isolate the parasites responsible for ill health. By 1860, the French chemist and microbiologist **Louis Pasteur** (b. 1822; d. 1895) had proposed an overall **theory of germs** and discovered the pasteurization process still used today to rid certain foods of bacteria.

In Lesson #1, students will learn to use a microscope.

In Lesson #2, students will examine epithelial cells under the microscope.

In Lesson #3, student will examine muscle and connective tissue under the microscope.

In Lesson #4, students will list the organ systems of the human body and the organs they contain.

ANSWERS TO THE HOMEWORK PROBLEMS

Any dictionary will provide definitions that students can use to find and deduce the major function of each organ system. The term "excretory" may not be present in an elementary dictionary; but the term "excrete" will be there. Students should be able to write a brief descriptive sentence about the function of each system: skeletal—provides structure and protection; muscular—executes movement; digestive—breaks down nutrients; excretory—eliminates wastes; circulatory—transports nutrients; respiratory—exchanges gases; nervous—senses and responds; endocrine—uses hormones to control other systems; immune—defends against germs; reproductive—perpetuates the species.

ANSWERS TO THE END-OF-THE-WEEK REVIEW QUIZ

1. C	6. E	11. cells; tissues; organs; organ systems
2. J	7. D	12. Students may choose from the following list of basic activities: sense,
3. I	8. H	move, respire, ingest, excrete, grow, and repair. An individual human
4. G	9. A	need not reproduce in order to survive, although the perpetuation of
5. B	10. F	the species depends upon a few human beings able to accomplish
		that task.

HB1 FACT-SHEET

CELLS, TISSUES, ORGANS, AND ORGAN SYSTEMS

CLASSWORK AGENDA FOR THE WEEK

(1)   Learn to use a microscope.
(2)   Examine epithelial cells under the microscope.
(3)   Examine muscle and connective tissue under the microscope.
(4)   List the organ systems of the human body and the organs they contain.

Like all living things, human beings have *basic needs*. Because we are all members of the same species—named *homo sapiens*—we all have the same basic needs. All of us need **energy**, **water**, **oxygen**, and a specific **temperature range** that will allow chemical reactions to take place in our bodies. We need to protect ourselves against drastic changes in temperature (e.g., seasonal change) in order to insure that our bodies continue to work properly. The word **metabolism** refers to all the chemical reactions that take place inside us. Our ability to keep our metabolic activities in proper balance is called **homeostasis**.

Humans perform *basic activities* common to all living things. Humans can **sense** their environment, **move** around in it, **respire** (e.g., breathe), **ingest** (e.g., eat), **excrete** (e.g., get rid of waste products), **grow**, **repair injuries**, and **reproduce**. A **unicellular** (e.g., one-celled) organism such as an ameba can perform the same activities. But humans have evolved more complex ways of performing these tasks. We are **multicellular** (e.g., many-celled) organisms.

Our cells are designed to perform special jobs. Muscle cells can contract; red blood cells carry oxygen; white blood cells can recognize and kill bacteria. Nerve cells can send signals. Any group of similar cells that work together to perform an important body function is called a **tissue**. Skin, muscle, and nerves are examples of tissues. Different tissues work together to perform more complex activities. A collection of tissues that works together to perform a specific set of activities is called an **organ**. Our heart is an organ that pumps blood. Our stomach is an organ that digests food.

Organ systems in the human body are collections of organs that work together to help us satisfy our basic biological needs. Humans have a **skeletal system**, a **muscular system**, a **digestive system**, an **excretory system**, a **circulatory system**, a **respiratory system**, a **nervous system**, an **endocrine system**, an **immune system**, and a **reproductive system**.

When our cells, tissues, organs, and organ systems are working properly we can live a healthy and happy life. When they are not we fall ill and may die. There are a variety of factors that can cause us to get sick. Illness is normally due to an invasion of the body by germs; and poor diet can certainly cause disease. Our mental health depends upon these and a variety of other factors. With proper hygiene, nutrition, and "friendly" surroundings the human body has little trouble maintaining a proper balance of bodily functions.

Homework Directions

Using any source available to you (i.e., dictionary, friends, relatives, etc.) find the function of each of the organ systems mentioned above. Write a brief sentence to summarize what you found out about each organ system.

Assignment due: _____

_____ _____ ____/____/____
Student's Signature   Parent's Signature   Date

CELLS, TISSUES, ORGANS, AND ORGAN SYSTEMS

Work Date: _____/_____/_____

LESSON OBJECTIVE

Students will learn how to use a microscope.

Classroom Activities

On Your Mark!

Begin with a brief lecture about the contributions made by **Hippocrates** (b. 460 B.C.; d. 377 B.C.) and the other scientists mentioned in the Teacher's Classwork Agenda and Content Notes to our understanding of the human body's **basic needs** and **levels of organization** (e.g., cells form tissues, tissues form organs, organs form organ systems).

Get Set!

Give a discussion of the history of the **science of optics** and its impact on the science of biology resulting from the invention of the microscope by **Anton van Leeuwenhoek** (b. 1632; d. 1723). Then perform this simple demonstration to illustrate the basic laws of optics at work in the microscope. (1) Place a straw in a glass or beaker of water and point out how the straw appears to bend. (2) Explain that light waves bend or "refract" as they pass from one medium (e.g., the water) into another medium (e.g., the glass, then air). (3) Give an eyedropper with water to each student. (4) Instruct students to place a droplet of water on any letter of their Fact Sheet. (5) Ask them to report their observations of the letter's image. They will report that the letter under the droplet becomes magnified. Explain that the "bending" of light waves reflecting off the surface of the letter as they pass across the curved surfaces of the water droplet into the air causes the image of the letter to appear larger.

Display a microscope and identify its parts shown on Journal Sheet #1. Have students copy the names of each part and describe its function as you lecture: (1) The **base** and **support arm** support the body of the microscope. Students should walk slowly when carrying the microscope to their observation station, holding the scope with two hands—one grasping the arm, with the other under the base—close to the center of their bodies. (2) Instruct them to use the **coarse focus knob** to raise the **objective lenses** (or lower the stage) so that the lenses are out of the way. (3) After securing a prepared slide on the **stage** under the **stage clips** they can (4) use the **light** or **mirror** to send light up through the hole in the stage. (5) Viewing the stage and slide *from the side*, student should use the coarse focus knob again to bring the *lowest power objective* as close to the slide as possible <u>without touching it</u>. (6) Viewing the object through the **eyepiece**, they can then *focus away from the slide* until the object comes into focus. This procedure prevents the objective lens from smashing into the slide. (7) Students can adjust the **diaphragm** to control the intensity of light passing through their slide. (8) They can use the **fine focus knob** to add clarity to the image. Instruct students to repeat steps #5 through #8 when changing objectives to a higher or lower power.

Go!

Give students ample time to complete the activity described in Figure A on Journal Sheet #1.

Materials

microscopes, microscope slides, microscope cover slips, eyedroppers, water, newspaper, beakers, straws

HB1 Journal Sheet #1

CELLS, TISSUES, ORGANS, AND ORGAN SYSTEMS

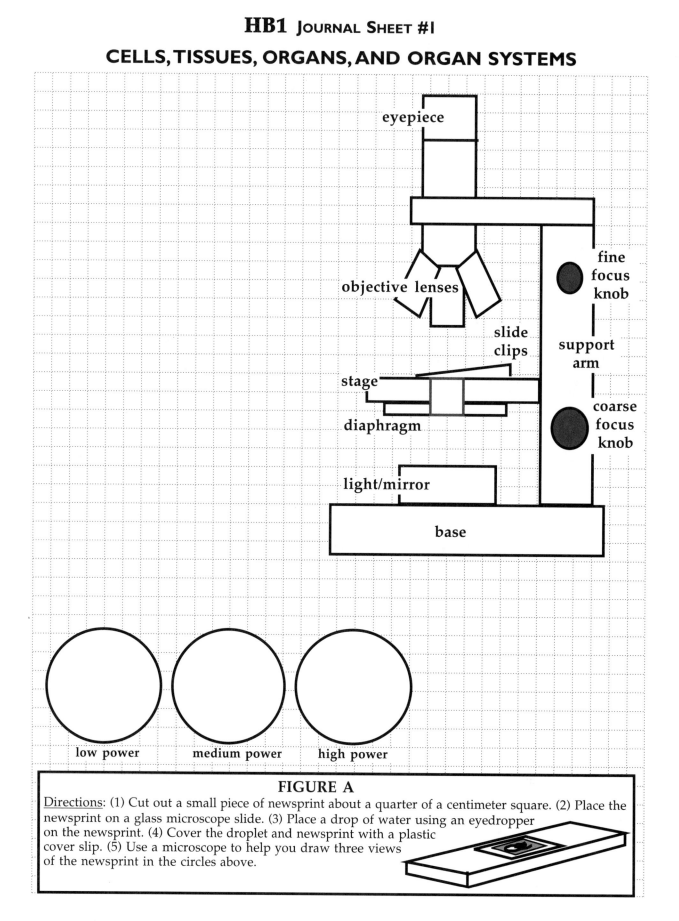

eyepiece

fine focus knob

objective lenses

slide clips

support arm

stage

coarse focus knob

diaphragm

light/mirror

base

low power   medium power   high power

FIGURE A

Directions: (1) Cut out a small piece of newsprint about a quarter of a centimeter square. (2) Place the newsprint on a glass microscope slide. (3) Place a drop of water using an eyedropper on the newsprint. (4) Cover the droplet and newsprint with a plastic cover slip. (5) Use a microscope to help you draw three views of the newsprint in the circles above.

CELLS, TISSUES, ORGANS, AND ORGAN SYSTEMS

Work Date: ____/____/____

LESSON OBJECTIVE

Students will examine epithelial cells under the microscope.

Classroom Activities

On Your Mark!

Prepare for class by purchasing or preparing solutions of methylene blue or Lugol's solution for staining. Lugol's solution can be prepared by dissolving 10 grams of potassium iodide (e.g., KI) in 100 ml of distilled water, then adding 5 grams of iodine crystals. Both stains will make the cell nucleus evident under medium power.

Draw Illustration A on the board and have students copy your drawing on Journal Sheet #2. Using the information in the Teacher's Classwork Agenda and Content Notes review the cell theory proposed by **Theodor Schwann** (b. 1810; d. 1882) and **Matthias Jakob Schleiden** (b. 1804; d. 1881) in 1838. Point out that much of the animal biology research done in the 19th and early 20th centuries was done on developing chicken **embryos** (e.g., chicks still in the egg). Scientists cut open a small hole in the shell of an egg and studied the

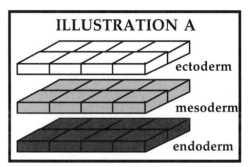

ILLUSTRATION A

ectoderm

mesoderm

endoderm

chick under the microscope as the bird developed. This research allowed **embryologists** to see how cells became different—or **differentiated**—to form the tissues and organs of a newborn chicken. They discovered that cells divide to form three distinct tissues called the **ectoderm** (e.g., meaning "outside skin"), **mesoderm** (e.g., meaning "middle skin"), and **endoderm** (e.g,., meaning "inside skin"). The cells of each layer differentiate further to form the organ systems that make up the human body. The ectoderm becomes the skin and nervous system. The mesoderm becomes the skeletal, muscular, and circulatory system. The endoderm becomes the organs of the digestive system. The same processes of **division** and **differentiation** take place in all other animals.

Get Set!

Explain that **epithelial** cells are "covering" cells. The skin, hair and inner lining of the mouth and digestive tract are epithelial cells. Point out that most cells and tissues are transparent and difficult to see under a microscope. For this reason, scientists "stain" cells with a variety of colored dyes to make them visible. The art and science of staining cells and tissues is called **histology** (e.g., meaning "tissue").

Go!

Give students ample time to complete the activities described in Figure B on Journal Sheet #2. Use preprepared slides of varying types of cells if available. Slide kits can be purchased through most laboratory supply houses.

Materials

microscopes, microscope slides, microscope cover slips, eyedroppers, water, scissors, methylene blue or Lugol's iodine solution (see above), flat-end toothpicks, cotton swabs

HB1 JOURNAL SHEET #2

CELLS, TISSUES, ORGANS, AND ORGAN SYSTEMS

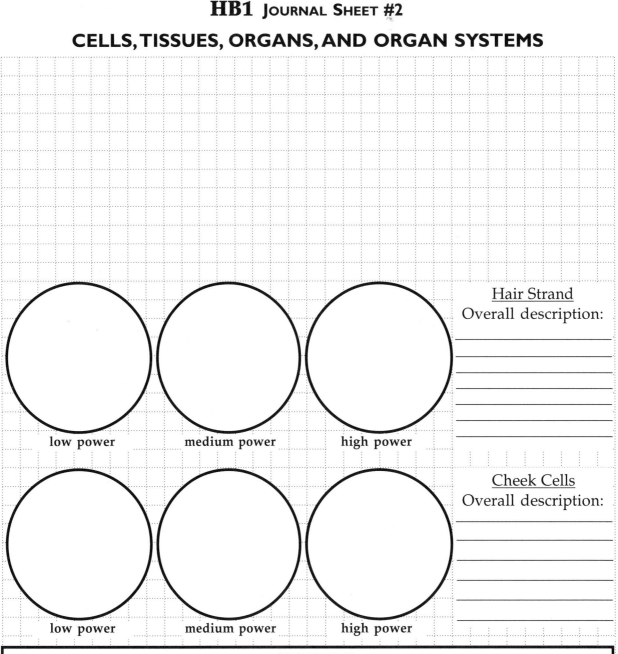

low power   medium power   high power

Hair Strand
Overall description:
_____
_____
_____
_____
_____
_____
_____

low power   medium power   high power

Cheek Cells
Overall description:
_____
_____
_____
_____
_____
_____
_____

FIGURE B

Directions for viewing strands of hair: (1) Use a scissor to carefully snip a centimeter length of a single strand of hair from your head. DO NOT PULL THE HAIR OUT BY THE ROOT. This can lead to an infection if the wound is not properly cleaned. (2) Place the hair strand on a microscope slide and cover it with a drop of plain water and a cover slip. (3) Draw your observations in the circles above.

Directions for viewing dead cheek cells: (1) Gently scrape the lining of your cheek with the flat side of a toothpick. (2) Smear the dead cheek cells onto a microscope slide. (3) Stain the specimen with a drop of methylene blue or Lugol's iodine solution provided by your instructor. (4) Draw your observations in the circles above.

GENERAL HEALTH PRECAUTIONS

Do not touch another student's specimens. Rinse and dry all microscope slides thoroughly and discard specimens, toothpicks, and cover slips. Your instructor will sterilize any equipment to be reused.

HB1 Lesson #3

CELLS, TISSUES, ORGANS, AND ORGAN SYSTEMS

Work Date: ____/____/____

LESSON OBJECTIVE

Students will examine muscle and connective tissue under the microscope.

Classroom Activities

On Your Mark!

Prepare for class by purchasing raw chicken parts (e.g., wings, legs, etc.) with skin. Wash the parts to be used thoroughly with soap and water. Before the start of class, separate out pink muscle tissue from a piece of chicken and cut the muscle into as many small microscope samples as needed (e.g., no piece larger than several cubic millimeters in size). Cut sections of clear connective tissue found adhering to the underside of the skin and surrounding muscle bundles. The soft white tendons attached to the ends of muscle bundles can also be used.

Begin class with a review of the information discussed in Lesson #2.

Get Set!

Explain that **muscle cells** have specialized proteins that allow the cells to contract. Students may be able to see these proteins as darkly stained "bands" running across muscle fibers in well-stained sections. They will also be able to see the nuclei of muscle cells in well-stained samples. Point out that **connective tissue** protects organs and holds organs in place. Explain the role of **tendons** (e.g., tissue connecting muscles to bones) if you use them. Students will be able to make out the nuclei of connective cells in well-stained samples.

Go!

Give students ample time to complete the activities described in Figure C on Journal Sheet #2. Use preprepared slides of varying types of cells if available. Slide kits can be purchased through most laboratory supply houses.

Materials

raw chicken parts with skin, microscopes, microscope slides, microscope cover slips, eyedroppers, water, methylene blue or Lugol's iodine solution (see Lesson #2), dissection kits (e.g., dissecting needles and forceps)

Name: _____ Period: _____ Date: ___/___/___

HB1 JOURNAL SHEET #3

CELLS, TISSUES, ORGANS, AND ORGAN SYSTEMS

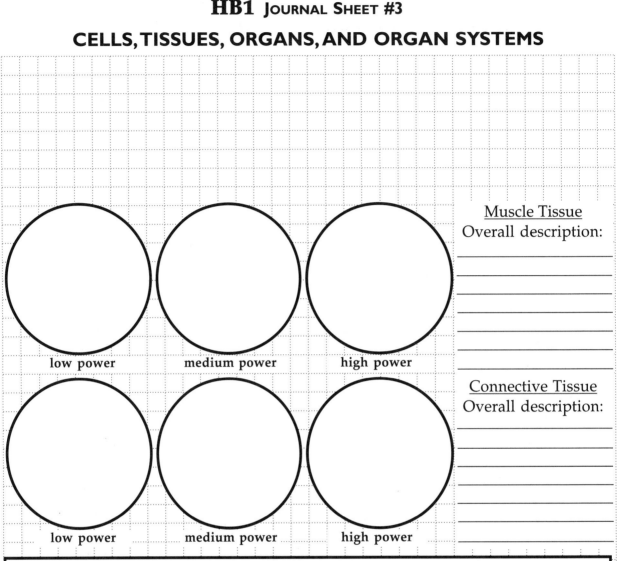

low power   medium power   high power

Muscle Tissue
Overall description:
_____
_____
_____
_____
_____
_____
_____

low power   medium power   high power

Connective Tissue
Overall description:
_____
_____
_____
_____
_____
_____
_____

FIGURE C

<u>Directions for viewing chicken muscle tissue</u>: (1) Your instructor will provide you with a small sample of chicken muscle. DO NOT HANDLE IT WITH BARE FINGERS. WEAR PLASTIC SURGICAL GLOVES AND GOGGLES. (2) Using forceps, place the sample on a microscope slide. (3) Use forceps and a dissecting needle to tease the sample into thin strands. (4) Stain the specimen with a drop of methylene blue or Lugol's iodine solution provided by your instructor and cover the sample with a cover slip. Touch the corner of a piece of tissue to the edge of the cover slip to draw off excess stain. (5) Draw your observations in the circles above.

<u>Directions for viewing chicken connective tissue</u>: (1) Your instructor will provide you with a small sample of chicken connective tissue. DO NOT HANDLE IT WITH BARE FINGERS. WEAR PLASTIC SURGICAL GLOVES AND GOGGLES. (2) Using forceps, place the sample on a microscope slide. (3) Use forceps and a dissecting needle to gently spread the sample into a thin sheet without tearing it. (4) Stain the specimen with a drop of methylene blue or Lugol's iodine solution provided by your instructor and cover the sample with a cover slip. Touch the corner of a piece of tissue to the edge of the cover slip to draw off excess stain. (5) Draw your observations in the circles above.

GENERAL HEALTH PRECAUTIONS

Do not touch another student's specimens. Rinse and dry all microscope slides thoroughly and discard specimens, and cover slips. Your instructor will sterilize any equipment to be reused.

CELLS, TISSUES, ORGANS, AND ORGAN SYSTEMS

Work Date: _____/_____/_____

LESSON OBJECTIVE

Students will list the organ systems of the human body and the organs they contain.

Classroom Activities

On Your Mark!

Refer students to their Fact Sheet and have them list the **basic human needs** mentioned—which are the same as the needs of other living things—and the **basic activities** performed by human beings. Point out the difference between a **unicellular** (e.g., ameba) and a **multicellular** (e.g., human being) organism.

Get Set!

Instruct students to scan the list of **organs** on Journal Sheet #4 and compare them to the list of **organ systems** mentioned in the Fact Sheet. Quiz students orally on their knowledge of the function of some of the organs and organ systems defined for homework.

Go!

Give students ample time to perform the activity described in Figure D on Journal Sheet #4. Circulate around the room to make sure students are placing the organs in their appropriate circles. Point out that some organs can be considered as belonging to more than one organ system. The reproductive organs (e.g., testes and ovaries) can be considered part of the endocrine system because they manufacture hormones to control the function of other organs. The tongue could be considered part of both the muscular system and the nervous system as it is capable of movement and has sensory receptors for taste. Point out that the appendix is a "vestigial organ" having no known use in humans.

Materials

Journal Sheet #4

HB1 JOURNAL SHEET #4

CELLS, TISSUES, ORGANS, AND ORGAN SYSTEMS

BASIC HUMAN NEEDS   BASIC HUMAN ACTIVITIES

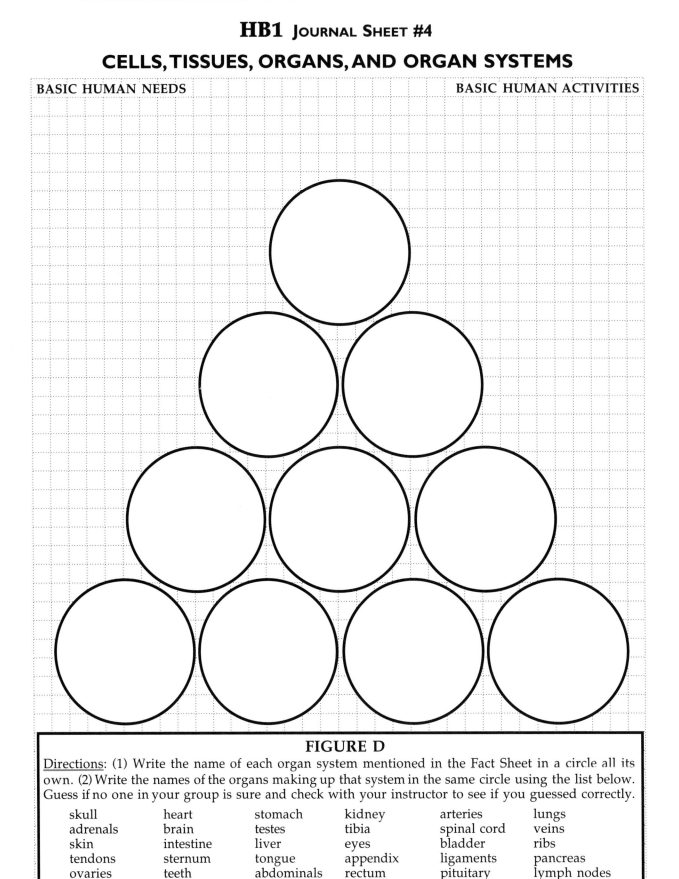

FIGURE D

<u>Directions</u>: (1) Write the name of each organ system mentioned in the Fact Sheet in a circle all its own. (2) Write the names of the organs making up that system in the same circle using the list below. Guess if no one in your group is sure and check with your instructor to see if you guessed correctly.

skull	heart	stomach	kidney	arteries	lungs
adrenals	brain	testes	tibia	spinal cord	veins
skin	intestine	liver	eyes	bladder	ribs
tendons	sternum	tongue	appendix	ligaments	pancreas
ovaries	teeth	abdominals	rectum	pituitary	lymph nodes

HB1 REVIEW QUIZ

Directions: Keep your eyes on your own work.
Read all directions and questions carefully.
THINK BEFORE YOU ANSWER!
Watch your spelling, be neat, and do the best you can.

CLASSWORK	(~40): _____
HOMEWORK	(~20): _____
CURRENT EVENT	(~10): _____
TEST	(~30): _____
TOTAL	(~100): _____

(A ≥ 90, B ≥ 80, C ≥ 70, D ≥ 60, F < 60)

LETTER GRADE: _____

TEACHER'S COMMENTS: _____
_____

CELLS, TISSUES, ORGANS, AND ORGAN SYSTEMS

MATCHING: Choose the letter of the word or phrase that best describes the major function of each organ system. *20 points*

_____ 1. skeletal
_____ 2. muscular
_____ 3. digestive
_____ 4. excretory
_____ 5. circulatory
_____ 6. respiratory
_____ 7. nervous
_____ 8. endocrine
_____ 9. immune
_____ 10. reproductive

A. defense against germs

B. transports nutrients

C. structure and protection

D. senses and responds

E. exchanges gases

F. perpetuates the species

G. eliminates wastes

H. uses hormones to control other systems

I. breaks down nutrients

J. executes movement

HB1 Review Quiz (cont'd)

Directions: Fill in the blanks as directed in the spaces provided.

11. Describe the organization of a living organism from the simplest to the more complex using the following terms: tissues, cells, organ systems, and organs. *4 points*

   _____ → _____ → _____ → _____

12. List six of the basic activities that must be performed by all humans in order for them to survive. *6 points*

   _____   _____   _____

   _____   _____   _____

THE SKELETAL SYSTEM

TEACHER'S CLASSWORK AGENDA AND CONTENT NOTES

Classwork Agenda for the Week

1. Students will identify bones of the axial and appendicular skeleton.

2. Students will identify different types of joints.

3. Students will dissect a long bone to examine its internal and external structure.

4. Students will lay out an anatomical chart of the human body beginning with the skeletal system.

Content Notes for Lecture and Discussion

Much of what we know about human behavior and the probable behavior of our ancestors comes from the study of bones. The **theory of evolution by means of natural selection** formulated by the English naturalist **Charles Robert Darwin** (b. 1809; d. 1882) and independently in the same decade by Welch naturalist **Alfred Russel Wallace** (b. 1823; d. 1913) was a major breakthrough in biology, particularly the field of paleontology. Darwin's theory suggested a mechanism by which life on our planet has expanded with such diversity, stressing that the survival of any species—including man—depends on how well that species solves basic biological problems in the face of a constantly changing environment. The skeletal structure of any animal provides clues to how that animal is adapted to its given habitat.

Darwin's publication of *The Origin of Species* in 1859 sent 19th century paleontologists in search of evidence of human origins: evidence which—like that of most other fossil evidence—can only be interpreted with a sufficient knowledge of bones. Since the first discovery of "prehominid" remains made in Indonesia by Dutch paleontologist **Marie Eugéne François Thomas Dubois** (b. 1858; d. 1940) in 1891 the search has led to the discovery of a number of "manlike" species. Although it is technically incorrect to say that our own species is the direct descendent of any one of these—just as it is incorrect to say that any living species is the descendent of any other living species—few scientists doubt that our ancestors evolved through a series of phases that can be physically differentiated on the basis of fossil evidence. The common ancestor of ourselves, other hominids, and prehominids (e.g., Neanderthals, Astralopithecines) was most probably a short, small-brained biped. Much of the valuable work done in this field is credited to the husband and wife team of paleontologists **Louis Seymour Bazett Leakey** (b. 1903; d. 1972) and **Mary Douglas Leakey** (b. 1913; d. 1966). One of the most complete prehominid skeletons—named "Lucy"—was unearthed in Ethiopia by American physical anthropologist **Donald Carl Johanson** (b. 1943) in 1978 and was dated at 3.5 million years old. More recent finds have dated closer to 4 million years. Although it is convenient to use terms such as "primitive" and "advanced" when discussing fossil evidence, it is important to realize that all living things solve life's most essential problems in one way or another or they perish. Our prehominid relatives were successful in their own way until selection pressures eliminated them from the gene pool.

The structure of the bones and skeleton hints at ways an organism solves the puzzles posed by the environment. A skeleton not only dictates the general shape of an animal but also provides clues to the way the animal moved and the tasks it was able to perform. The shape and orientation of a gorilla's pelvis and that of a human reflect basic principles of locomotion. The pelvis of a gorilla is long, thin, and tilted toward the horizontal. The skeletal structure of this animal makes it impossible for the creature to rise off its forelimbs for any extended period of time. It is essentially a quadruped. The pelvis of a human, on the other hand, is broader and oriented toward the vertical. Humans are bipeds. The arrangement of bones in the human hand allow for an "opposable thumb" that facilitates the grasping and manipulation of tools, a feat a chimpanzee accomplishes with little dexterity. The human cranium suggests a basic evolutionary advance over our ancestors. Our relatively larger brain permits us to perform a wider, more complex range of behaviors. The study of the skeletal system is more than mere anatomy.

In Lesson #1, students will identify bones of the axial and appendicular skeleton.

In Lesson #2, students will identify different types of joints.

In Lesson #3, students will dissect a long bone to examine its internal and external structure.

In Lesson #4, students will lay out an anatomical chart of the human body beginning with the skeletal system.

Lesson #4 is a preparatory lesson that begins a longterm project to be accomplished as part of this Human Biology & Health curriculum. At the end of their studies students will have created a lifesize multilayered diagram of human organs and organ systems that clearly illustrates their understanding of how the human body works.

ANSWERS TO THE HOMEWORK PROBLEMS

Students' charts will vary but should demonstrate their understanding of the relationships between the joints and the bones that comprise them (see Lesson #2).

ANSWERS TO THE END-OF-THE-WEEK REVIEW QUIZ

1. about 200
2. appendicular
3. axial
4. true
5. true

6. do
7. dairy
8. proteins
9. true
10. true

11. C
12. B
13. E
14. A
15. D

16. cranium
17. mandible
18. vertebrae
19. humerus
20. radius/ulna

21. pelvis
22. phalanges
23. femur
24. tibia/fibula
25. metatarsals

HB2 Fact Sheet

THE SKELETAL SYSTEM

CLASSWORK AGENDA FOR THE WEEK

(1)   Identify bones of the axial and appendicular skeleton.
(2)   Identify different types of joints.
(3)   Dissect a long bone to examine its internal and external structure.
(4)   Lay out an anatomical chart of the human body beginning with the skeletal system.

The bones of the **skeletal system** have five important functions: (1) they give the body shape and support, (2) they allow movement but cannot move by themselves, (3) they protect tissues and organs, (4) they produce red blood cells, and (5) they store minerals such as calcium and phosphorus that the body needs to carry on life functions.

The average human skeleton has **206 bones** that can be divided into two main groups. One group of bones makes up the **axial skeleton**. The axial skeleton includes the **skull**, **ribs**, **sternum** (e.g., breastbone), and **vertebral column**. The word "axial" comes from the word "axis." An axis such as the "axis of the Earth" is an imaginary straight line around which something rotates or turns. The axis of the human skeleton is an imaginary straight line running down from the top of the head through the body. The other group of bones makes up the **appendicular skeleton**. The appendicular skeleton includes the **shoulders**, **hips**, **arms** and **hands**, **legs** and **feet**. The word "appendicular" comes from the verb "to append." To append means to attach something as an extra part to another object. Like the "appendix" added to the back of a book, arms and legs are added to a skeleton. Arms and legs are **appendages**.

Bones are connected to muscles and other bones by **connective tissue**. The connective tissue that connects bones to other bones is called **ligament**. The connective tissue that connects muscle to a bone is called **tendon**.

Bones are made of cells rich in **protein** like all of the other organs of the body but owe their hardness and strength to **minerals**. The important minerals found in bone are **calcium** and **phosphorous**. These elements are mostly found in foods such as dairy products and vegetables. Soft bone containing less calcium than hard bone is called **cartilage**. Cartilage is a flexible connective tissue found in many parts of the body such as the ears and nose. Cartilage supports harder bone and helps to cushion the skeleton against shock. The bones of a newborn child are made of cartilage. The bones harden after birth and bone cells are added to the ends of long bones during a person's life, causing that individual to grow. In a plastic model or "bleached-bone" skeleton the bones appear white. However, bones are made of living tissue that must be supplied with oxygen and nutrients like other tissues of the body. Nerves and blood vessels can be seen under a microscope between bone cells making up bone tissue. In old age, people's bones tend to lose mass, become more porous (e.g., meaning "filled with holes"), and may bend or break easily. This condition is called **osteoporosis**. Osteoporosis can also result from lack of exercise or prolonged weightlessness during spaceflight. Exercise and a diet containing sufficient amounts of calcium (e.g., milk and cheese) are the best prevention against the disease.

Bones are organs composed of several layers of tissue. **Compact bone** is found in the hollow shaft of a bone and has a high concentration of hardening minerals. **Spongy** bone is found at the ends of a bone and contains tiny marrow-filled chambers that increase the volume and strength of the bone without increasing its mass. **Marrow** is reddish-yellow tissue that produces blood cells and stores fat. A bone is surrounded by an **outer membrane** containing bone-forming cells, blood vessels, and nerves.

A **joint** is a place where two bones come together. There are five kinds of joints. **Fixed joints** found in the skull are immovable. A **pivot joint** allows your neck to **rotate** on its axis. **Ball-and-socket joints** allow your arms to swing in a circle at your shoulders and your legs to swing in a circle at your hips. Your knee and elbow move back and forth on a **hinge joint**. Your hands can slide across your forearms at the wrists and your feet can slide across the bottoms of your legs at the ankles on **sliding joints**.

HB2 Fact Sheet (cont'd)

Any bone can be fractured or dislocated. A **fracture** is a crack or break in a bone. A **dislocation** involves the tearing of ligaments when a bone is torn out of a socket. Both types of injury can be repaired by surgery.

Homework Directions

Refer to the diagram of the skeleton on Journal Sheet #1. Make a chart to describe the location of ten (10) joints, naming the type of joint and the bones that form that joint.

For example:

	joint	type of joint	bones
1.	elbow	hinge	humerus connected to radius/ulna
2.	..	..	..

Assignment due: _____

_____   _____   ____/____/____
Student's Signature   Parent's Signature   Date

18

THE SKELETAL SYSTEM

Work Date: ____/____/____

LESSON OBJECTIVE

Students will identify bones of the axial and appendicular skeleton.

Classroom Activities

On Your Mark!

Prepare for this unit several days in advance of Lesson #1. Dissect clear of muscles, tendon, and ligament as many chicken long bones as needed for group examination; clean and immerse them in strong vinegar for 5–7 days in advance of Lesson #3 to leach out minerals and soften the bone. Change the solution every day. A one molar solution of HCl will work as well or better (e.g., in 3–5 days).

At the start of Lesson #1, display both a model skeleton, if one is available, and the soaking chicken bones. Point out that bones are made of **protein**—like all other body tissues—with extra **minerals** (e.g., **calcium** and **phosporus**) to give them hardness. A mild acid dissolves and "leaches out" the minerals in the bone leaving the soft protein intact. In Lesson #3, students will examine the bones after they have soaked in acid for about a week. Explain that heating dried bones in an oven at high temperatures breaks down the proteins but leaves the hard minerals intact. Proteins together with minerals give bones their strength.

Get Set!

Using the information in the Teacher's Classwork Agenda and Content Notes, give a brief lecture on how paleontologists can tell something from looking at bones about the way an animal is shaped and about how it behaves. Use the example comparison of the gorilla and human pelvis to show how scientists determine whether a fossilized skeleton belonged to a "quadruped" or "biped." Give students a chance to examine the bones of the skeleton. Have them note the "rough" surfaces along the mostly smooth length of the long bones. Muscle tendons attach to these rough regions. Paleontologists can, therefore, deduce the size and strength of an animal from its bone structure by examining the extent of muscle attachments. Ask students to note the function of each of their teeth (e.g., front incisors for cutting, pointed canines and bicuspids for tearing and holding, back molars for grinding). Point out that herbivores (e.g., cows and horses) have molars only, flat teeth for grinding grass straws. Ask: "Do you think you would be able to deduce the diet of an animal by examining its fossilized skeleton?" Answer: Yes, with a little thought and skill. Refer students to their Fact Sheet to identify the major bones of the **axial** and **appendicular skeletons**.

Go!

Give students ample time to complete the activity described in Figure A on Journal Sheet #1. Circulate around the room to make sure that students are correctly identifying each of the individual bones in the diagram. The chart has more spaces than are needed to complete each list.

Materials

model skeleton (if available), chicken long bones, vinegar or one molar HCl, beakers

HB2 Journal Sheet #1

THE SKELETAL SYSTEM

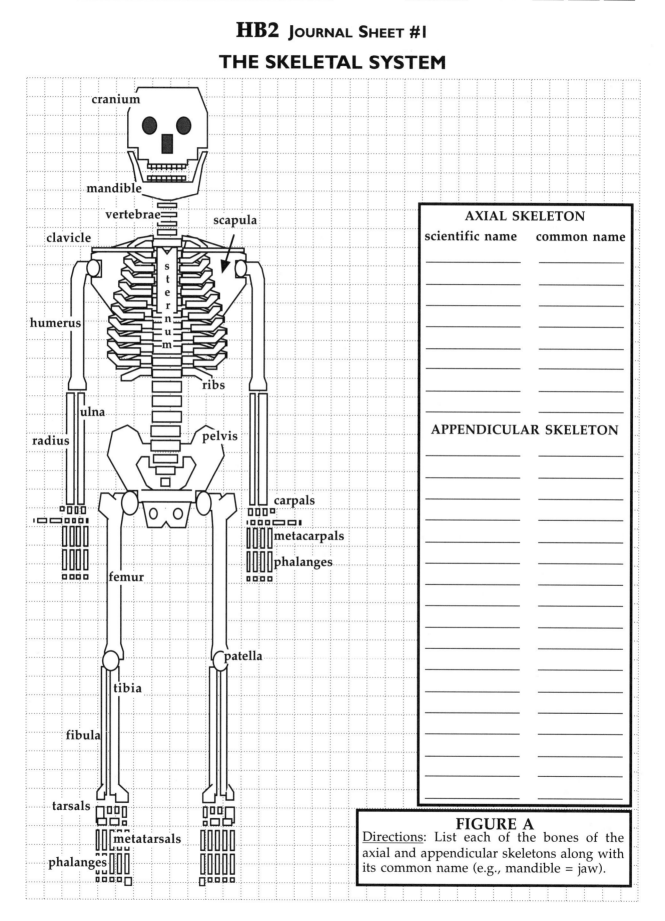

cranium

mandible

vertebrae

clavicle

scapula

sternum

humerus

ribs

ulna

radius

pelvis

carpals

metacarpals

phalanges

femur

patella

tibia

fibula

tarsals

metatarsals

phalanges

AXIAL SKELETON	
scientific name	common name
_____	_____
_____	_____
_____	_____
_____	_____
_____	_____
_____	_____
_____	_____

APPENDICULAR SKELETON	

FIGURE A

Directions: List each of the bones of the axial and appendicular skeletons along with its common name (e.g., mandible = jaw).

THE SKELETAL SYSTEM

Work Date: ____/____/____

LESSON OBJECTIVE

Students will identify different types of joints.

Classroom Activities

On Your Mark!

Begin class by pointing out that bones are joined by **ligaments**. Draw Illustration A on the board and have students copy your drawing on Journal Sheet #2 to identify the anatomy of a typical joint. Ask students if they have ever heard of a condition called "water on the knee." This condition results from a rupture of the **synovial membrane** resulting in the leakage of liquid from the synovial cavity. Ask students to explain any difficulties a person with this condition might encounter. Point out that **synovial fluid** cushions the ends of bones against shock. Explain that **arthritis** is a disease that strikes the joints of millions of people, young and old. Arthritis is an inflammation of the joints brought on by any number of causes and is still being researched in medical laboratories. Arthritis affects the joints, connective tissue, and other supporting tissues. It is a **rheumatic** or **connective tissue disease**.

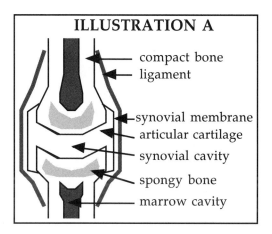

ILLUSTRATION A

- compact bone
- ligament
- synovial membrane
- articular cartilage
- synovial cavity
- spongy bone
- marrow cavity

Get Set!

Refer students to their Fact Sheet in order to identify the different types of joints: **fixed**, **pivot**, **ball-and-socket**, **hinge**, and **sliding joint**. Clarify and demonstrate the direction of movement allowed by the bones at several joints. Define an **extension** as an increase in the angle at a joint (e.g., as in an "extension" of the arm at the elbow joint). Define a **flexion** as a decrease in the angle at a joint (e.g., as in a "flexion" of the arm at the elbow joint). Explain that some people are "double jointed." This term refers to the ability to **hyperextend** or **dislocate** a joint where the ends of the bones are flattened or abnormally formed. Most people are "double jointed" somewhere in their body.

Go!

Give students ample time to complete the activity described in Figure B on Journal Sheet #2. Point out the "fixed joints" of the cranium (e.g., the shadow line) where bones "knit together" soon after birth. Explain that a newborn has a "soft spot" at the top of the cranium for several weeks after birth until these bones become fused.

Materials

model skeleton (if available)

HB2 JOURNAL SHEET #2

THE SKELETAL SYSTEM

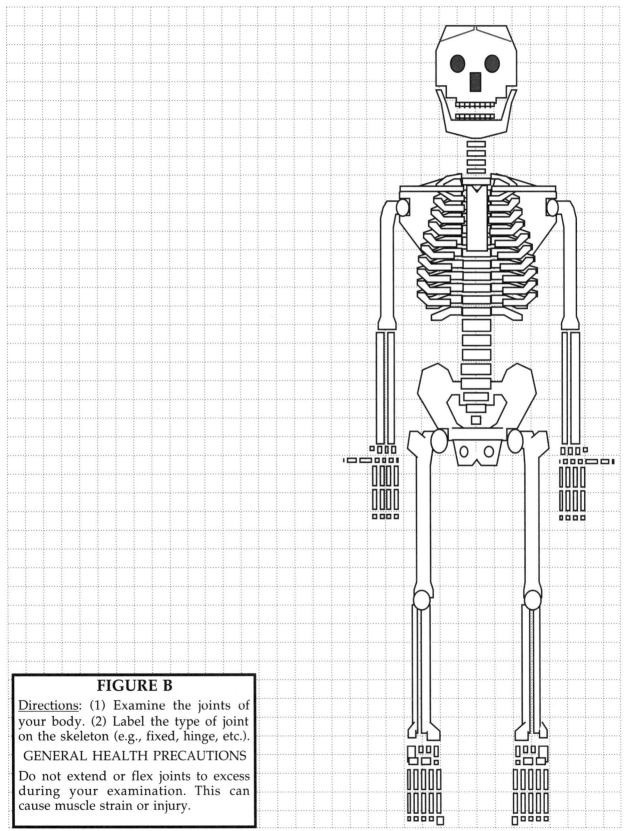

FIGURE B

Directions: (1) Examine the joints of your body. (2) Label the type of joint on the skeleton (e.g., fixed, hinge, etc.).

GENERAL HEALTH PRECAUTIONS

Do not extend or flex joints to excess during your examination. This can cause muscle strain or injury.

THE SKELETAL SYSTEM

Work Date: ____/____/____

LESSON OBJECTIVE

Students will dissect a long bone to examine its internal and external structure.

Classroom Activities

On Your Mark!

Begin by pointing out that bones obviously have different shapes. Bones can be **flat** (e.g., cranial bones), **long** (e.g., arm bones, leg bones, phalanges), **short** (e.g., carpals, metacarpal, tarsals, and metatarsals), **sesamoid** (e.g., patella), or **irregular** (e.g., vertebrae).

Get Set!

Explain that long bones are hollow. Draw Illustration B on the board—omitting labels—and have students copy your drawing on Journal Sheet #3. Have them label the parts of the bone using the Fact Sheet.

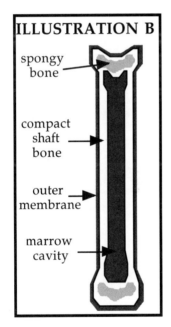

ILLUSTRATION B

spongy bone

compact shaft bone

outer membrane

marrow cavity

Go!

Distribute the long bones that have been soaking in mild acid. Give students ample time to complete the activity described in Figure C on Journal Sheet #3 employing the "Common Sense Health Guidelines" mentioned in the Appendix: Techniques and Tips for Laboratory Dissections.

Materials

preprepared chicken long bones, dissection trays and kits, paper towels, dissecting scope or magnifying glass

HB2 JOURNAL SHEET #3

THE SKELETAL SYSTEM

FIGURE C

<u>Directions for dissecting a chicken long bone</u>: (1) Be sure your bone is washed thoroughly with soap and water, rinsed, and dried. (2) Examine the bone. Why is it soft? Explain your answer in one brief sentence. (3) Use a scissor to cut the bone in half and examine it with a magnifying glass or under a dissecting scope. (4) Draw your observations. (5) Use the scalpel—on soft tissue only—or a scissor to cut off the end of the bone. (6) Examine it with a magnifying glass or under a dissecting scope. (7) Draw your observations.

GENERAL HEALTH PRECAUTIONS

Wear goggles, surgical gloves, and an apron. Exercise standard safety precautions when using the instruments in your dissection kit. Clean up as directed by your instructor.

THE SKELETAL SYSTEM

Work Date: ____/____/____

LESSON OBJECTIVE

Students will lay out an anatomical chart of the human body beginning with the skeletal system.

Classroom Activities

On Your Mark!

Explain to students that they are about to begin a long-term project that will continue for most of their study of Human Biology & Health. When the project is complete they will have constructed a series of lifesize charts with diagrams representing the major organ systems of the human body. Most of the work on this project will be done in class during one period of the week until the project is complete. Give the students the option to do some of the work at home. But stress the point that they will have to bring their materials to class when instructed to do so in order to show the work they have accomplished. Set aside a large cardboard box that can store the rolled-up posters of every student (e.g., like the cubicle box in a poster shop).

Get Set!

Briefly review the major bones of the axial and appendicular skeletons.

Go!

Give students ample time to complete the activity described in Figure D on Journal Sheet #4. Discourage students from designing three-dimensional structures as their project will be difficult to store in the weeks ahead.

Materials

butcher paper, construction paper, scissors, crayon or felt tip markers

HB2 Journal Sheet #4

THE SKELETAL SYSTEM

FIGURE D

THE PROJECT YOU ARE ABOUT TO BEGIN IS A LONG-TERM PROJECT.
MAKE ARRANGEMENTS TO KEEP YOUR POSTER IN A SECURE PLACE AS YOU WILL NEED
TO WORK ON IT AT LEAST ONCE A WEEK UNTIL IT IS COMPLETE.

Directions: (1) Lay on the floor the large piece of butcher paper given to you by your instructor. (2) Lie down on the paper flat on your back, hands at your sides, and have a classmate trace your body on the paper. (3) Use the materials provided by your instructor to draw pictures of the individual bones of the body so that they can be placed in their proper positions on the butcher paper diagram. (4) Use small sections of tape no more than a centimeter in length to secure the paper parts. DO NOT SECURE THEM PERMANENTLY! You may have to change their position slightly to add additional structures later on during the course of this activity. (5) Roll up the chart neatly and wrap it with a rubber band before securing it in the box provided by your instructor. (6) Use this Journal Sheet to record any tasks you might need to accomplish at home to enhance the look of this project.

Name: _____   **Period:** _____   **Date:** ____/____/____

HB2 REVIEW QUIZ

Directions: Keep your eyes on your own work.
Read all directions and questions carefully.
THINK BEFORE YOU ANSWER!
Watch your spelling, be neat, and do the best you can.

TEACHER'S COMMENTS: _____
_____

THE SKELETAL SYSTEM

TRUE–FALSE FILL-IN: If the statement is true, write the word TRUE. If the statement is false, change the underlined word to make the statement true. *10 points*

_____ 1. The human skeleton has about <u>500</u> bones.

_____ 2. The <u>axial</u> skeleton includes the arms and legs.

_____ 3. The <u>appendicular</u> skeleton includes the skull and ribs.

_____ 4. Bones are held together by <u>ligaments</u>.

_____ 5. <u>Tendons</u> connect muscle to the bone.

_____ 6. Bones <u>do not</u> contain nerves and blood vessels.

_____ 7. The elements that give bone their hardness can best be found in foods such as <u>meat</u> products and vegetables.

_____ 8. Putting a bone in weak acid will dissolve its minerals and leave soft <u>carbohydrates</u>.

_____ 9. Heating a bone in a hot oven will remove the soft tissue and leave the hard <u>minerals</u>.

_____ 10. Soft bone having less calcium than hard bone is called <u>cartilage</u>.

MATCHING: Choose the letter of the word or phrase that best describes each type of joint. *10 points*

_____ 11. hinge joint   (A) immovable

_____ 12. ball-and-socket joint   (B) swing around in a circle

_____ 13. pivot joint   (C) back and forth

_____ 14. fixed joint   (D) slips across

_____ 15. sliding joint   (E) rotates on an axis

PROBLEM

Directions: Name the bones indicated by filling in the blanks. *10 points*

16. _____

17. _____

18. _____

19. _____

20. _____

21. _____

22. _____

23. _____

24. _____

25. _____

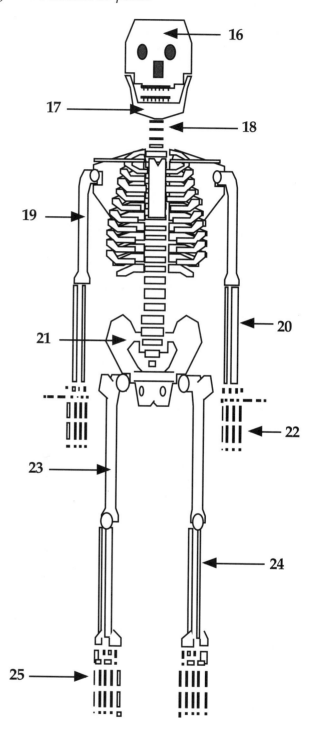

_____   _____   ___/___/___
   Student's Signature   Parent's Signature   Date

THE MUSCULAR SYSTEM

TEACHER'S CLASSWORK AGENDA AND CONTENT NOTES

Classwork Agenda for the Week

1. Students will examine major muscles of the skeleton to identify the movements they control.

2. Students will begin the dissection of a chicken wing to identify tissues associated with muscles.

3. Students will complete the dissection of a chicken wing and compare the muscle bundles present to those in a human arm.

4. Students will illustrate the major muscles of the torso and appendages to be added to the human body chart project.

Content Notes for Lecture and Discussion

Two of the most important activities performed by living things are the ability to **sense** and **move**. In ancient times philosophers such as the Greek physician **Galen** (b. 129; d. 200) debated the origins of **sensibility** (e.g., sensation) and **irritability** (e.g., movement). The two concepts raised issues in the debate over the origins of consciousness. Is an organism's irritability (e.g., its capacity to respond to environmental stimuli) preceded by the perception of that stimuli (e.g., consciousness)? Or can an organism respond without prior sensibility of a stimulus? Philosophers were aware of the "involuntary" actions of the heart and digestive tract but believed those actions to be derived from the sensibilities of "the soul." In 1752, the Swiss physiologist **Albrecht von Haller** (b. 1708; d. 1777) examined the problem using laboratory animals. In his book entitled *A Dissertation on the Sensible and Irritable Parts of Animals* he suggested that the nervous system was the site of sensibility and dependent upon the actions of "the soul." Irritability was the product of muscular contraction resulting from a direct stimulus applied to a muscle. In 1786, the Italian physiologist **Luigi Galvani** (b. 1737; d. 1798) discovered that touching a piece of metal during a lightning storm to a frog's leg dissected free of the animal itself caused the leg to twitch and flex. This demonstration supported the notion that muscular action could be free of the "sensible" aspects of an organism. The overall controversy is evident in the unresolved "mind-body duality problem" which still exists today in the field of philosophy. Since the start of the 19th century following the acceptance of cell theory, however, irritability has been considered an attribute of all living things regardless of their sensibility. Contractility is an attribute specific to muscle fiber and bundles.

Following Galvani's discovery, physiologists searched for the mechanisms responsible for muscular contraction. By the end of the 19th century the principles of reflex action had been elucidated by the English neurophysiologist **Charles Robert Sherrington** (b. 1857; d. 1952). Sherrington discovered that all muscle fibers were the targets of as many nerve fibers: a typical muscle bundle containing nearly as many "sensory nerves" as "motor nerves." Sensory nerve fibers relay the status of muscle contraction to sites in the brain which Sherrington also identified. Sherrington demonstrated that when a muscle is activated, its "antagonist" is inhibited. The theory became known as **Sherrington's Law of Reciprocal Innervation**. The contraction of a muscle fiber is initiated by the release of a **chemical neurotransmitter** (e.g., acetylcholine) which alters the ionic imbalance existing across a muscle cell membrane. The electrical potential across the cell membrane is "depolarized" causing the proteins actin and myosin to alter shape and contract the fiber.

The vertebrate muscle system is grouped into *somatic* and *visceral* muscles. **Somatic muscles** are muscles of the trunk and appendages that control the voluntary and reflexive (e.g., spinal reflex) movement of the skeleton. **Visceral muscles** are the muscles of the digestive tract under the automatic control of the **autonomic nervous system**. The actions of the latter will be discussed in other applicable units of this text. As Sherrington found, the somatic muscles of the skeleton are arranged in pairs, one muscle countering or reversing the action of its antagonist. For example: the bicep is the antagonist of the tricep. Skeletal muscles are the force behind the "lever action" of the bones: each bone attached by tendons to **flexors** that decrease the angle at a given joint and **extensors** that increases it.

In Lesson #1, students will examine major muscles of the skeleton to identify the movements they control.

In Lesson #2, students will begin the dissection of a chicken wing to identify tissues associated with muscles.

In Lesson #3, students will complete the dissection of a chicken wing and compare the muscle bundles present to those in a human arm.

In Lesson #4, students will illustrate the major muscles of the torso and appendages to be added to the human body chart project.

ANSWERS TO THE HOMEWORK PROBLEMS

Students' charts will vary but should demonstrate their understanding of the relationships between a number of skeletal muscles and their antagonists.

ANSWERS TO THE END-OF-THE-WEEK REVIEW QUIZ

1. muscle	6. lactic	11. true	16. C
2. nerves	7. reflex	12. true	17. E
3. bundles	8. true	13. cardiac	18. B
4. true	9. true	14. visceral/involuntary	19. A
5. too little	10. true	15. diaphragm	20. D

DIAGRAM: The shadow lines illustrate the general manner in which each muscle can be connected to the bones in order to counter the action of its antagonist in causing a flexion or extension at the joint. Students' drawings should reflect their understanding that muscles can only contract (e.g., become shorter).

DIAGRAM: The shadow lines illustrate one way that muscles can be connected to the vertebrae in order to cause its rotation. Students' drawings should reflect their understanding that muscles can only contract (e.g., become shorter).

HB3 FACT SHEET

THE MUSCULAR SYSTEM

CLASSWORK AGENDA FOR THE WEEK

(1) Examine major muscles of the skeleton to identify the movements they control.
(2) Begin the dissection of a chicken wing to identify tissues associated with muscles.
(3) Complete the dissection of a chicken wing and compare the muscle bundles present to those in a human arm.
(4) Illustrate the major muscles of the torso and appendages to be added to the human body chart project.

   Muscle cells are the only cells in the body that have the unique ability to contract. A muscle cell contains two proteins called **actin** and **myosin**. Actin and myosin change shape under the appropriate chemical conditions. The chemical conditions that cause muscle cells to contract, then relax, are created by the nerves that control muscles. When a nerve directs a muscle cell to contract the cell shortens along its entire length, then relaxes. Many muscle cells form **muscle fibers** that group together into **muscle bundles**. Nerves can cause some or all of the muscle fibers in a muscle bundle to contract so that the muscle can do work. When you tighten a muscle such as the **bicep** (e.g., flexor of the arm) more than a million muscle fibers are contracting and relaxing every millisecond to keep the muscle in a tight bundle. Muscles require a lot of oxygen to do their work and lack of oxygen from overwork (e.g., oxygen debt) causes lactic acid to build up in muscle cells. The build up of lactic acid in muscle cells causes muscle fibers to contract or "cramp" uncontrollably.

   There are two major categories of muscles: *voluntary* and *involuntary* muscles. All **voluntary muscles** are under "conscious" control. That is, you can cause voluntary muscles to contract simply by thinking about it. Voluntary muscles are connected to the bones of the skeleton by **tendons** and cause bones to change position around a joint. All voluntary muscles work in pairs, one muscle opposing another. When one muscle contracts the other relaxes. This allows you to flex or extend an arm or leg, rotate your head, make funny faces, or tighten the muscles of your **torso** (e.g., trunk of the body excluding the arms, legs, head and neck). **Involuntary muscles** are not under conscious control. That is, they are controlled by a part of the brain that works automatically to keep your heart beating and food moving through your digestive tract. Voluntary muscles are also referred to as **skeletal muscles**. The muscles of the heart are called **cardiac muscles**. The muscles of the digestive tract are called smooth or **visceral muscles**.

   A few muscles are under both voluntary and "reflexive" control. The muscles of the **diaphragm**—which helps the chest cavity to expand and contract as you breathe—is controlled by the automatic parts of the brain. However, you can consciously cause your diaphragm to contract when you blow air out of your lungs. You can also stop the diaphragm from working and hold your breath. After a few moments, however, your brain will force you to start breathing again.

   The tearing of muscle fibers during vigorous activity is called a **sprain.** Sprains are the most common type of muscle injury. Less common injuries include the tearing of tendons which in many cases must be repaired by surgery.

Homework Directions

Refer to the diagram of the muscles on Journal Sheet #1. Make a chart to describe the location of ten (10) joints, naming the muscles that cause flexion and extension at that joint.

For example:

	joint	flexor	extensor
1.	elbow	bicep	tricep
2.	..	..	..

Assignment due: _____

_____   _____   ____/____/____
Student's Signature   Parent's Signature   Date

THE MUSCULAR SYSTEM

Work Date: ____/____/____

LESSON OBJECTIVE

Students will examine major muscles of the skeleton to identify the movements they control.

Classroom Activities

On Your Mark!

Perform the following demonstration of a simple "knee-jerk reflex." (1) Ask a student volunteer to sit on a chair in front of the class. (2) Have the student cross legs so that the top leg hangs down loosely, able to swing freely at the knee joint. (3) Instruct the student to relax the muscles of the leg. (4) Gently tap the tendon just below the patella with a rubberheaded mallet or the handle of a screwdriver to show how the foot kicks forward. Point out that this simple reflex is tested by physicians during thousands of medical exams everyday. Draw Illustration A on the board and have students copy your drawing on Journal Sheet #1. Explain that **sensory nerves** in the shin muscle (e.g., tibialis anterior) relay information to the spinal cord that the muscle is being stretched. The spinal cord relays information back to the muscle on top of the thigh (e.g., rectus femoris) to extend the knee. Ask the volunteer to place the palm of the hand under the bottom of the thigh and prevent the knee reflex from occurring as you tap. Ask the student to report what happened to the muscle on the underside of the thigh when he or she prepared to stop the reflex. The report will be that the muscle (e.g., biceps femoris) along with other leg muscles tightened.

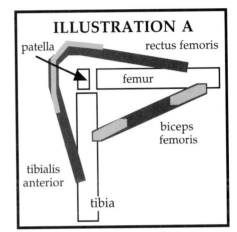

ILLUSTRATION A

patella
rectus femoris
femur
biceps femoris
tibialis anterior
tibia

Get Set!

Explain the concept of **antagonistic muscles** and explain the **law of reciprocal innervation** discovered by English neurophysiologist **Charles Robert Sherrington** (b. 1857; d. 1952) as described in the Teacher's Classwork Agenda and Contents Notes. Give students several minutes to quietly read their Fact Sheet before orally quizzing them on their understanding of the difference between **voluntary** and **involuntary muscles**.

Go!

Give students ample time to complete the activity described in Figure A on Journal Sheet #1. Reiterate the directions to "gently palpate" or probe each muscle to identify its approximate location. Circulate around the room to make sure that students are identifying each of the individual muscles shown in the diagram. Make sure they are clear about the difference between a **flexion** and an **extension**.

Materials

rubberheaded mallet or screwdriver

HB3 JOURNAL SHEET #1

THE MUSCULAR SYSTEM

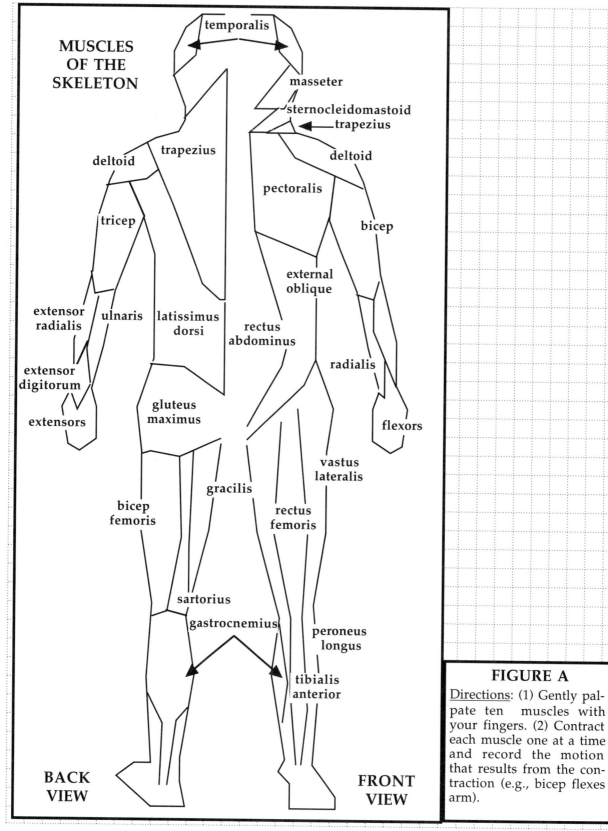

MUSCLES OF THE SKELETON

temporalis
masseter
sternocleidomastoid
trapezius
trapezius
deltoid
deltoid
pectoralis
tricep
bicep
external oblique
extensor radialis
ulnaris
latissimus dorsi
rectus abdominus
radialis
extensor digitorum
gluteus maximus
flexors
extensors
vastus lateralis
bicep femoris
gracilis
rectus femoris
sartorius
gastrocnemius
peroneus longus
tibialis anterior

BACK VIEW

FRONT VIEW

FIGURE A

Directions: (1) Gently palpate ten muscles with your fingers. (2) Contract each muscle one at a time and record the motion that results from the contraction (e.g., bicep flexes arm).

THE MUSCULAR SYSTEM

Work Date: ____/____/____

LESSON OBJECTIVE

Students will begin the dissection of a chicken wing to identify tissues associated with muscles.

Classroom Activities

On Your Mark!

Display a model human skeleton if available and/or draw the bottom illustration appearing on Journal Sheet #2 on the board. Using the skeleton and/or drawing, compare and contrast the bones of the human arm to that of a chicken wing. Point out that the arrangement of the bones (e.g., humerus, radius, ulna, carpals, metacarpals, and phalanges) are essentially the same in both animals although the size and shape of individual bones is different. The arm of a person and the wing of a bird are **homologous structures**. That is, they have the same embryological origin, albeit different functions.

Get Set!

Go over the use of dissection tools and common sense health guidelines mentioned in the *Appendix: Techniques and Tips For Laboratory Dissections*. Preview the dissection procedure described in Figure B on Journal Sheet #2, so that students are clear on the proper way to use the T-pins, scissors, and scalpel. Explain that the dissection to be done in this lesson is a superficial examination of the muscles and connective tissues of the chicken wing. In Lesson #3, students will do a more thorough dissection to analyze the connections of muscles to bones and bones joints.

Go!

Distribute the chicken wings. Instruct students to take turns doing the dissection. Only one person at a time should handle dissection tools. Others should observe until it is their turn. Give students ample time to complete the activity described in Figure B on Journal Sheet #2. Circulate around the room to make sure students are employing appropriate dissection techniques while observers make drawings as directed. Make sure students add alcohol to their ziplock® baggies before placing them in a tray that can be refrigerated until Lesson #3.

Materials

chicken wings, ethyl or isopropyl (e.g., rubbing) alcohol, ziplock® baggies, dissection trays and kits, paper towels, refrigerator

HB3 JOURNAL SHEET #2

THE MUSCULAR SYSTEM

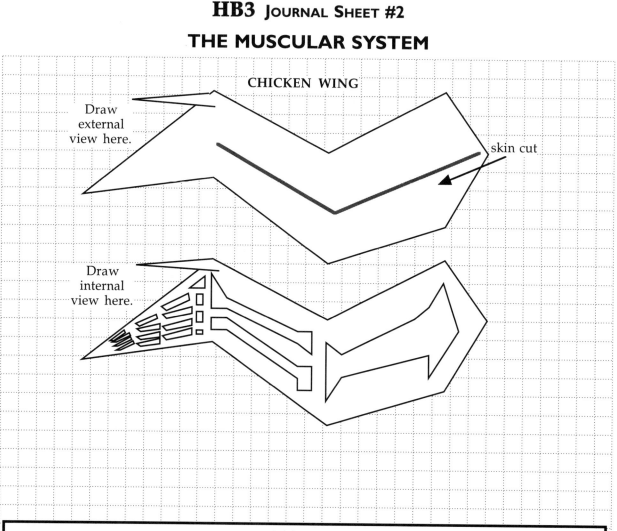

CHICKEN WING

Draw external view here.

skin cut

Draw internal view here.

FIGURE B

<u>Directions for dissecting a chicken wing</u>: (1) Wash the wing thoroughly with soap and water. Rinse and dry it. (2) Examine the wing to identify the **dorsal** (e.g., top or back) and **ventral** (e.g., bottom or front) sides. The dorsal side is covered by a thick layer of "goose-pimpled" skin. There may be a small feather or two sticking out of the skin. The skin on the ventral side is nearly transparent. You can see muscles and blood vessels running under the skin. (3) Place the wing in the dissecting tray with the ventral side facing up. (4) Secure the wing with T-pins as directed by your instructor, pinning the specimen down at the "hand" and "upper arm". (5) Draw the details of this view in the schematic diagram above. (6) Use forceps and a scissor to hold and cut the skin along the midline of the wing as shown in the top diagram. (7) Hold one of the skin flaps with forceps and gently lift it away from the underlying muscles. Hold a scalpel with the sharp edge facing up and—with a sideways scraping motion—clear away the connective tissue attaching the skin to the muscle. As you scrape back the connective tissue the skin flap will pull up easily from the top of the humerus to the wrist. Perform the same operation on the other skin flap before pinning both flaps back with T-pins. (8) Draw the details of the internal view in the schematic diagram above. (9) Use the names of the muscles in the diagram of human muscles on Journal Sheet #1 to name the muscles of this chicken appendage. (10) When you complete this phase of the dissection, remove the insect pins and place the wing in a ziplock® baggie. Add 30-40 ml of alcohol to the baggie before sealing it. (11) Clean all dissecting tools as instructed.

GENERAL HEALTH PRECAUTIONS

Wear goggles, surgical gloves, and an apron. Exercise standard safety precautions when using the instruments in your dissection kit.

THE MUSCULAR SYSTEM

Work Date: ____/____/____

LESSON OBJECTIVE

Students will complete the dissection of a chicken wing and compare the muscle bundles present to those in a human arm.

Classroom Activities

On Your Mark!

Review the use of dissection tools and common sense health guidelines mentioned in the *Appendix: Techniques and Tips For Laboratory Dissections.*

Get Set!

Go over the dissection procedure described in Figure C on Journal Sheet #3, so that students are clear on the proper way to use the dissection tools. Explain that you will be circulating around the room and asking questions as they separate and examine different muscles of the chicken arm. They should be able to compare two or three of the muscles in the wing to those present in a human arm. They can refer to the drawing they made in Lesson #2 or explain their observations by direct examination of their dissected specimen.

Go!

Distribute the chicken wings. Instruct students to take turns doing the dissection. Only one person at a time should handle dissection tools. Others should observe until it is their turn. Give students ample time to complete the activity described in Figure C on Journal Sheet #3. Circulate around the room to make sure students are employing appropriate dissection techniques. Quiz groups on their knowledge of the muscles and bones of the chicken wing and human arm. When the dissection is completed discard the chicken remains according to district biohazard guidelines.

Materials

chicken wings from Lesson #2 preserved in ethyl or isopropyl (e.g., rubbing) alcohol, dissection trays and kits, paper towels

HB3 Journal Sheet #3

THE MUSCULAR SYSTEM

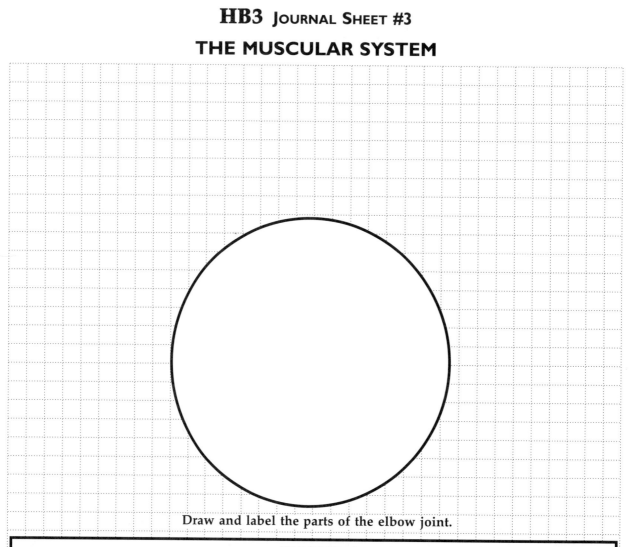

Draw and label the parts of the elbow joint.

FIGURE C

Directions for dissecting a chicken wing: (1) Remove the wing from the baggie and wash it thoroughly with soap and water. Rinse and dry it. (2) Place the wing in the dissecting tray with the ventral side facing up. (3) Secure the wing and skin flaps with T-pins as directed by your instructor. (4) Use forceps and a wooden/plastic probe to separate muscles from one another. Leave them attached to the bones. Each muscle bundle is "wrapped" in a sheath of clear tissue and connected to a bone or another muscle by "fibrous white" tendons. (5) Examine the red blood vessels and yellow or white nerves supplying these muscles. Blood vessels and nerves are usually found running alongside long bones. (6) Examine the muscle bundles one at a time and discuss with your groupmates the movement you think would occur if a particular muscle contracted. Can you identify the antagonist of that muscle? (7) Use scissors to cut the tendons and forceps to remove the muscles. Place the muscles off to the side in the tray. (8) Identify the bones of the upper and lower arms and examine the smooth white ligaments connecting the bones. (9) Use scissors to cut through the ligaments of the elbow joint and examine the ends of the bones joined together at the synovial cavity. (10) Make a drawing of the dissected joint. (11) When you complete the dissection and drawing of the joint remove the insect pins and wrap the remains of the wing in a paper towel before placing it in a ziplock® baggie. (12) Clean all dissecting tools and discard the tissue remains as instructed.

GENERAL HEALTH PRECAUTIONS

Wear goggles, surgical gloves, and an apron. Exercise standard safety precautions when using the instruments in your dissection kit.

THE MUSCULAR SYSTEM

Work Date: ____/____/____

LESSON OBJECTIVE

Students will illustrate the major muscles of the torso and appendages to be added to the human body chart project.

Classroom Activities

On Your Mark!

Review the positions and names of the muscles illustrated in the diagram on Journal Sheet #1. Explain to students that they will continue the long-term project begun in the previous unit.

Get Set!

Distribute posters and art materials.

Go!

Give students ample time to complete the activity described in Figure D on Journal Sheet #4. Discourage students from designing three-dimensional structures as their project will be difficult to store in the weeks ahead.

Materials

butcher paper, construction paper, scissors, crayon or felt tip markers

HB3 JOURNAL SHEET #4

THE MUSCULAR SYSTEM

FIGURE D

<u>Directions</u>: (1) Continue working on your HUMAN BODY CHART. (2) Use the materials provided by your instructor to draw pictures of the individual muscles of the body so that they can be placed in their proper positions, connected to the appropriate bones on the butcher paper diagram. You will need to lift the ribs and vertebrae and some of the bones of the appendages to position the muscles of the dorsal (e.g., back) side of the body. (3) Use small sections of tape <u>no more than a centimeter in length</u> to secure the paper parts. DO NOT SECURE THEM PERMANENTLY! You may have to change their position slightly to add additional structures later on during the course of this activity. (4) Roll up the chart neatly and wrap it with a rubber band before securing it in the box provided by your instructor. (5) Use this Journal Sheet to record any tasks you might need to accomplish at home to enhance the look of this project.

HB3 Review Quiz

Directions: Keep your eyes on your own work.
Read all directions and questions carefully.
THINK BEFORE YOU ANSWER!
Watch your spelling, be neat, and do the best you can.

CLASSWORK	(~40): _____
HOMEWORK	(~20): _____
CURRENT EVENT	(~10): _____
TEST	(~30): _____
TOTAL	(~100): _____

(A ≥ 90, B ≥ 80, C ≥ 70, D ≥ 60, F < 60)

LETTER GRADE: _____

TEACHER'S COMMENTS: _____

_____

THE MUSCULAR SYSTEM

TRUE–FALSE FILL-IN: If the statement is true, write the word TRUE. If the statement is false, change the underlined word to make the statement true. *15 points*

_____ 1. <u>All</u> cells contains two proteins called actin and myosin.

_____ 2. The chemical conditions that cause muscle cells to contract are created by <u>other muscles</u>.

_____ 3. Muscle fibers group together into muscle <u>cells</u>.

_____ 4. Muscles require a lot of <u>oxygen</u> to do their work.

_____ 5. Oxygen debt is the result of <u>too much</u> oxygen in muscle cells.

_____ 6. The acid that builds up in tired muscles is called <u>sulfuric</u> acid.

_____ 7. The automatic contraction of a muscle is called a <u>seizure</u>.

_____ 8. All <u>voluntary</u> muscles are under conscious control.

_____ 9. Voluntary muscles are connected to the bones of the skeleton by <u>tendons</u>.

_____ 10. <u>All</u> voluntary muscles work in pairs, one muscle opposing another.

_____ 11. <u>Involuntary</u> muscles are not under conscious control.

_____ 12. Voluntary muscles are also referred to as <u>skeletal</u> muscles.

_____ 13. The muscles of the heart are called <u>visceral</u> muscles.

_____ 14. The muscles of the digestive tract are called smooth or <u>cardiac</u> muscles.

_____ 15. One of the muscles that is under both voluntary and "reflexive" control is the <u>heart</u>.

HB3 Review Quiz *(cont'd)*

MATCHING: Choose the letter of the contracting muscle on the right that will cause the consequence described on the left. *10 points*

_____	16. bend elbow	(A)	masseter
_____	17. elevate chin	(B)	rectus femorus
_____	18. raise knee	(C)	bicep
_____	19. clench jaw	(D)	gastrocnemius
_____	20. point toes	(E)	trapezius

DIAGRAM: Draw two muscles connected to the two long bones (e.g., solid rectangles) to show how flexion and extension can occur at the joint (e.g., space between the rectangles). *2 points*

DIAGRAM: Draw two muscles connected to the vertebrae (e.g., circle) and collar bones (e.g., solid rectangles) to show how the neck rotates. NOTE: This is a view from the top of the head. *3 points*

NUTRITION AND THE DIGESTIVE SYSTEM

TEACHER'S CLASSWORK AGENDA AND CONTENT NOTES

Classwork Agenda for the Week

1. Students will identify major organs of the digestive system and set up a daily chart record of the foods they will eat this week.

2. Students will test food samples for the presence of protein and starch.

3. Students will convert starch to simple sugar.

4. Students will illustrate the major organs of the digestive system to be added to the human body chart project.

Content Notes for Lecture and Discussion

Dietary theories began with the Greek authorities **Hippocrates** (b. 460 B.C.; d. 377 B.C.) and **Galen** (b. 129; d. 200). Their teachings comprised the first documented guides to physicians on the use of food to conserve health and fight disease. Hippocrates taught that all habits, including eating and drinking habits, were to be exercised with moderation. Patients were instructed to expose themselves to the freshness of the air, to exercise, and let nature take its course in balancing the body "humours." Galen adopted Hippocrates's ideas and began classifying food according to its physical qualities such as temperature and moistness. This was consistent with the notion that the health of the body was determined by the flow of the body's humoral fluids. An imbalance of these fluids—phlegm, blood, choler, and yellow bile—were used to describe the resulting states of illness. In the 16th century, Galen's ideas were challenged by the work of the Belgian physician **Andreas Vesalius** (b. 1514; d. 1564) whose anatomical studies published in 1543 contradicted Galen's grasp of anatomy. In 1628, the English physician **William Harvey** (b. 1578; d. 1657) demonstrated how the heart and blood vessels circulated blood throughout the body which allowed physicians to discard the humoral hypothesis altogether.

With the advancement of the science of chemistry in the 18th and 19th centuries the physiology of digestion became the emphasis of dietary research allowing scientists the opportunity to view dietary laws in light of food substances involved in the body's **metabolism**. The Swiss physiologist **Albrecht von Haller** (b. 1708; d. 1777) discovered bile to be the chemical agent responsible for the digestion of fats. The French naturalist **René de Réaumur** (b. 1683; d. 1757) demonstrated the effects of gastric juices on food. The young American physiologist **John R. Young** (b. 1782; d. 1804) discovered that saliva and gastric juices were released simultaneously with the introduction of food into the mouth. The English chemist **William Prout** (b. 1785; d. 1850)—for whom the proton is named—identified the active ingredient in gastric juice to be hydrochloric acid. The most classic study of digestion was performed in 1822–23 by the American army surgeon **William Beaumont** (b. 1785; d 1853). One of his patients, an animal trapper, was shot in the stomach and treated by Beaumont. The muscles of the patient's abdominal wall did not heal properly, leaving a gastric fistula leading to the lumen of the stomach. Beaumont was able to observe the actions of the stomach and its juices on food either swallowed or placed directly into the organ. In 1833, he published his *Experiments and Observations on the Gastric Juice and Physiology of Digestion* describing the results of these and other observations. The German chemist **Justus von Liebig** (b. 1803; d. 1873) examined excreted products like urea and carbon dioxide in relation to ingested proteins and plant sugar. The French physiologist **Claude Bernard** (b. 1813; d. 1878) demonstrated the functions of the pancreas and showed how the liver broke down foods in the synthesis of glycogen. Bernard is considered the "father of experimental medicine." The importance of amino acids as the building blocks of proteins was demonstrated by the American nutritionist and biochemist **Elmer Verner McCollum** (b. 1879; d. 1967). McCollum also elucidated the role of fats, vitamins, and minerals present in the diet of animals.

The role of vitamins and minerals is largely an enzymatic one. Both serve as "coenzymes" or "cofactors" in the regulation of chemical reactions involved in growth and normal body functioning. **Vitamin A** (a.k.a., retinol) maintains healthy eyes, skin, and the linings of the digestive tract. **Vitamin D** (a.k.a., cholecalciferol) maintains healthy bones. Vitamin D deficiency results in poorly formed bones, a condition called "rickets." **Vitamin E** (a.k.a., alpha-tocopherol) protects cells from damage by oxygen. Vitamin E deficiency results in the degeneration of nerve and muscle tissue. **Vitamin K** promotes healthy blood clotting. **Vitamin A**, **D**, **E**, and **K** are "fat soluble" vitamins stored in fat tissue. **Vitamins B complex** and **Vitamin C** are "water soluble" vitamins that cannot be stored in the body. **Vitamin B complex** consists of several related vitamins needed for general health maintenance. Excess vitamins C and vitamin B complex are washed out of the body and must be ingested on a daily basis. **Vitamin C** is needed for the production of the body's energy reserves (e.g., tricarboxylic acid or Kreb's Cycle). Vitamin C deficiency results in "scurvy." Symptoms of scurvy include bleeding gums, swollen joints, skin bruises, and overall weakness. **Minerals** like the ions of **sodium**, **chlorine**, **calcium**, and **iodine** are also needed for the maintenance of a healthy body. Like vitamins, minerals help regulate **cellular metabolism**.

In Lesson #1, students will identify major organs of the digestive system and set up a daily chart record of the foods they will eat this week.

In Lesson #2, students will test food samples for the presence of protein and starch.

In Lesson #3, students will convert starch to simple sugar.

In Lesson #4, students will illustrate the major organs of the digestive system to be added to the human body chart project.

ANSWERS TO THE HOMEWORK PROBLEMS

Student charts will vary but should demonstrate their ability to keep accurate records for a period of several days and an attempt to relate the data gathered to the information presented in the *Recommended Daily Allowance Chart of Nutrients* on Journal #1.

ANSWERS TO THE END-OF-THE-WEEK REVIEW QUIZ

1. digestion	11. true	21. complete
2. mouth	12. true	22. incomplete
3. saliva/the mouth	13. small	23. B
4. true	14. rectum	24. E
5. true	15. anus	25. A
6. peristalsis/muscles	16. true	26. C
7. stomach	17. true	27. G
8. true	18. carbohydrates	28. F
9. liver	19. fats	29. D
10. true	20. proteins	30. H

HB4 FACT SHEET

NUTRITION AND THE DIGESTIVE SYSTEM

CLASSWORK AGENDA FOR THE WEEK

(1) Identify major organs of the digestive system and set up a daily chart record of the foods you will eat this week.
(2) Test food samples for the presence of protein and starch.
(3) Convert starch to simple sugar.
(4) Illustrate the major organs of the digestive system to be added to the human body chart project.

A healthy diet is essential to a healthy life. The Greek physician **Hippocrates** (b. 460 B.C.; d. 377 B.C.) was aware of the need to eat healthy foods to maintain good health. The word "diet" comes from the Greek work *diaita* meaning "way of life." The body needs a balanced diet of proper nutrients to carry on metabolic activity and to grow healthy cells and tissues. **Nutrients** are the usable substances in food that help us to accomplish these important functions. The six nutrients required by all living things—including humans—are *carbohydrates, fats, proteins, vitamins, minerals,* and *water.*

Carbohydrates are a primary source of energy. Carbohydrates (e.g., sugars and starches) are found in fruits, vegetables, and grain products. Plants produce sugar during photosynthesis. Starches are complex chains of sugar molecules that comprise the cell walls of plant cells. When we eat plants those starches are broken down into simple sugars during digestion. During respiration we "burn" sugar molecules to release their stored energy. Energy from respiration gives the cell the power to do work. There are about four calories of energy in one gram of carbohydrate. One "small" **calorie** is the energy needed to raise the temperature of one gram of water one degree Celsius. One **Food Calorie** is equal to 1,000 "small" calories. **Fats** insulate and protect body organs and make up cell membranes. Fats are also a secondary source of energy. Fats are found in nuts, butter, cheese, and meat. **Proteins** are the "building blocks" of life. They are made of long **amino acid** chains that are linked together according to the instructions of **DNA** molecules (e.g., genes and chromosomes). Proteins make up the structure of our skin, hair, muscle tissue, and more. There are eight essential amino acids found in food. Red meat, fish, poultry, dairy products, and eggs are sources of **complete proteins** that contain all the necessary amino acids. Plants such as rice, cereal, and vegetables are **incomplete proteins** that are missing one or more of the essential amino acids. Proteins are broken down into their individual amino acids by digestion before the cells of the body can put them to good use. Proteins can also be burned for their energy if carbohydrates and fats are unavailable. One gram of protein releases approximately four calories of energy. **Vitamins** are "coenzymes" that regulate the chemical reactions involved in growth and normal body functioning. **Minerals** such as the ions of sodium, chlorine, calcium, and iodine are also needed for the maintenance of a healthy body. Like vitamins, minerals help regulate cellular metabolism. **Water** provides the "medium" in which all the body's chemical reactions can take place. That is why water is so essential for life. The blood plasma that carries nutrients to the body's individual cells is 92% water. Because water stores heat energy better than most other substances it helps the body to maintain a regular temperature of about 98.6° Fahrenheit (e.g., 37° Celsius).

Digestion is the process of breaking down food into simple nutrients. Foods are broken down by the physical action of the teeth and muscles of the digestive tract. This physical action is called **mechanical digestion**. Food is also broken down by enzymes. **Enzymes** are molecules that speed up chemical reactions that would normally take hours or days to occur on their own. This is called **chemical digestion**.

Both mechanical and chemical digestion begin in the **mouth**. **Salivary glands** release **saliva** containing the enzyme **ptyalin** as the **teeth** tear, crush, and grind food so that it can be swallowed. Ptyalin breaks down **starches** into simple **sugars**. Food then enters a tube called the **esophagus** that transports it to the **stomach**. The cells lining the stomach release **gastric juices** including **hydrochloric acid** and **pepsin**. Pepsin is an enzyme that breaks down proteins into amino acids. A rhythmic muscular contraction of the muscles of the digestive tract called **peristalsis** moves the food through the entire digestive system. Food moves from the stomach into the **small intestine**. Peristalsis pushes food through the small intestine as it is digested by both mechanical and chemical action. Three organs attached to the small intestine supply it with **intestinal juices** that help break down food. One of the many functions of the **liver** is to break down worn out **red blood cells** to produce **bile**. Bile is made of a chemical molecule called **cholesterol** that aids in the digestion of fats. Bile is stored in the **gall bladder**. The **pancreas** releases **pancreatic juices** which break down proteins, starches, and fats. By the time food reaches the end of the small intestine it is ready to be absorbed into the bloodstream. Nutrients are absorbed into the blood through microscopic structures called **villi**. Villi are shaped like tiny fingers sticking out of the intestinal wall. Inside each **villus** are microscopic blood vessels that absorb the simple nutrients our cells need to do their work. Excess water and undigested substances leave the small intestine and move into the **large intestine**. There they are prepared for excretion. Waste products are stored in the **rectum** and eliminated from the body by the muscles of the **anus**.

Homework Directions

Make a chart of the foods you eat each day during the course of the week. With the help of the chart on Journal Sheet #1 (e.g., *Recommended Daily Allowance of Nutrients*) list the kind and amount of nutrients that were in each food. Nutrition labels give the "recommended daily allowances" of vitamins and minerals as a percentage of the total amount required to maintain good health. Record and add up these percentages to see if you are getting 100% of the nutrients needed. Estimate gram amounts of carbohydrates, fats, and proteins for foods that did not come with a nutrition label (e.g., fast foods). You can do this by keeping in mind that 1 kilogram (e.g., 1,000 grams) equals about 2 pounds (e.g, 2.2 lbs.) and that 1 gram is about the mass of a paper clip.

Assignment due: _____

_____	_____	___/___/___
Student's Signature	Parent's Signature	Date

NUTRITION AND THE DIGESTIVE SYSTEM

Work Date: ____/____/____

LESSON OBJECTIVE

Students will identify major organs of the digestive system and set up a daily chart record of the foods they will eat this week.

Classroom Activities

On Your Mark!

Give students 10 minutes to read their Fact Sheet. Discuss and list the primary function of each of the nutrients described in the Fact Sheet and have students copy that information on Journal Sheet #1. Have them orally describe some of the consequences of having a poor diet.

Get Set!

Have students distinguish between the organs of the **digestive tract** or **alimentary canal** (e.g., mouth, esophagus, stomach, small intestine, large intestine, rectum, and anus) and the organs that assist in the digestion of foods by producing digestive juices (e.g., salivary glands, liver, pancreas, gall bladder). Have them draw two circles on Journal Sheet #1 and group the two sets of organs separately in the circles.

Go!

Distribute "Nutrition Facts" labels that appear by law on every food package and assist students in creating an "example table" on Journal Sheet #1 that they can use in completing the Homework Assignment. Their table can be set up just like the "Nutrition Facts" label. Explain how to estimate the amounts of nutrients in preprepared foods they eat at fast food restaurants or at home. They can do this by remembering that there are 2.2 pounds in one kilogram. A large hamburger (i.e., a quarter-pounder), therefore, contains about 115 grams of food, although not all of it is pure protein. Each gram of food, containing carbohydrate or protein, yields about 4 food calories. Point out that thiamin, riboflavin, and niacin are vitamins B1, B2, and B3, respectively.

Materials

Journal Sheet #1, "Nutrition Facts" labels from cereal or other food products

HB4 Journal Sheet #1

NUTRITION AND THE DIGESTIVE SYSTEM

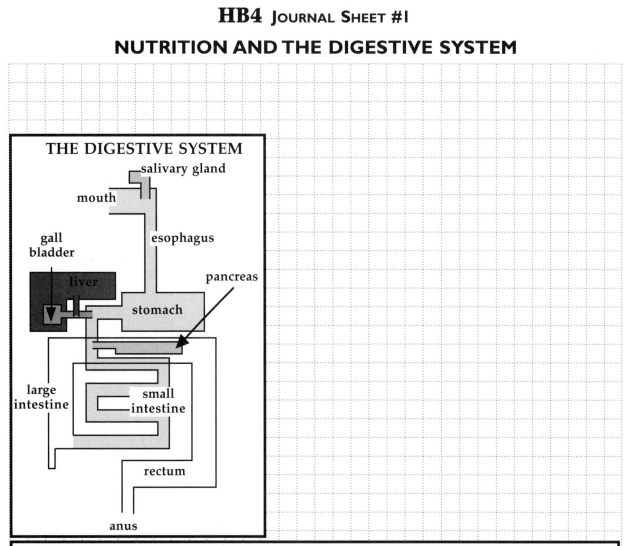

THE DIGESTIVE SYSTEM

salivary gland
mouth
esophagus
gall bladder
liver
pancreas
stomach
large intestine
small intestine
rectum
anus

RECOMMENDED DAILY ALLOWANCE OF NUTRIENTS											
	age	weight (kg)†	Food calories	protein (g)	Vitamin A*	Vitamin B1	Vitamin B2	Vitamin B3	Vitamin C	Vitamin D*	Vitamin E*
males	10-12	35	2500	45	4500	1.3	1.3	17	40	400	20
	12-14	43	2700	50	5000	1.4	1.4	18	45	400	20
	14-18	59	3000	60	5000	1.5	1.5	20	55	400	25
females	10-12	35	2250	50	4500	1.1	1.3	15	40	400	20
	12-14	44	2300	50	5000	1.2	1.4	15	45	400	20
	14-16	52	2400	55	5000	1.2	1.2	16	50	400	25
	16-18	54	2300	55	5000	1.2	1.5	15	50	400	25

* The amounts of vitamins A, D, and E are given in International Units. The amounts of vitamins B1, B2, B3, and C are given in milligrams.
† To obtain your weight in kilograms divide your weight in pounds by 2.2. There are 2.2 pounds in one kilogram.

NUTRITION AND THE DIGESTIVE SYSTEM

Work Date: ____/____/____

LESSON OBJECTIVE

Students will test food samples for the presence of protein and starch.

Classroom Activities

On Your Mark!

Before the start of class prepare the following solutions: (1) a 3% copper sulphate (CuSO₄) solution is prepared by dissolving 3 grams of copper sulphate in 97 ml of water; (2) a 10% potassium hydroxide (KOH) solution is prepared by dissolving 10 grams of potassium hydroxide in 97 ml of warm water on a hot plate. Keep the two solutions separate until used; (3) a beaker of Lugol's solution is prepared by dissolving 5 grams of potassium iodide (KI) in 1,000 ml of water, then adding 2 grams of resublimed iodine crystals or tincture of iodine. Set aside samples of lean ground beef, bread, egg white and corn starch, margarine, and plain sugar.

Begin by pointing out that strong alkalies like potassium hydroxide turn blue-violet in the presence of copper sulphate and the bonds that link amino acids together to form proteins. Explain that starch is a carbohydrate composed of linked sugars molecules. In the presence of starch, Lugol's solution turns light blue or green. If time permits, students can boil the bread and meat samples before they place them in their petri dishes. Warmed starch changes color more quickly than raw starch.

Get Set!

Discuss the procedure used to identify proteins and starch in the food samples provided as described in Figure A on Journal Sheet #2. Have students create their own table on Journal Sheet #2 to record which food items contain protein, starch, or both as a result of their observations.

Go!

Assist students in completing the experiments described in Figure A on Journal Sheet #2. When they are finished give them time to review their Homework Assignment which requires a daily reporting of the nutritional value of yesterday's "menu."

Materials

hot plate, balance, copper sulphate, potassium hydroxide, potassium iodide, resublimed iodine crystals or tincture of iodine, water, beakers, medicine droppers, lean ground beef, lard or margarine, eggs, sugar, petri dishes, bread, corn starch

HB4 Journal Sheet #2

NUTRITION AND THE DIGESTIVE SYSTEM

FIGURE A

Directions to test for the presence of proteins: (1) Place several grams (i.e., a teaspoon) of lean ground beef, lard or margarine, egg white, and sugar in 4 separate petri dishes. (2) Mix together in a small beaker the 3% copper sulphate and 10% potassium hydroxide solutions given to you by your instructor. (3) Use a medicine dropper to place several drops of the light blue mixture onto each sample. (4) Record your observations. The mixed reagent called Biuret reagent turns blue-violet in the presence of protein.

Directions to test for the presence of starch: (1) Place several grams (i.e., a teaspoon) of lean ground beef, bread, egg white, and corn starch in 4 separate petri dishes. (2) Use a medicine dropper to place on each sample several drops of the solution given to you by your instructor. (3) Record your observations. The reagent called Lugol's reagent turns blue-black in the presence of starch.

GENERAL SAFETY PRECAUTIONS

Wear goggles. Avoid direct skin contact with the food samples or the chemical solutions. Uncooked food contains bacteria and the chemical solutions used are caustic.

NUTRITION AND THE DIGESTIVE SYSTEM

Work Date: ____/____/____

LESSON OBJECTIVE

Students will convert starch to simple sugar.

Classroom Activities

On Your Mark!

Benedict's solution is a sodium citrate, sodium carbonate, copper sulphate solution that can be purchased from any laboratory supply house. In the presence of glucose, the solution turns an orange or yellowish-red color.

Begin the lesson by reviewing the composition of **starch** as a complex chain of sugar molecules. Explain that Benedict's solution turns an orange or yellowish-red color in the presence of simple sugars (e.g., glucose) but not in the presence of starch.

Get Set!

Discuss the procedure used to identify sugar in the experiment described in Figure B on Journal Sheet #3. Be sure students know exactly how to handle **hot test tubes** with heat-resistant gloves or tongs. Warn them to avoid inhaling any of the gases or hot vapors (i.e., steam) produced by the experiment.

Go!

Assist students in completing the experiment described in Figure B on Journal Sheet #3. Circulate around the room to make sure students are following the step-by-step directions and that all Bunsen burner flames are set <u>VERY LOW</u>! The solutions in the test tubes will boil easily and splatter if the flames are too high! When they are finished give them time to review their Homework Assignment to date which requires a daily reporting of the nutritional value of yesterday's "menu."

Materials

Bunsen burners, matches, ring stands and clamps, large test tubes, test tube tongs, sodium carbonate pellets, concentrated hydrochloric acid (i.e., 37%), Benedict's solution, water, corn starch

HB4 JOURNAL SHEET #3

NUTRITION AND THE DIGESTIVE SYSTEM

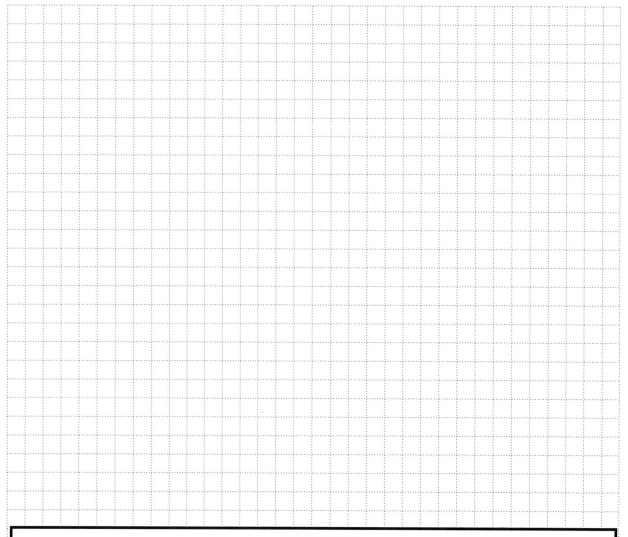

FIGURE B

Directions: (1) Pour 5 ml of water into a large test tube. (2) Place a "pinch" of corn starch into the water. (3) Light the Bunsen burner and heat the test tube to boiling on VERY LOW FLAME! (4) Have your instructor add one drop of concentrated hydrochloric acid to your test tube. (5) Turn off the Bunsen burner and use a test tube holder to transfer your test tube to the sink. (6) Hold the test tube over the sink and add several pellets of the sodium carbonate provided by your instructor, and continue adding several pellets one at a time until the bubbles disappear. (7) Add to the test tube a drop of the Benedict's solution provided by your instructor. (8) Secure the test tube over the Bunsen burner, light the burner, and reheat again on a VERY LOW FLAME! (9) Record your observations. Benedict's solution turns orange (or yellow-red) in the presence of simple sugar (e.g., glucose).

corn starch solution

VERY LOW FLAME

GENERAL SAFETY PRECAUTIONS

Wear goggles, an apron, and use heat-resistant gloves or tongs. Use extreme caution in the handling of equipment that is hot.

NUTRITION AND THE DIGESTIVE SYSTEM

Work Date: _____/_____/_____

LESSON OBJECTIVE

Students will illustrate the major organs of the digestive system to be added to the human body chart project.

Classroom Activities

On Your Mark!

Review the positions and names of the organs illustrated in the diagram on Journal Sheet #1. Explain to students that they will continue working on their long-term project of the human body chart.

Get Set!

Distribute posters and art materials.

Go!

Give students ample time to complete the activity described in Figure C on Journal Sheet #4. As in previous lessons, discourage students from designing three-dimensional structures as their project will be difficult to store in the weeks ahead.

Materials

butcher paper, construction paper, scissors, crayon or felt tip markers

HB4 JOURNAL SHEET #4

NUTRITION AND THE DIGESTIVE SYSTEM

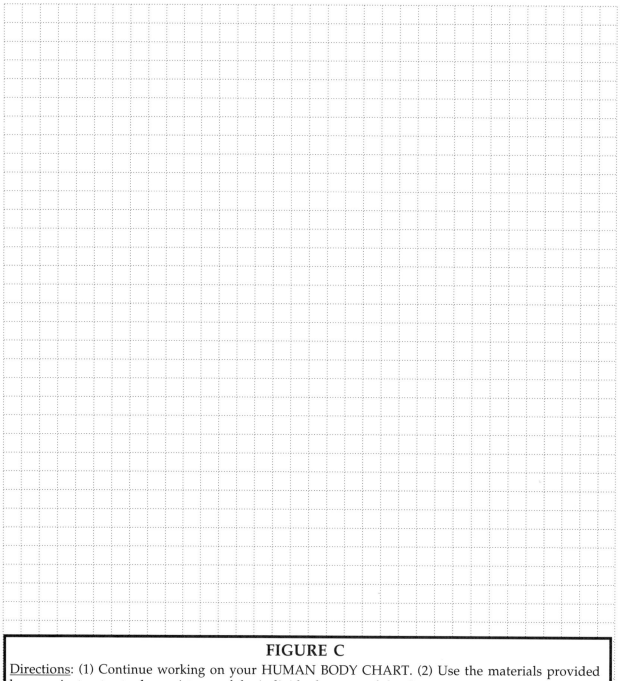

FIGURE C

<u>Directions</u>: (1) Continue working on your HUMAN BODY CHART. (2) Use the materials provided by your instructor to draw pictures of the individual organs of the digestive system so that they can be placed in their proper positions on the butcher paper diagram in relation to the bones and muscles of the body. You will need to lift the muscles of the abdomen and chest to position the digestive organs; then replace those muscles in their appropriate positions. (3) Use small sections of tape <u>no more than a centimeter in length</u> to secure the paper parts. DO NOT SECURE THEM PERMANENTLY! You will have to change their positions again to add additional structures later on during the course of this activity. (4) Roll up the chart neatly and wrap it with a rubber band before securing it in the box provided by your instructor. (5) Use this Journal Sheet to record any tasks you might need to accomplish at home to enhance the look of this project.

HB4 Review Quiz

Directions: Keep your eyes on your own work.
Read all directions and questions carefully.
THINK BEFORE YOU ANSWER!
Watch your spelling, be neat, and do the best you can.

CLASSWORK   (~40): _____
HOMEWORK   (~20): _____
CURRENT EVENT (~10): _____
TEST   (~30): _____

TOTAL   (~100): _____
(A ≥ 90, B ≥ 80, C ≥ 70, D ≥ 60, F < 60)

LETTER GRADE: _____

TEACHER'S COMMENTS: _____
_____

NUTRITION AND THE DIGESTIVE SYSTEM

TRUE–FALSE FILL-IN: If the statement is true, write the word TRUE. If the statement is false, change the underlined word to make the statement true. *22 points*

_____ 1. The process of breaking down food into usable substances is called <u>dissection</u>.

_____ 2. The process of breaking down food begins in the <u>stomach</u>.

_____ 3. Ptyalin is an enzyme found in <u>the stomach</u>.

_____ 4. The digestion of food by enzymes is called <u>chemical</u> digestion.

_____ 5. The physical action of breaking down food is called <u>mechanical</u> digestion.

_____ 6. Food is forced down the esophagus by <u>gravity</u>.

_____ 7. The <u>esophagus</u> releases gastric juices like hydrochloric acid, mucus, and pepsin.

_____ 8. Food moves from the stomach to the <u>small</u> intestine.

_____ 9. An intestinal juice called bile is produced in the <u>pancreas</u> and stored in the gallbladder.

_____ 10. Bile is an enzyme that breaks down <u>fats</u>.

_____ 11. The <u>pancreas</u> produces an intestinal juice that digests proteins, starches, and fats.

_____ 12. Digested foods are absorbed into the bloodstream through "fingerlike" structures called <u>villi</u>.

_____ 13. By the time digested food reaches the end of the <u>large</u> intestine most nutrients have been absorbed into the bloodstream.

_____ 14. Undigested food is stored in the <u>anus</u> before excretion.

_____ 15. Food wastes are eliminated from the body through the <u>rectum</u>.

_____ 16. <u>Nutrients</u> are the usable substances in food.

_____17. <u>Carbohydrates</u> are an organism's primary source of energy.

_____18. Sugars and starches are the two main types of <u>minerals</u>.

_____19. <u>Proteins</u> are a secondary source of energy found in nuts, butter, cheese, and meat.

_____20. <u>Vitamins</u> are long amino acid chains that link together according to the instructions of the DNA molecules.

_____21. Red meat, fish, poultry, dairy products, and eggs are sources of <u>incomplete</u> proteins which contain all the necessary amino acids.

_____22. Plants such as rice, cereal, and vegetables are <u>complete</u> proteins that are missing one or more of the essential amino acids.

PROBLEM

Directions: Read statement #23 through #30. Write the letters A, B, C, D, E, F, G, and H in the spaces provided to put the events describing the digestive process in their proper order. *8 points*

_____ 23. The epiglottis closes over the windpipe allowing the food to pass safely into the esophagus.

_____ 24. Food moves into the small intestine.

_____ 25. Teeth grind food into smaller pieces as saliva breaks down starch.

_____ 26. Food moves down the esophagus by peristalsis.

_____ 27. Digested nutrients are absorbed by villi into the bloodstream.

_____ 28. Bile and pancreatic fluid digest fats, proteins, and carbohydrates.

_____ 29. Food is churned and mixed with gastric juices.

_____ 30. Excess water is removed from waste products.

_____   _____   ____/____/____
Student's Signature   Parent's Signature   Date

THE SKIN AND EXCRETORY SYSTEM

TEACHER'S CLASSWORK AGENDA AND CONTENT NOTES

Classwork Agenda for the Week

1. Students will determine factors that affect the balance of fluids between the inside and the outside of cells.

2. Students will identify the layers of the skin and how it helps to control body temperature.

3. Students will identify the excretory organs of the urinary tract.

4. Students will illustrate the organs of the excretory system to be added to the human body chart project.

Content Notes for Lecture and Discussion

The "humoural hypothesis" of the Greek authorities **Hippocrates** (b. 460 B.C.; d. 377 B.C.) and **Galen** (b. 129; d. 200) dominated western medical thought for nearly 1500 years. Although the work of the Belgian physician **Andreas Vesalius** (b. 1514; d. 1564), the English physician **William Harvey** (b. 1578; d. 1657), and the French physiologist and founder of experimental medicine **Claude Bernard** (b. 1813; d. 1878) led to the toppling of that idea, the notion that the stability of the internal environment was essential to the health of an organism was maintained. Bernard—who demonstrated the functions of the pancreas and liver—showed that nerves in the skin contracted and dilated blood vessels to regulate body temperature. This led him to the concept of the *milieu intérieur* (e.g., meaning "internal environment") that stimulated research for years to come.

Research into the nature of the cellular milieu received its first scientific treatment by the French physicist **Jean Nollet** (b. 1700; d. 1770) in 1748. Nollet investigated the phenomenon of **osmosis**: the passage of solvent (e.g., water) through a semipermeable barrier (e.g., treated cellophane or goldbeater's membrane) resulting from an unequal concentration of solute on different sides of the barrier. Osmosis should not be confused with diffusion which is the more general dilution of solutes in fluids. Osmosis is more specifically the passage of water across a membrane that is permeable only to water. The German botanist **Wilhelm Friedrich Philipp Pfeffer** (b. 1845; d. 1920) elucidated the osmotic process by developing a device to measure osmotic pressure in 1877. He showed that osmotic pressure was dependent upon both the temperature and salt concentrations of the solutions surrounding the semipermeable membrane.

In 1926, the American physiologist **Walter Bradford Cannon** (b. 1871; d. 1945) coined the term **homeostasis** to describe an organism's capacity to maintain internal equilibrium in the face of environmental change. Cannon studied the effects of hormones on sugar metabolism and thermoregulation and the role of the nervous system in controlling heart rate, respiratory rate, and the "flight or fight" response. His extensive research on the mechanisms of the autonomic nervous system were published in 1939 in his book entitled the *Wisdom of the Body*.

The involvement of the major excretory organs in the elimination of toxic wastes from the body was apparent with the first gross dissections made by physicians and surgeons of the 16th and 17th centuries. However, the manner in which fluids were filtered at the cellular level was not understood until advances in microscopy and physiology were made in the 19th century. The English surgeon and histologist **Sir William Bowman** (b. 1816; d. 1892) discovered that urine was a byproduct of blood filtration performed by the kidneys. He identified the **nephron** as the basic unit of kidney function to which the German anatomist and histologist **Friedrich Gustav Jacob**

Henle (b. 1809; d. 1885) added the tubelike structures leading to the renal vein known today as Henle's loop. A more thorough understanding of the filtering process led to the invention of the first kidney dialysis machine in 1943.

In Lesson #1, students will determine factors that affect the balance of fluids between the inside and the outside of cells.

In Lesson #2, students will identify the layers of the skin and how it helps to control body temperature.

In Lesson #3, students will identify the excretory organs of the urinary tract.

In Lesson #4, students will illustrate the organs of the excretory system to be added to the human body chart project.

ANSWERS TO THE HOMEWORK PROBLEMS

Students' answers will vary but should stress the pertinent points of each answer.

(1) Drinking pure distilled water has the opposite effect of drinking seawater. Pure distilled water—not the mineral-containing "distilled" water that can be purchased at the supermarket—dilutes the salt concentration of the extracellular medium of the stomach. The result is a swelling of the cells of the stomach lining: "If the salt concentration inside the cell is greater than the salt concentration outside the cell, then water will flow into the cell to dilute the intracellular salt."

(2) During a fever the blood vessels of the hypodermis expand to increase blood flow and loss of heat. This is evidenced by a redness of the skin during a fever. In addition, sweat glands will excrete excess water to promote cooling by evaporation at the body's surface. The fever created by the overactivity of cells fighting the illness will drop. Most fevers "break" after a period of extensive sweating.

(3) Kidney stones clogging the ureter cause urine to backflow into the kidneys. Since urine is toxic, the kidneys can suffer permanent damage unless the stones are quickly removed.

ANSWERS TO THE END-OF-THE-WEEK REVIEW QUIZ

1. water	6. high
2. true	7. pores
3. true	8. cools
4. osmosis	9. urea
5. low	10. true

Answers #11, #12, and #13 may be in any order.

11. The skin protects the body against invasion by germs and ultraviolet radiation from the sun.
12. The skin is waterproof.
13. The skin acts like a "thermostat" or heat regulator that controls the conservation and elimination of body heat produced by the metabolic activity of cells.

14. F	18. A
15. D	19. B
16. G	20. E
17. C	

HB5 FACT SHEET

THE SKIN AND EXCRETORY SYSTEM

CLASSWORK AGENDA FOR THE WEEK

(1) Determine factors that affect the balance of fluids between the inside and the outside of cells.
(2) Identify the layers of the skin and how it helps to control body temperature.
(3) Identify the excretory organs of the urinary tract.
(4) Illustrate the organs of the excretory system to be added to the human body chart project.

All animals including human beings are made mostly of water. The average adult human—weighing about 70 kilograms (e.g., 154 pounds)—is about 49 kilograms (e.g., liters) water. About 70% of that water is inside cells. The rest is between cells or in the bloodstream. The fluid inside cells is called **intracellular fluid**. The fluid outside cells is called **extracellular fluid**. Both intracellular and extracellular fluids contain salt (e.g., sodium and chloride ions) and protein. The membranes of cells serve the important function of keeping the correct amount of salts and proteins in balance inside and outside of cells. The balance of materials is called **osmotic balance** because the flow of water across the cell membrane is called **osmosis**. The amount of water that flows in or out of a cell is affected by the amount of salt and protein in the intracellular and extracellular fluids. If the salt concentration inside a cell is greater than the salt concentration outside the cell, then water will flow into the cell to dilute the intracellular salt. If the salt concentration inside a cell is lower than the salt concentration outside the cell, then water will flow out of the cell to dilute the extracellular salt. The importance of maintaining a healthy osmotic balance is the reason it is dangerous to drink sea water. A high concentration of saltwater in the stomach can cause the cells of the stomach lining to shrivel and die (e.g., lose intracellular fluid). The skin and organs of the excretory system are especially designed to help maintain the balance of water, salt, and proteins in the body. In addition, the organs of the excretory system filter waste products out of the blood and eliminate them from the body.

The **skin** has several functions. (1) The skin protects the body against invasion by germs and ultraviolet radiation from the sun. (2) The skin is waterproof. And, (3) the skin acts like a "thermostat" or heat regulator that controls the conservation and elimination of body heat produced by the metabolic activity of cells. When the temperature outside is low, blood vessels in the lower layers of the skin shrink to reduce blood flow and heat loss. When the temperature outside is high, the same blood vessels widen to allow more blood flow and greater heat loss. When the temperature outside is very high—or excess internal heat is produced by exercise—the sweat glands of the skin filter water from surrounding tissue and leak it through **skin pores** to the surface. The evaporation of sweat from the surface of the skin cools the body surface. The skin is made of three main layers. The top layer of the skin is the **epidermis** or covering. The middle layer is the **dermis**, containing **oil** and **sweat glands**, **sensory nerves**, **hair** and **hair muscle roots**. The inner layer of the skin is the **hypodermis**, containing blood vessels and fatty tissue.

The blood contains many waste products resulting from cell metabolism. The liver, for example, removes excess **amino acids** from the blood and transforms those chemical molecules into **urea**. Urea is a poisonous chemical that must be removed from the body. The job of the **excretory system** is to filter urea, excess water, salt, and other waste products from the blood and eliminate them from the body. The kidneys are the major organs of the excretory system. The **kidneys** are the filtering units that keep the blood free of impurities. The **renal artery** delivers blood to the kidneys; the **renal vein** returns it to the circulation after it is filtered. Each of the two kidneys contains millions of microscopic filtration factories called **nephrons**. Inside every nephron, waste substances are filtered out of the bloodstream. Liquid waste called **urine** flows from the kidneys through a tube called the **ureter** to a storage organ called the **bladder**. Then, the urine is expelled from the body by the bladder through a tube called the **urethra**.

Homework Directions

Directions: Answer each of the following questions in one or two short, clear sentences.

(1) A scientist boiled some water and captured the hot water vapor. He then cooled the vapor to produce 100% pure liquid water that contained no salt or other impurities. Explain why it would be unhealthy to drink water that pure.

(2) A person who is ill sometimes develops a "fever." Explain how the skin helps to reduce a fever. Be specific regarding the events that take place in the blood vessels of the hypodermis.

(3) Kidney stones are small, hard clumps of mineral waste that can become stuck in the ureter. Explain why it is essential to remove kidney stones when they develop.

Assignment due: _____

_____   _____   ___/___/____
Student's Signature   Parent's Signature   Date

THE SKIN AND EXCRETORY SYSTEM

Work Date: ____/____/____

LESSON OBJECTIVE

Students will determine factors that affect the balance of fluids between the inside and outside of cells.

Classroom Activities

On Your Mark!

Give students several minutes to read the first paragraph of their Fact Sheet. Test their comprehension of the reading by orally quizzing them for definitions of **intracellular fluid**, **extracellular fluid**, and **osmosis**. Define the term **diffusion** as the spreading or diluting of a substance into another substance such as food coloring diffusing in water or perfume diffusing in air. Explain that osmosis is a special case of diffusion. Define osmosis as the movement of water through a barrier that is "selectively permeable" to only water.

Get Set!

Have students set up the experiment described in Figure A on Journal Sheet #1 before continuing with the lecture. Draw Illustration A on the board and have students copy your drawing on Journal Sheet #1. Explain how the German botanist **Wilhelm F. P. Pfeffer** (b. 1845; d. 1920) used the device to measure osmotic pressure. When the sugar or salt concentration inside the pot was greater than the concentration on the outside, water flowed through the membrane into the pot causing the liquid mercury in the tube to rise. The opposite occurred when the concentration of solutes was reversed.

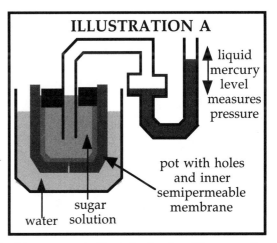

ILLUSTRATION A

liquid mercury level measures pressure

pot with holes and inner semipermeable membrane

water sugar solution

Go!

Give students ample time to examine the potato slices after 15 minutes and write a paragraph to explain their observations as requested in the Activity directions.

Materials

100 ml beakers, table salt, fresh potatoes, plastic or butter knives, water

HB5 JOURNAL SHEET #1

THE SKIN AND EXCRETORY SYSTEM

FIGURE A

<u>Directions</u>: (1) Mix 20 grams of table salt in 100 milliliters of water. (2) Set aside a second 100 ml beaker filled with 100 ml of plain tapwater. (3) Cut a fresh potato into 4 slices, each slice about 5 millimeters thick. (4) Place 2 of the slices in the saltwater and other 2 slices in the plain water. (5) Wait 15 minutes, then remove and examine the condition of the slices. How are they different? Explain how osmosis is involved in causing the changes you observe in the potato slices.

THE SKIN AND EXCRETORY SYSTEM

Work Date: ____/____/____

LESSON OBJECTIVE

Students will identify the layers of the skin and how it helps to control body temperature.

Classroom Activities

On Your Mark!

Ask students to explain why soap is useful in removing dirt from the skin. Explain that soap is a product of animal fat (e.g., lard). Then assist students in performing the following simple demonstration: (1) Distribute paper cups and have students fill the cups nearly to the rim with water. (2) Distribute eyedroppers filled with cooking oil and have students place several drops of the oil on the surface of the water. (3) Instruct them to use the end of the eyedropper to push the oil drops closer to one another until the drops fuse. Ask students to explain why the oil droplets fuse. Point out that fatty vegetable and animal oil molecules **cohere** (e.g., stick together) in the same way that water molecules cohere to other water molecules to form droplets. Point out that cell membranes are made of **fatty lipids** that are water repellant (e.g., oil and water do not mix). Skin cells like all other cells have cell membranes. The animal fat in soap that we rub on our skin attracts the fatty lipids in the cell membranes of dead skin cells. Rinsing with water flushes the dead skin cells and dirt off the body.

Get Set!

Give students several minutes to read the second paragraph of their Fact Sheet. Refer students to the illustration on Journal Sheet #2 and assist them in identifying the structures in the three layers of the skin. Point out that the **Epidermis** is actually a series of layers containing **dead skin cells** on the top and **basal cells** down on the bottom layer that form new skin cells. The **Dermis** contains **sensory nerves**, **hair roots** connected to **muscles** that contract and cause the hair to "stand on end," and two types of glands: **sweat glands** that extract water and release it through the **skin pores**, and **sebaceous glands** that produce oil that makes its way to the surface along strands of hair. The **Hypodermis** contains fat tissue and blood vessels. Point out how the arteries and veins are connected to one another and that arteries deliver fresh blood to the cells while veins take waste materials away from the cells.

Go!

Give students ample time to complete the activities described in Figure B and Figure C on Journal Sheet #2. Encourage them to use the Fact Sheet before discussing with their groupmates what they are going to draw in each situation posed by the activity.

Materials

paper cups, cooking oil, eyedroppers, water

HB5 JOURNAL SHEET #2

THE SKIN AND EXCRETORY SYSTEM

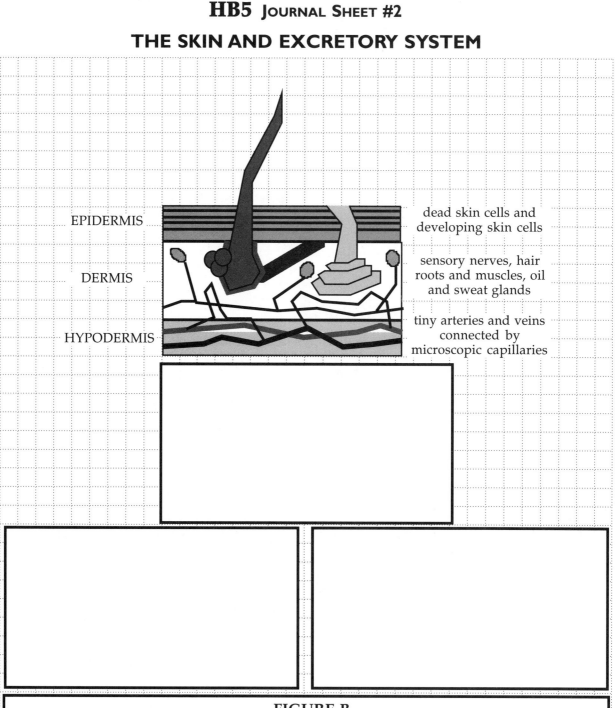

EPIDERMIS

dead skin cells and developing skin cells

DERMIS

sensory nerves, hair roots and muscles, oil and sweat glands

HYPODERMIS

tiny arteries and veins connected by microscopic capillaries

FIGURE B

Directions: (1) Study the top diagram of the layers of the skin. (2) Draw a picture to explain what happens when the air temperature outside is high. (3) Draw a picture to explain what happens when the air temperature outside is low. (4) Draw a picture to explain what happens when skin hairs "piloerect" (e.g., meaning to "stand up").

FIGURE C

Directions: (1) Pour a teaspoon of rubbing alcohol on the top of your hand. (2) Blow on the liquid as it evaporates. (3) Record your observations. Does your hand feel cooler or warmer? Explain how sweating cools off the surface of the skin.

THE SKIN AND EXCRETORY SYSTEM

Work Date: _____/_____/_____

LESSON OBJECTIVE

Students will identify the excretory organs of the urinary tract.

Classroom Activities

On Your Mark!

Use the information in the Teacher's Classwork Agenda and Content Notes to review the concept of osmosis and give a brief lecture of the concept of **homeostasis** introduced by the American physiologist **Walter Bradford Cannon** (b. 1871; d. 1945) in 1926. Define homeostasis as the tendency of an organism to maintain uniformity and stability in its internal environment in the face of external change. Write the definition on the board and have students copy it onto Journal Sheet #3.

Get Set!

Give students several minutes to read paragraph #3 on the Fact Sheet. Draw Illustration B on the board and have students copy your schematic diagram on Journal Sheet #3. Label the organs of the "urinary tract" and discuss the function of each organ.

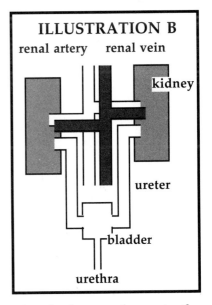

ILLUSTRATION B
renal artery   renal vein
kidney
ureter
bladder
urethra

Go!

Give students ample time to brainstorm and complete the activity described in Figure D on Journal Sheet #3. Encourage them to use the information in paragraph #1 of the Fact Sheet and the illustration (e.g., Illustration A) they copied on Journal Sheet #1 to solve the problem presented. As you circulate around the room hint at the importance of the salt concentration in the pot shown in the illustration. Adding salt to the pot would cause water to flow into it through the semipermeable membrane. Adding fresh water to the pot would dilute the salt concentration and cause water to flow out of the pot through the membrane. The solution to the problem is a device similar to the one in Illustration A with additional pipes that can add either salt or water to the inner pot lined with a semipermeable membrane. Discuss the solution to the problem after everyone has attempted to solve it.

Materials

Journal Sheet #1 and Journal Sheet #3

HB5 JOURNAL SHEET #3

THE SKIN AND EXCRETORY SYSTEM

FIGURE D

The kidney dialysis machine was invented in 1943. The machine filters water and waste materials out of the blood in people with damaged kidneys. Brainstorm with your groupmates and, using the information you have learned this week, draw a diagram of a machine that can filter water out of the blood and put it back into the blood.

THE SKIN AND EXCRETORY SYSTEM

Work Date: ____/____/____

LESSON OBJECTIVE

Students will illustrate the organs of the excretory system to be added to the human body chart project.

Classroom Activities

On Your Mark!

Review the positions and names of the organs illustrated in the diagram on Journal Sheet #3. Explain to students that they will continue working on their long-term project of the human body chart.

Get Set!

Distribute posters and art materials.

Go!

Give students ample time to complete the activity described in Figure E on Journal Sheet #4. As in previous lessons, discourage students from designing three-dimensional structures as their project will be difficult to store in the weeks ahead.

Materials

butcher paper, construction paper, scissors, crayon or felt tip markers

HB5 JOURNAL SHEET #4

THE SKIN AND EXCRETORY SYSTEM

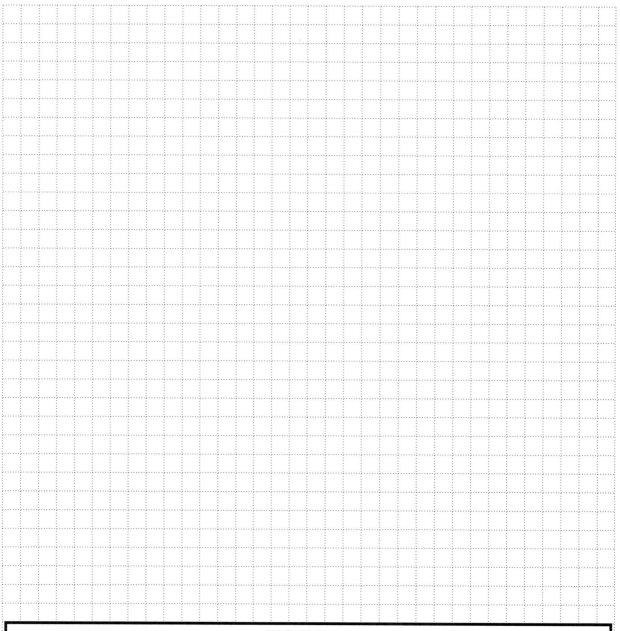

FIGURE E

<u>Directions</u>: (1) Continue working on your HUMAN BODY CHART. (2) Use the materials provided by your instructor to draw pictures of the individual organs of the excretory system so that they can be placed in their proper positions on the butcher paper diagram in relation to the other organs of the body. You will need to lift the organs of the digestive system to place the organs of the excretory system in their proper location at the back of the torso. The right kidney should be placed slightly lower than the left to make room for the liver above it. (3) Use small sections of tape <u>no more than a centimeter in length</u> to secure the paper parts. DO NOT SECURE THEM PERMANENTLY! You will have to change their positions again to add additional structures later on during the course of this activity. (4) Roll up the chart neatly and wrap it with a rubber band before securing it in the box provided by your instructor. (5) Use this Journal Sheet to record any tasks you might need to accomplish at home to enhance the look of this project.

HB5 REVIEW QUIZ

Directions: Keep your eyes on your own work.
Read all directions and questions carefully.
THINK BEFORE YOU ANSWER!
Watch your spelling, be neat, and do the best you can.

CLASSWORK   (~40): _____
HOMEWORK   (~20): _____
CURRENT EVENT   (~10): _____
TEST   (~30): _____

TOTAL   (~100): _____
(A ≥ 90, B ≥ 80, C ≥ 70, D ≥ 60, F < 60)

LETTER GRADE: _____

TEACHER'S COMMENTS: _____
_____

THE SKIN AND EXCRETORY SYSTEM

TRUE–FALSE FILL-IN: If the statement is true, write the word TRUE. If the statement is false, change the underlined word to make the statement true. *20 points*

_____   1. All animals including human beings are made mostly of <u>salt</u>.

_____   2. The fluid inside cells is called <u>intracellular</u> fluid.

_____   3. The fluid outside cells is called <u>extracellular</u> fluid.

_____   4. The flow of water across the cell membrane is called <u>a leak</u>.

_____   5. When the temperature outside is <u>high</u>, blood vessels in the skin shrink to reduce blood flow and heat loss.

_____   6. When the temperature outside is <u>low</u>, blood vessels widen to allow more blood flow and greater heat loss.

_____   7. During strenuous exercise the sweat glands filter water from surrounding tissue and leak it through skin <u>hairs</u> to the surface.

_____   8. The evaporation of sweat from the surface of the skin <u>warms</u> the body surface.

_____   9. One of the functions of the liver is to remove excess amino acids from the blood and transforms those chemical molecules into <u>urine</u>.

_____   10. Each of the two kidneys contains millions of microscopic filtration factories called <u>nephrons</u>.

ESSAY: List three important functions of the skin. *3 points*

11. _____

12. _____

13. _____

MATCHING: Choose the letter of the phrase that best describes the function of each organ of the excretory system. *7 points*

_____ 14. kidney   (A) allows urine to flow to a storage organ

_____ 15. renal artery   (B) stores urine

_____ 16. renal vein   (C) microscopic filtering unit

_____ 17. nephron   (D) delivers blood to filtering organs

_____ 18. ureter   (E) eliminates urine from the body

_____ 19. bladder   (F) one of a pair of filtering organs

_____ 20. urethra   (G) removes blood from filtering organs

THE CIRCULATORY SYSTEM

TEACHER'S CLASSWORK AGENDA AND CONTENT NOTES

Classwork Agenda for the Week

1. Students will identify the organs of the circulatory system and use a pie graph to identify the components of blood.

2. Students will observe blood flow in the tail capillaries of a goldfish.

3. Students will examine the effects of exercise on pulse rate.

4. Students will illustrate the organs of the circulatory system to be added to the human body chart project.

Content Notes for Lecture and Discussion

Hippocrates (b. 460 B.C.; d. 377 B.C.) and **Aristotle** (b. 384 B.C.; d. 322 B.C.) believed that the heart was the major organ of feelings and intelligence. Able to hear the heartbeat of the unborn through the abdominal wall of a pregnant woman, Aristotle also believed that the heart was the first organ to develop and that it supplied the body with the necessary "animal heat" required for life. The Greek physician **Herophilus of Chalcedon** (c. 330 B.C.; c. 260 B.C.) who lived and worked in ancient Alexandria distinguished arteries from veins. He recorded detailed observations of many dissections which—according to some resources—were performed on living criminals condemned to death. The Greek physician **Erasistratus** (c. 304 B.C.; c. 250 B.C.)—considered the founder of physiology—accurately described the function of heart valves and discovered the general route that blood takes through the circulatory system. However, he described that circulation in the wrong direction. **Galen** (b. 129; d. 200) dissected the hearts of living animals and cadavers and described the passage of blood from the right side of the heart to the left side believing that the blood passed through tiny pores in the septum. The comments of the Egyptian physician **Ibn Al-Nafis** (b. 1205; d. 1288) contradicted those of Galen by describing the passage of blood from the right side of the heart to the left side via the pulmonary artery, lungs, and pulmonary vein. Al-Nafis's work remained controversial, however, for many physicians and surgeons throughout the Middle Ages. The work of the English physician **William Harvey** (b. 1578; d. 1657) settled the controversy. By examining the circulatory systems of mammals Harvey determined that blood was carried to the heart by veins and out to the organs of the body by arteries. He confirmed the role of the pulmonary artery, lungs, and pulmonary vein described by Al-Nafis. The brilliance of Harvey's work is appreciated largely for his mathematical approach to the problems of the circulation. He determined the variable nature of heart rate resulting from a variety of activities and the amount of blood pumped by the heart with every systolic (e.g., ventricular) beat. He calculated the amount of blood pumped throughout the system every hour and from his analysis concluded that the blood was being circulated and recirculated rather than being produced anew by the liver as many of his predecessors had thought. In 1661, the Italian physician **Marcello Malpighi** (b. 1628; d. 1694) discovered capillaries, the microscopic channels between arteries and veins.

Although the invention of the **stethoscope** in 1816 by the French inventor **René Théophile Hyacinthe Laënnec** (b. 1781; d. 1826) permitted physicians to listen closely to the rhythmic beating of the living human heart, early 19th century physicians measured blood pressure by inserting tubes directly into the arteries. In 1896, the Italian physician **S. Riva Rocci** (b. 1863; d. 1936) invented the **sphygmomanometer**, allowing physicians to take less invasive measurements. The German physician **Wilhelm His, Jr.** (b. 1863; d. 1934) and the Scottish anatomist **Arthur Keith** (b. 1866; d. 1955) described the nerves innervating the right side of the heart that initiated cardiac contractions. The Dutch physician **Willem Einthoven** (b. 1860; d. 1927) invented the **electrocardiogram** (e.g., ECG or EKG) and demonstrated that some cardiac disorders were the product of an irregular heartbeat due to an irregularity in the "electrical" activity of heart muscles. In 1901, the American immunologist **Karl Landsteiner** (b. 1868; d. 1943) discovered the existence of the A, B, and O blood groups, thereby facilitating blood transfusions which had been largely unsuccessful since the start of the 19th century.

In Lesson #1, students will identify the organs of the circulatory system and use a pie graph to identify the components of blood.

In Lesson #2, students will observe blood flow in the tail capillaries of a goldfish.

In Lesson #3, students will examine the effects of exercise on pulse rate.

In Lesson #4, students will illustrate the organs of the circulatory system to be added to the human body chart project.

ANSWERS TO THE HOMEWORK PROBLEMS

Beginning at the left ventricle the blood travels in order through the following structures: left ventrical, aorta, arteries, organ capillary beds, veins, right atrium, right ventrical, pulmonary artery, lungs, pulmonary vein, and left atrium.

ANSWERS TO THE END-OF-THE-WEEK REVIEW QUIZ

1. blood	6. lungs	11. B	16. C
2. oxygen	7. aorta	12. F	17. D
3. carbon dioxide	8. true	13. I	18. E
4. circulatory	9. true	14. G	19. J
5. heart/cardiac	10. true	15. A	20. H

ESSAY: Any of the following solid materials is acceptable as well as other materials that students can logically defend (e.g., germs): red blood cells, white blood cells, platelets, carbohydrates (e.g., sugars), lipids (e.g., fats), minerals, proteins, and other chemical nutrients and messengers. Note that plasma is the general term used to describe the liquid portion of the blood made mostly of water.

HB6 FACT SHEET

THE CIRCULATORY SYSTEM

CLASSWORK AGENDA FOR THE WEEK

(1) Identify the organs of the circulatory system and use a pie graph to identify the components of blood.
(2) Observe blood flow in the tail capillaries of a goldfish.
(3) Examine the effects of exercise on pulse rate.
(4) Illustrate the organs of the circulatory system to be added to the human body chart project.

The function of the **circulatory system** is to transport important nutrients throughout the body in a liquid solution called **blood**. Among the materials carried in the blood by the circulatory system are **oxygen, carbon dioxide, water, disease-fighting cells** and **proteins**, and other **chemical nutrients and messengers**.

All cells use oxygen to burn food for energy. Carbon dioxide is the waste product of that "burning" process called **respiration**. Supplying cells with oxygen and removing carbon dioxide from the cells of the body is one main function of the circulatory system.

Blood is pumped to all the organs of the body by the **heart**. Oxygen-rich blood from the lungs arrives on the left side of the heart and is pumped throughout the rest of the body through a major blood vessel called the **aorta**. "Used" blood from the body that is rich in carbon dioxide travels back to the right side of the heart and is pumped to the lungs where it is "refueled" with fresh oxygen. At the same time, carbon dioxide is "dumped" into the lungs where it can be eliminated from the body by exhaling.

The heart has **four chambers** that keep "oxygen-rich" and "carbon dioxide-rich" blood separated. A wall of tissue called the **septum** divides the left side of the heart from the right side. The two upper chambers of the heart, called **atria**, collect the blood for pumping into the larger lower chambers of the heart. The two lower chambers called **ventricles** do all the hard pumping, forcing blood through the **blood vessels** of the entire body. **Valves** between the atria and the ventricles keep blood from flowing backward inside the heart.

Arteries are blood vessels that carry blood away from the heart. They are lined with smooth muscle tissue to help them do their job. **Veins** are thin-walled blood vessels that carry blood back to the heart. They contain valves to prevent blood from flowing backward in the circulatory system. Arteries carry blood away from the heart. Veins carry blood back to the heart.

Capillaries are microscopic blood vessels that connect arteries to veins. Capillaries surround all the cells of the body and allow nutrients to pass from the bloodstream to the cells and from the cells back into the bloodstream.

Blood contains four main components: **plasma, white blood cells, red blood cells,** and **platelets**. **Plasma** is a fluid that is 90% water and 10% dissolved carbohydrates, fats, salts, gases, and proteins. Some of the proteins in plasma are **antibodies** that fight disease. **White blood cells** destroy dying cells and germs. **Red blood cells** carry oxygen and carbon dioxide. **Platelets** cause the blood to clot when you have a cut. White blood cells, red blood cells, and platelets make up the solid portion of the blood.

There are many types of **disease** that can cause damage to the circulatory system. A thickening of the inner lining of arteries is called **atherosclerosis**. High blood pressure against the inner linings of the arteries is called **hypertension**. Both of these diseases make the heart work harder and can damage both the heart and blood vessels. A healthy diet low in fat helps the blood vessels of the circulatory system to remain free of clogs that can impair circulation.

Homework Directions

Write a paragraph explaining the route that blood takes in the circulatory system by referring to the diagram drawn in Lesson #1. Begin your description at the left ventricle.

Assignment due: _____

_____   _____   ____/____/____
Student's Signature   Parent's Signature   Date

THE CIRCULATORY SYSTEM

Work Date: ____/____/____

LESSON OBJECTIVE

Students will identify the organs of the circulatory system and use a pie graph to identify the components of blood.

Classroom Activities

On Your Mark!

Use the information in the Teacher's Classwork Agenda and Content Notes to give a brief lecture about ancient views of the circulatory system according to **Hippocrates** (b. 460 B.C.; d. 377 B.C.) and **Aristotle** (b. 384 B.C.; d. 322 B.C.). Point out how their views were changed by the work of **Ibn Al-Nafis** (b. 1205; d. 1288) and **William Harvey** (b. 1578; d. 1657).

Get Set!

Draw Illustration A on the board and assist students in labelling the schematic diagram that appears on Journal Sheet #1. Point out the **septum** dividing the heart in two, separating the right and left sides of the heart. Have students note the **valves** between the atria and ventricles that prevent the backward flow of blood. Explain that both atria contract together pumping blood into the larger lower ventricles

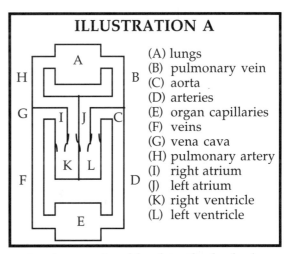

ILLUSTRATION A

(A) lungs
(B) pulmonary vein
(C) aorta
(D) arteries
(E) organ capillaries
(F) veins
(G) vena cava
(H) pulmonary artery
(I) right atrium
(J) left atrium
(K) right ventricle
(L) left ventricle

(e.g., diastole). Then the ventricles contract, pumping blood to the body (e.g., left ventricle) and lungs (e.g., right ventricle). All arteries take blood away from the heart and veins take blood toward the heart. The **pulmonary artery**, returning blood from the body, is the only artery with purple carbon dioxide-rich blood. The **pulmonary vein**, returning blood from the lungs, is the only vein with red oxygen-rich blood.

Go!

Give students ample time to examine the table listing the *Components of the Blood* on Journal Sheet #1 and assist them in completing the pie graph activity described in Figure A.

Materials

Journal Sheet #1, protractors, lamb or sheep heart (if available)

HB6 JOURNAL SHEET #1

THE CIRCULATORY SYSTEM

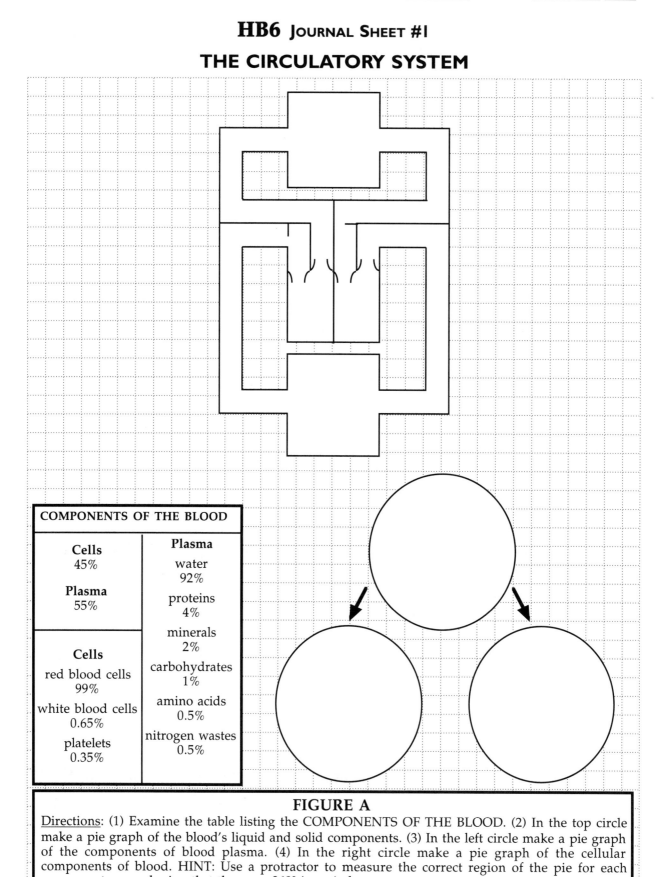

COMPONENTS OF THE BLOOD

Cells	Plasma
Cells 45%	water 92%
Plasma 55%	proteins 4%
	minerals 2%
Cells	carbohydrates 1%
red blood cells 99%	amino acids 0.5%
white blood cells 0.65%	nitrogen wastes 0.5%
platelets 0.35%	

FIGURE A

<u>Directions</u>: (1) Examine the table listing the COMPONENTS OF THE BLOOD. (2) In the top circle make a pie graph of the blood's liquid and solid components. (3) In the left circle make a pie graph of the components of blood plasma. (4) In the right circle make a pie graph of the cellular components of blood. HINT: Use a protractor to measure the correct region of the pie for each component remembering that there are 360° in a circle.

THE CIRCULATORY SYSTEM

Work Date: ____/____/____

LESSON OBJECTIVE

Students will observe blood flow in the tail capillaries of a goldfish.

Classroom Activities

On Your Mark!

Prepare for this lesson by purchasing small goldfish (e.g., feeders) from a local fish store. The fish can be kept alive in a fishtank or in the bag supplied by the store if air is bubbled into the bag using a small air pump.

Review the route that blood takes in its circulation around the body as described in Lesson #1. Draw Illustration B on the board and have students copy your drawing on Journal Sheet #2. Mention that while **William Harvey** (b. 1578; d. 1657) accurately described the circulation of the blood he was not sure how blood passed through organs from arteries to veins. Point out that the Italian physician **Marcello Malpighi** (b. 1628; d. 1694) discovered the existence of microscopic **capillaries** that surround each cell that make up the tissues and organs of the body.

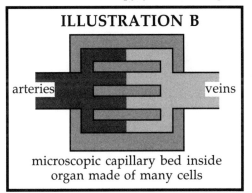

ILLUSTRATION B

arteries / veins

microscopic capillary bed inside organ made of many cells

Get Set!

Mention that the blood comprises about 6% of the body's weight. A person weighing 70 kilograms (e.g., 154 pounds) has about 25 trillion (e.g., 25,000,000,000,000) red blood cells. One cubic millimeter (e.g., one microliter) of blood contains about 5,000,000 red blood cells and about 7,500 white blood cells. An average "drop" of blood is about 25 cubic millimeters in volume. Explain that blood flows through arteries into smaller and smaller vessels called **arterioles.** Arterioles branch into smaller capillaries. Nutrients and oxygen **diffuse** across the cell membranes lining the walls of the capillaries and across the cell membranes of individual cells. Waste products and carbon dioxide diffuse back across the cell membranes and capillary walls back into the bloodstream. The capillaries join together (e.g., like lanes merging in a highway) combining to form larger **venules** that join to form larger veins.

Go!

Give students ample time to complete the activity described in Figure B on Journal Sheet #2. Stress the importance of treating the goldfish gently as they will survive this ordeal without harm if treated with care.

Materials

small goldfish (e.g., feeders), petri dishes, cotton balls, water, glass slide, microscopes

HB6 JOURNAL SHEET #2

THE CIRCULATORY SYSTEM

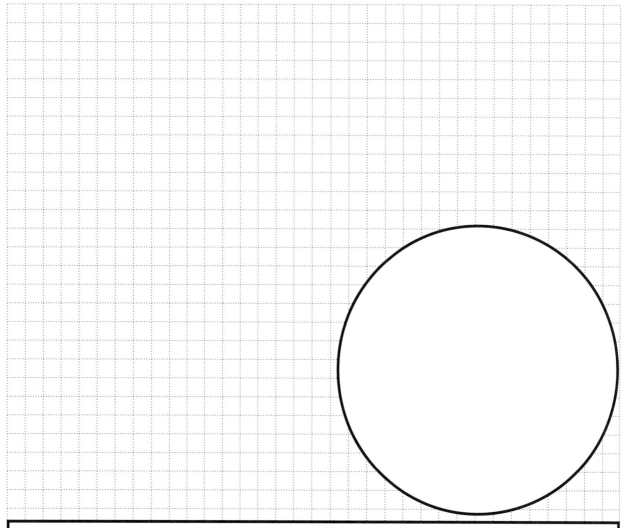

FIGURE B

<u>Directions</u>: (1) Place the small goldfish provided by your instructor on its side in a petri dish. (2) Soak a cotton ball in water and cover the body of the fish above the tail with the wet cotton. The water in the cotton has dissolved oxygen that the fish will absorb through its gills to stay alive. (3) Place the slide flat over the fish's tail. (4) Place the dish on the microscope stage and focus on the tail using low power. You may need to move the dish around until you see tiny dots (e.g., red blood cells) moving along invisible tubes (e.g., capillaries) through the fish's tail. (5) When you see a flow of tiny dots raise the objective lens and focus again using a higher power. (6) Quickly sketch your observations at low or medium power. (7) Put the fish back into the tank or baggie as instructed by your teacher.

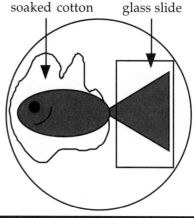

soaked cotton   glass slide

GENERAL HEALTH AND SAFETY GUIDELINES

Wash your hands with soap and water when you are finished handling the fish. Remember to treat all animals with care and respect. With proper handling the goldfish will survive this temporary ordeal without injury.

THE CIRCULATORY SYSTEM

Work Date: ____/____/____

LESSON OBJECTIVE

Students will examine the effects of exercise on pulse rate.

Classroom Activities

On Your Mark!

Draw Illustration C on the board and have students copy your drawing on Journal Sheet #3. Explain that a "pulse" marks the swelling of a vein where a valve is opening and closing with each **systolic** (e.g., ventricular) **beat** of the heart. In drawing "A" the heart beats and forces the valve open allowing blood to flow through the vein. In "B" the blood flows back against the valve forcing it to close, thereby preventing "backflow" in the circulatory system. This occurs during the **diastolic** (e.g., atrial) **beat** when the ventricles relax and the atria pump blood into them.

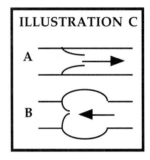

Get Set!

Demonstrate how to take a pulse: (1) Hold the hand palm up. (2) Press the middle finger of the other hand gently against the wrist at the base of the radius (e.g., base of the thumb). Feel around until you locate the pulse. (3) Count the number of beats during a 15 second interval and multiply by 4 to get the number of ventricular beats (e.g., pulse rate) per minute. Point out that other pulses can be detected at the back of the knee and under the chin at the back of the jaw (e.g., jugular pulse).

Go!

Check your list of students to be sure that all students are physically able to complete the activity described in Figure C on Journal Sheet #3. ANY STUDENT WITH ASTHMA OR OTHER RESPIRATORY OR HEART PROBLEMS SHOULD BE EXCUSED FROM PERFORMING THE ACTIVITY! Give students ample time to complete the activity described in Figure C on Journal Sheet #3. They will observe the degree to which exercise accelerates pulse rate.

Materials

second hand or stopwatches

HB6 Journal Sheet #3

THE CIRCULATORY SYSTEM

EFFECTS OF EXERCISE ON PULSE RATE		
name	rate before exercise	rate after exercise
average rates		

FIGURE C

<u>Directions</u>: (1) Place your middle finger on the pulse of your wrist. (2) Count the number of pulse beats in a 30 second interval and multiply by 2. This is the number of times your heart beats in one minute. (3) Jog in place at a leisurely pace for two minutes and repeat Steps #1 and #2. (4) Collect the same information from 10 classmates and average the "before" and "after" set of measures. Explain your observations.

THE CIRCULATORY SYSTEM

Work Date: _____/_____/_____

LESSON OBJECTIVE

Students will illustrate the organs of the circulatory system to be added to the human body chart project.

Classroom Activities

On Your Mark!

Display textbook illustrations of the four-chambered human heart and compare the structures in the illustration to the schematic drawing on Journal Sheet #1. The position of the heart is directly beneath the sternum with the upper chambers (e.g., the atria) tilted slightly toward the left side of the body. Explain to students that they will continue working on their long-term project of the human body chart.

Get Set!

Distribute posters and art materials.

Go!

Give students ample time to complete the activity described in Figure D on Journal Sheet #4. As in previous lessons, discourage students from designing three-dimensional structures as their project will be difficult to store in the weeks ahead.

Materials

butcher paper, construction paper, scissors, crayon or felt-tip markers

HB6 JOURNAL SHEET #4

THE CIRCULATORY SYSTEM

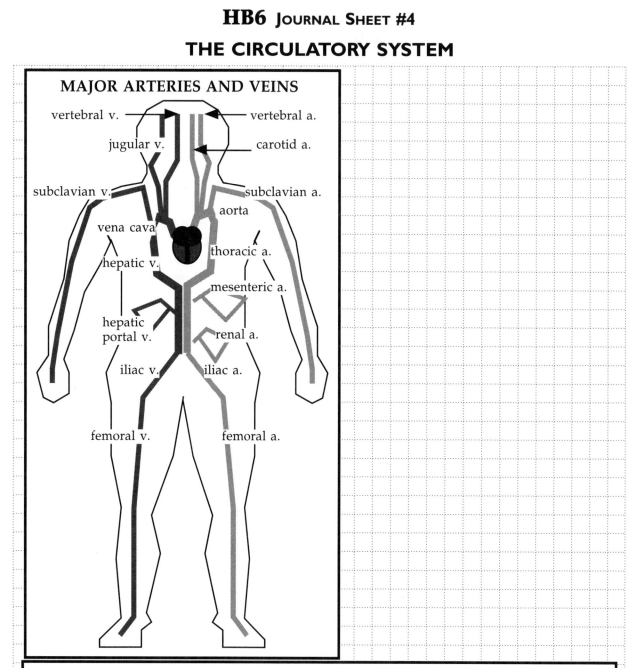

MAJOR ARTERIES AND VEINS

FIGURE D

Directions: (1) Continue working on your HUMAN BODY CHART. (2) Use the materials provided by your instructor to draw pictures of the individual organs of the circulatory system so that they can be placed in their proper positions on the butcher paper diagram. You will need to lift the sternum and rib cage to place the heart in its proper position beneath the sternum. (3) Use the diagram above to position the major blood vessels beneath the skeletal muscles and digestive tract remembering that—unlike this diagram—both arteries and veins run on both sides of the body. The pulmonary artery and pulmonary vein will be added in the next unit on the respiratory system. (4) Use small sections of tape no more than a centimeter in length to secure the paper parts. DO NOT SECURE THEM PERMANENTLY! You will have to change their positions again to add additional structures later on during the course of this activity. (5) Roll up the chart neatly and wrap it with a rubber band before securing it in the box provided by your instructor. (6) Use the remainder of this Journal Sheet to record any tasks you might need to accomplish at home to enhance the look of this project.

HB6 Review Quiz

Directions: Keep your eyes on your own work.
Read all directions and questions carefully.
THINK BEFORE YOU ANSWER!
Watch your spelling, be neat, and do the best you can.

CLASSWORK   (~40): _____
HOMEWORK   (~20): _____
CURRENT EVENT   (~10): _____
TEST   (~30): _____

TOTAL   (~100): _____
(A ≥ 90, B ≥ 80, C > 70, D > 60, F < 60)

LETTER GRADE: _____

TEACHER'S COMMENTS: _____
_____

THE CIRCULATORY SYSTEM

TRUE–FALSE FILL-IN: If the statement is true, write the word TRUE. If the statement is false, change the underlined word to make the statement true. *10 points*

_____ 1. The function of the circulatory system is to transport important nutrients throughout the body in a liquid solution called <u>urea</u>.

_____ 2. All cells use <u>carbon dioxide</u> to burn food for energy.

_____ 3. <u>Oxygen</u> is the waste product of a "burning" process called respiration.

_____ 4. Supplying cells with oxygen and removing carbon dioxide from the cells of the body is one main function of the <u>excretory</u> system.

_____ 5. Blood is pumped to all the organs of the body by the <u>skeletal</u> muscles.

_____ 6. Oxygen-rich blood from the <u>kidneys</u> arrives on the left side of the heart.

_____ 7. Oxygen-rich blood is pumped throughout the rest of the body through a major blood vessel called the <u>artery</u>.

_____ 8. The heart has <u>four</u> chambers that keep "oxygen-rich" and "carbon dioxide-rich" blood separated.

_____ 9. <u>Arteries</u> are blood vessels that carry blood away from the heart.

_____ 10. <u>Veins</u> are thin-walled blood vessels that carry blood back to the heart.

ESSAY: List 5 solid substances present in blood. *10 points*

_____   _____   _____   _____   _____

HB6 Review Quiz *(cont'd)*

Directions: Begin with oxygen entering the lungs. Then write the letters A, B, C, D, E, F, G, H, I, and J in blanks #11 through #20 to describe how blood circulates around the body. The letter "J" should be the structure that sends blood back to the lungs. *10 points*

Oxygen enters the blood in the tiny air sacs of the lungs, then goes to the _____

_____ 11.   left atrium

_____ 12.   capillaries

_____ 13.   right ventricle

_____ 14.   veins

_____ 15.   pulmonary vein

_____ 16.   left ventricle

_____ 17.   aorta

_____ 18.   arteries

_____ 19.   pulmonary artery

_____ 20.   right atrium

THE RESPIRATORY SYSTEM

Teacher's Classwork Agenda and Content Notes

Classwork Agenda for the Week

1. Students will identify the organs of the respiratory system and make a model of the lungs to show how we breathe.

2. Students will demonstrate the presence of carbon dioxide in exhaled air.

3. Students will demonstrate the effect of exercise on the air capacity of the lungs.

4. Students will illustrate the organs of the respiratory system to be added to the human body chart project.

Content Notes for Lecture and Discussion

The ancient Greeks, including **Hippocrates** (b. 460 B.C.; d. 377 B.C.), thought that breathing served to cool the body made warm by the "animal heat" produced by the heart. The English physician **William Harvey** (b. 1578; d. 1657), having shown how the circulatory system recycles blood in the body, showed that blood was "reinvigorated" to a healthy red color in the lungs, then passed via the pulmonary vein to the left atrium and ventricle for distribution to the body. The English physicist and chemist **Robert Boyle** (b. 1627; d. 1691) and his young contemporary English physician **John Mayow** (b. 1841; d. 1879) showed that air was necessary for life. The Swiss physician and "founder of neurology" **Albrecht von Haller** (b. 1708; d. 1777) discovered the function of the diaphragm in regulating the mechanics of breathing; but exactly how the air was absorbed into the blood through the lungs remained a mystery until the Italian physician **Marcello Malpighi** (b. 1628; d. 1694) discovered pulmonary capillaries under the microscope in thin sections of human and animal lung tissue. It remained for the French chemist **Antoine Lavoisier** (b. 1743; d. 1794) to make the connection between air and combustion and draw the analogy between combustion and respiration at about the same time that oxygen was being isolated in 1774 by the English chemist **Joseph Priestley** (b. 1733; d. 1804).

The pioneering work of German chemists **Julius Lothar Meyer** (b. 1830; d. 1895), **Otto Funke** (b. 1828; d. 1879), and **Ernst Felix Hoppe-Seyler** (b. 1825; d. 1895) resulted in the discovery of hemoglobin in addition to a variety of other organic compounds. Hemoglobin is the red-pigmented protein present in the red blood cells that attaches to molecular oxygen (e.g., O_2) and carbon dioxide. The protein containing several dozen amino acids and a porphyrin ring complex made of iron is produced in bone marrow. It is the iron ion that bonds loosely to an oxygen or a carbon dioxide molecule. The production of hemoglobin requires iron, vitamin B_{12} and folic acid.

The French physiologist **Pierre Jean Marie Flourens** (b. 1794; d. 1867) found the location of the brain region responsible for regulating respiratory rate in the brainstem or medulla oblongata.

In Lesson #1, students will identify the organs of the respiratory system and make a model of the lungs to show how we breathe.

In Lesson #2, students will demonstrate the presence of carbon dioxide in exhaled air.

In Lesson #3, students will demonstrate the effect of exercise on the air capacity of the lungs.

In Lesson #4, students will illustrate the organs of the respiratory system to be added to the human body chart project.

HB7 Content Notes *(cont'd)*

ANSWERS TO THE HOMEWORK PROBLEMS

Students' graphs will vary but should show that heart rate is greater than respiration rate at a ratio of about 4:1 in both cases.

ANSWERS TO THE END-OF-THE-WEEK REVIEW QUIZ

1. oxygen
2. true
3. respiratory
4. bronchi (pl.)/bronchus (s.)
5. alveoli (pl.)/alveolus (s.)

6. true
7. capillaries
8. diaphragm
9. epiglottis
10. less

11. larynx
12. trachea
13. bronchus
14. alveoli (pl.)/alveolus (s.)
15. diaphragm

ESSAY: habitual coughing, sore throat, bronchitis, emphysema, cancer

HB7 Fact Sheet

THE RESPIRATORY SYSTEM

CLASSWORK AGENDA FOR THE WEEK

(1) Identify the organs of the respiratory system and make a model of the lungs to show how we breathe.
(2) Demonstrate the presence of carbon dioxide in exhaled air.
(3) Demonstrate the effect of exercise on the air capacity of the lungs.
(4) Illustrate the organs of the respiratory system to be added to the human body chart project.

Chemical respiration combines oxygen and glucose (e.g., simple sugar) to produce energy. Water and carbon dioxide—a gas that can impair the metabolism of cells—is also created in the process. The major task of the **respiratory system** is to get oxygen into the body and carbon dioxide out of the body. The major organs of the respiratory system are the *nose, pharynx* (e.g., throat), *larynx* (e.g., voice box), *trachea, bronchi, lungs* and a strong muscle located at the bottom of the rib cage called the *diaphragm.*

When a person inhales the **diaphragm** contracts to expand the rib cage. At the same time, a tiny muscular flap called the **epiglottis** opens the **trachea**, the main air passage leading to the lungs. Air is forced into the lungs by atmospheric pressure. The diaphragm is a voluntary muscle like other skeletal muscles but is also under the automatic control of the nervous system. That is why it is extremely difficult for people to hold their breath for an extended period of time. Sensors in the blood vessels of the brain detect the rise of carbon dioxide in the bloodstream. When this happens the brain sends a message to the diaphragm to contract and force the person to start breathing. Holding your breath for an extended period of time can be very dangerous and should never be attempted. Resulting dizziness could cause a fall and serious injury.

Small hairs in the nose filter dust particles that could clog air passages as air flows into the body past the **pharynx**. The trachea is lined with a sticky protein called **mucus** and tiny hairs called **cilia** that trap and sweep dust and impurities back into the mouth as **phlegm**. The trachea divides into a left and right **bronchus**. One bronchus is attached to each lung. Each bronchus divides into smaller tubes called **bronchioles** that spread out into the lungs like the branches of a tree. Each bronchiole ends in a cluster of microscopic air sacs called **alveoli**. The exchange of oxygen for carbon dioxide occurs in the alveoli which are surrounded by networks of **capillaries**.

When the diaphragm relaxes the volume of the rib cage decreases expelling gases into the air. A person exhales four times as much carbon dioxide as they inhale. However, nitrogen and oxygen still make up the larger percentages of exhaled air. That is the reason it is possible to help an unconscious person breathe using **cardiopulmonary resuscitation** (e.g., **CPR**). CPR is also known as **artificial respiration**. CPR forces a lot more oxygen than carbon dioxide into an unconscious person's lungs. A person who exhales can also control the muscles inside the **larynx**, the organ of speech. The larynx—or "Adam's apple"—is made of cartilage and can be felt at the front of the neck.

Cigarette and cigar smoke contain tar, soot, and dust that clog the bronchioles and alveoli of the lungs. A habitual smoker destroys lung tissue at a regular rate until there are very few healthy alveoli helping the lungs to do their job. The most common ailments caused by smoking are **habitual coughing, sore throat, bronchitis, emphysema**, and **cancer**. Emphysema and cancer are major life-threatening diseases.

Homework Directions

Compare the increase in heart rate to the increase in respiratory rate during periods of relaxation and exercise. To take your heart rate while sitting in a relaxed position, (1) place your middle finger on the pulse of your wrist. (2) Count the number of pulse beats in a 30 second interval and multiply by 2. This is the number of times your heart beats in one minute. (3) Jog in place at a leisurely pace for 2 minutes and repeat Steps #1 and #2. (4) Wait 15 minutes, then measure your respiratory rate by (5) counting the number of breaths you inhale during a 30 second interval. Multiply by 2. This is your rate of respiration per minute. (6) Jog in place at a leisurely pace for 2 minutes and repeat Step #5. (7) Make a bar graph to compare the number of heart beats to the number of breaths you take while at rest and immediately after exercise.

Assignment due: _____

_____ _____ ____/____/____
Student's Signature   Parent's Signature   Date

THE RESPIRATORY SYSTEM

Work Date: ___/___/___

LESSON OBJECTIVE

Students will identify the organs of the respiratory system and make a model of the lungs to show how we breathe.

Classroom Activities

On Your Mark!

Before the start of class prepare the 1-holed rubber stopper-glass tube assembly shown in Figure A on Journal Sheet #1.

Use the information in the Teacher's Classwork Agenda and Content Notes to give a brief lecture about ancient views of the respiratory system according to **Hippocrates** (b. 460 B.C.; d. 377 B.C.). Draw Illustration A on the board and have students copy your drawing on Journal Sheet #1 as you give a brief history of the scientists whose discoveries led to our understanding of the system.

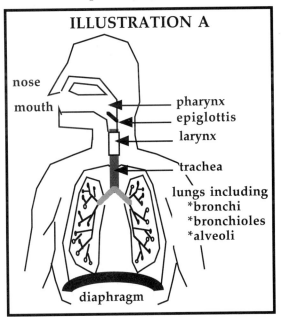

ILLUSTRATION A

nose

mouth

pharynx
epiglottis
larynx

trachea

lungs including
*bronchi
*bronchioles
*alveoli

diaphragm

Get Set!

Give students time to read the Fact Sheet as they label the parts of the respiratory system using that information. Circulate around the room to make sure they are labelling their drawing correctly.

Go!

Give students ample time to construct the model of the lungs and diaphragm as described in Figure A on Journal Sheet #1. Circulate around the room making sure that their paragraph explanation summarizes the mechanisms that allow us to breathe. They should mention that the diaphragm pulls down and increases the volume of the chest cavity, thereby allowing the atmosphere to force air into the lungs. Relaxing the diaphragm reduces the volume of the chest cavity, forcing air back out of the lungs.

Materials

2-liter plastic bottles, small and large balloons, tape, 1-holed rubber stoppers with glass tubing

HB7 JOURNAL SHEET #1

THE RESPIRATORY SYSTEM

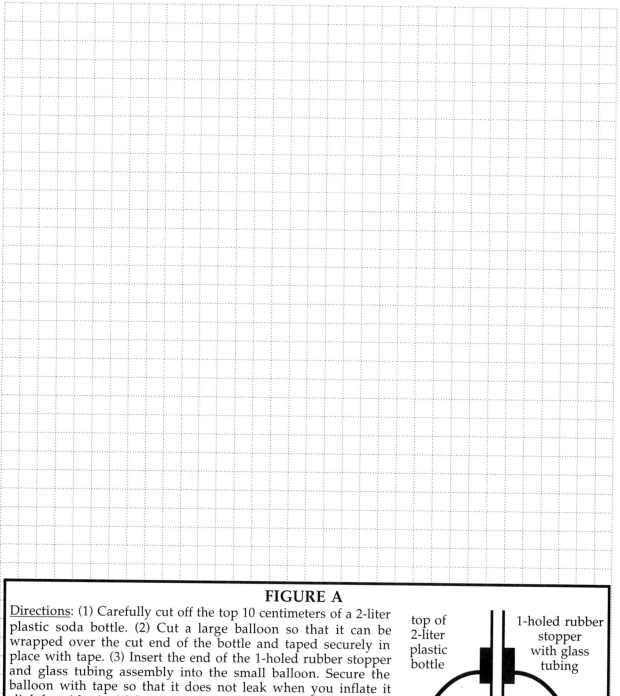

FIGURE A

<u>Directions</u>: (1) Carefully cut off the top 10 centimeters of a 2-liter plastic soda bottle. (2) Cut a large balloon so that it can be wrapped over the cut end of the bottle and taped securely in place with tape. (3) Insert the end of the 1-holed rubber stopper and glass tubing assembly into the small balloon. Secure the balloon with tape so that it does not leak when you inflate it slightly with air. (4) Insert the balloon and rubber stopper into the mouth of the bottle tight enough to prevent leaks. (5) Pull down on the large balloon (e.g., the diaphragm) and record your observations. (6) Press up on the large balloon and record your observations. (7) Close the top of the glass tubing with the tip of your index finger and repeat Steps #5 and #6. Write a brief paragraph explaining how the actions of the diaphragm make us breathe.

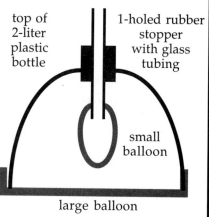

top of 2-liter plastic bottle

1-holed rubber stopper with glass tubing

small balloon

large balloon

THE RESPIRATORY SYSTEM

Work Date: ____/____/____

LESSON OBJECTIVE

Students will demonstrate the presence of carbon dioxide in exhaled air.

Classroom Activities

On Your Mark!

Prepare a weak sodium hydroxide (e.g., NaOH) solution and phenolphthalein solution. The former can be prepared by dissolving 4 grams of NaOH in 1,000 milliliters of water. The latter can be purchased in liquid form from a laboratory supply house or can be prepared by adding 1 gram of phenolphthalein powder to 40 ml of ethyl alcohol and 120 ml of distilled water. Together the two solutions will combine to form the "carbon dioxide indicator solution" students will use in the activity described in Figure B on Journal Sheet #2.

Use the information in the Teacher's Classwork Agenda and Content Notes to give a brief lecture about **hemoglobin**. Explain that the hemoglobin molecule is a chain of several dozen amino acids with an attached carbon (e.g., porphyrin) ring containing **iron** ions. The iron in hemoglobin can bond lightly to oxygen or carbon dioxide molecules depending upon the chemical characteristics of the surrounding solution (e.g., blood plasma). Rich red blood indicates the presence of oxygen bound to hemoglobin while purple blood indicates the presence of carbon dioxide bound to hemoglobin.

Get Set!

Explain that **sodium hydroxide** (e.g., a chemical base - NaOH) turns pink in the presence of a substance called **phenolphthalein**. When carbon dioxide (e.g., CO_2) is mixed with water (e.g., H_2O) the two molecules form an acid called **carbonic acid** (e.g., H_2CO_3). Acids neutralize bases to form salt and water. By breathing into a weak solution of NaOH that has been "stained" with phenolphthalein, carbonic acid will be produced to neutralize the sodium hydroxide. This will cause the pink solution to become clear. Write the chemical equations on the board and have students who have had an introduction to chemistry copy the equations.

$$CO_2 + H_2O \longrightarrow H_2CO_3$$
$$2NaOH + H_2CO_3 \longrightarrow Na_2CO_3 + 2H_2O$$

Go!

Give students ample time to complete the activity described in Figure B on Journal Sheet #2.

Materials

sodium hydroxide, phenolphthalein solution (or phenolphthalein powder and ethyl alcohol), water, straws, medicine droppers, 250 ml beakers

HB7 Journal Sheet #2

THE RESPIRATORY SYSTEM

FIGURE B

Directions: (1) Fill a beaker with 100 ml of water. (2) Add 5 drops of the phenolphthalein indicator. (3) Add a few drops of the sodium hydroxide solution until the solution turns a "rose" color and remains pink after light stirring with a plastic straw. (4) Gently blow into the solution using the plastic straw for up to a minute and record your observations. AVOID SPLATTERING THE SOLUTION!

GENERAL HEALTH AND SAFETY PRECAUTIONS.

Wear goggles. AVOID DRAWING ANY OF THE TEST SOLUTION UP THE STRAW. Phenolphthalein can cause illness if ingested and is toxic to skin.

THE RESPIRATORY SYSTEM

Work Date: ____/____/____

LESSON OBJECTIVE

Students will demonstrate the effect of exercise on the air capacity of the lungs.

Classroom Activities

On Your Mark!

Before the start of class prepare the 2-holed rubber stopper-rubber tubing assembly shown in Figure C on Journal Sheet #3.

Review the results of the activity performed in Lesson #3 in the last unit on *The Circulatory System*. Ask students to explain why heart rate increases during exercise. They should explain that the cells of the body require more nutrients (e.g., glucose) to provide energy for the body to do extra work. Explain that additional oxygen is also required to keep the cells healthy as they work.

Get Set!

Explain that **chemical respiration** occurring in the individual cells of the body is the burning of **glucose** by **oxygen** to produce **carbon dioxide** and **water**. Write the following chemical equation on the board and have students who have had an introduction to chemistry copy the equations.

$$C_6H_{12}O_6 + 6O_2 \longrightarrow 6CO_2 + 6H_2O$$

Go!

Check your list of students to be sure that all students are physically able to complete the activity described in Figure C on Journal Sheet #3. ANY STUDENT WITH ASTHMA OR OTHER RESPIRATORY OR HEART PROBLEMS SHOULD BE EXCUSED FROM PERFORMING THE ACTIVITY! Give the rest of the class ample time to complete the activity. When they are finished, have students spend several minutes brainstorming the effects that smoking would have on the capacity of the lungs to take in oxygen during vigorous exercise. Have them relate this information to the results of their Homework Assignment. Ask them if they think the results of the activity performed in Lesson #2 of this unit would change if they blew into the straw after exercise. Answer: It would take less time to clear the solution because there is more carbon dioxide in each exhaled breath during exercise.

Materials

plastic gallon bottles, 2-holed rubber stopper-rubber tubing assembly, 100 ml graduated cylinders, tissues or paper towels, 2 liter plastic soda bottles

HB7 JOURNAL SHEET #3

THE RESPIRATORY SYSTEM

EFFECTS OF EXERCISE ON LUNG CAPACITY

name	capacity before exercise	capacity after exercise
average capacity		

FIGURE C

Directions: (1) Fill a plastic gallon bottle with water. (2) Attach the rubber tubing to the glass tubes in the 2-holed rubber stopper provided by your instructor. (3) Cap the bottle securely to prevent air leaks. (4) Place the end of the long rubber tube into a 2 liter plastic soda bottle. (5) Cover the short rubber tube with a single-ply layer of tissue or paper towel and exhale into the short tube. (6) Measure the amount of water that spills into the 2 liter bottle using a 100 ml graduated cylinder. This represents the approximate capacity of your lungs. (7) Discard the tissue or paper towel to prevent the spread of germs. (8) Jog in place at a leisurely pace for two minutes and repeat Step #5 through #7. (9) Collect the same information from 10 classmates and average the "before" and "after" measures. Explain your observations.

THE RESPIRATORY SYSTEM

Work Date: ____/____/____

LESSON OBJECTIVE

Students will illustrate the organs of the respiratory system to be added to the human body chart project.

Classroom Activities

On Your Mark!

Display textbook illustrations of the respiratory or cardiopulmonary systems and compare the structures in the illustration to the schematic drawing on Journal Sheet #1. Explain to students that they will continue working on their long-term project of the human body chart.

Get Set!

Distribute posters and art materials.

Go!

Give students ample time to complete the activity described in Figure D on Journal Sheet #4. As in previous lessons, discourage students from designing three-dimensional structures as their project will be difficult to store in the weeks ahead.

Materials

butcher paper, construction paper, scissors, crayon or felt-tip markers

HB7 JOURNAL SHEET #4

THE RESPIRATORY SYSTEM

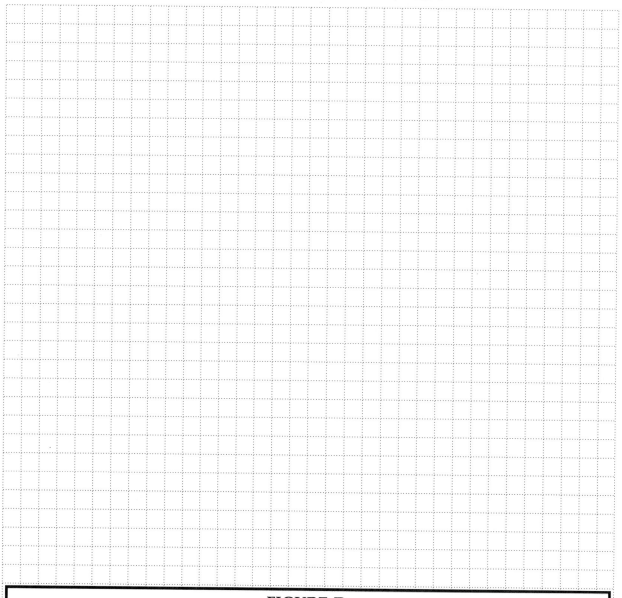

FIGURE D

<u>Directions</u>: (1) Continue working on your HUMAN BODY CHART. (2) Use the materials provided by your instructor to draw pictures of the individual organs of the respiratory system—adding the pulmonary arteries and pulmonary veins—so that they can be placed in their proper positions on the butcher paper diagram. You will need to lift the sternum and rib cage, heart, and major cardiac blood vessels to place the trachea, bronchi, and lungs in their proper position beneath the heart. (3) Don't forget to attach the pairs of pulmonary arteries and pulmonary veins that transport blood from the heart to the lungs and back to the heart. Attach the diaphragm to the bottom of the rib cage. (4) Use small sections of tape <u>no more than a centimeter in length</u> to secure the paper parts. DO NOT SECURE THEM PERMANENTLY! You will have to change their positions again to add additional structures later on during the course of this activity. (5) Roll up the chart neatly and wrap it with a rubber band before securing it in the box provided by your instructor. (6) Use the remainder of this Journal Sheet to record any tasks you might need to accomplish at home to enhance the look of this project.

HB7 Review Quiz

Directions: Keep your eyes on your own work.
Read all directions and questions carefully.
THINK BEFORE YOU ANSWER!
Watch your spelling, be neat, and do the best you can.

CLASSWORK	(~40): _____
HOMEWORK	(~20): _____
CURRENT EVENT	(~10): _____
TEST	(~30): _____
TOTAL	(~100): _____

(A ≥ 90, B ≥ 80, C ≥ 70, D ≥ 60, F < 60)

LETTER GRADE: _____

TEACHER'S COMMENTS: _____
_____

THE RESPIRATORY SYSTEM

TRUE–FALSE FILL-IN: If the statement is true, write the word TRUE. If the statement is false, change the underlined word to make the statement true. *10 points*

_____ 1. Chemical respiration combines <u>hydrogen</u> and glucose to produce energy.

_____ 2. In addition to energy, other products of respiration are water and <u>carbon dioxide</u>.

_____ 3. The main task of the <u>excretory</u> system is to get oxygen into the body and carbon dioxide out of the body.

_____ 4. The trachea divides into two <u>bronchioles</u>.

_____ 5. Bronchioles end in tiny air sacs called <u>ravioli</u>.

_____ 6. The human voice is produced in an organ called the <u>larynx</u>.

_____ 7. Tiny air sacs in the lungs are surrounded by <u>mucus</u> carrying red blood cells.

_____ 8. Movement of the <u>lung muscle</u> produces inhaling and exhaling.

_____ 9. Choking can occur if the <u>esophagus</u> fails to close as a person swallows food.

_____ 10. Exhaled air contains <u>more</u> carbon dioxide than oxygen.

ESSAY: List 5 ailments that are caused by smoking. *10 points*

_____   _____   _____   _____   _____

DIAGRAM: Fill in the blanks with the names of the organs of the respiratory system. *10 points*

11. _____

12. _____

13. _____

14. _____

15. _____

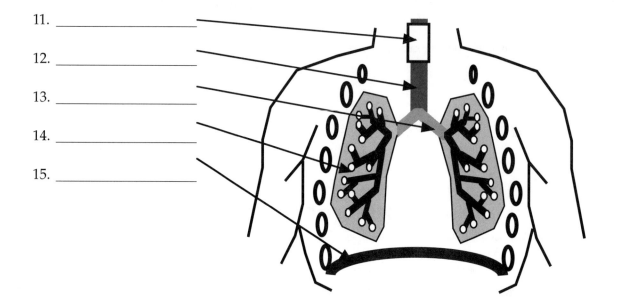

_____   _____   ____/____/____
   Student's Signature   Parent's Signature   Date

THE SENSE ORGANS

TEACHER'S CLASSWORK AGENDA AND CONTENT NOTES

Classwork Agenda for the Week

1. Students will identify the different types of sensory receptors of the skin.
2. Students will dissect a sheep's eye to identify the parts of the eye.
3. Students will identify the parts of the ear and the organ of balance.
4. Students will test the taste receptors of the tongue.

Content Notes for Lecture and Discussion

The Greek physician **Alcmeaon** (c. 500 B.C.) performed the first animal dissections in an attempt to discover the "sensory channels" leading to the brain. While **Hippocrates** (b. 460 B.C.; d. 377 B.C.) argued that the brain was the seat of sensibility (e.g., sensation, thought, and feeling) **Plato** (b. 427 B.C.; d. 347 B.C.) relegated sensations to that part of the soul residing in the heart. It was not until the Greek physicians **Herophilus of Chalcedon** (c. 330 B.C.; c. 260 B.C.) and **Erasistratus** (c. 304 B.C.; c. 250 B.C.) distinguished nerves in the course of their human dissections, tracing nerve fibers to the brain, that the direct link between sensory organs and the nervous system was established.

Despite their anatomical and physiological complexity the organs of sight, hearing, smell, taste, and touch give us a strictly limited view of the world around us. The eyes are sensitive to a restricted range of electromagnetic wavelengths from about 350 to 750 millimicrons (e.g., 10^{-9} meters). This range comprises the entire range of visible light perceived by animals and used by plants for photosynthesis. The ears are sensitive to mechanical vibrations at frequencies of 16 to 16,000 oscillations per second. The two chemical senses, smell and taste, rely on the ability of specialized cells to detect a particular variety of molecular structures. There are more "odorless" and "tasteless" substances than there are aromatic and palatable ones. Physiologists group odors into seven major categories: camphoraceous, ethereal, floral, musky, peppermint, pungent, and putrid. The taste buds of the tongue can discern bitter, sour, salty, and sweet but nothing more. The sensory cells of the skin can detect light and heavy pressure, heat and cold; but their placement around the approximately 2 square meters of skin that cover the human body permits varying degrees of discrimination. The tips of the fingers can discriminate objects a fraction of a millimeter apart. Similar judgments made about points of pressure exerted on the back are less exacting.

The senses are a window on the world; but it is the brain that "perceives" that world. The science of **psychophysiology** began with the work of **Sir Isaac Newton** (b. 1642; d. 1727) who established the basic laws of optics. Newton's work was continued by the English physician and Egyptologist **Thomas Young** (b. 1773; d. 1829). Young developed the **trichromatic theory of light** which asserts that the retina is differentially sensitive to three primary colors (e.g., red, green, and blue). The basic idea is that the eye is sensitive to three different kinds of electromagnetic vibrations and that all color sensation results from retinal cells being stimulated at varying degrees of strength. Paint pigments produce colors different from those of varying light frequencies when mixed. The German psychologists **Ernst Heinrich Weber** (b. 1795; d. 1878) and **Gustav Theodor Fechner** (b. 1801; d. 1887) developed the **Weber-Fechner law** in an attempt to resolve the traditional "mind-body problem." The law expresses the logarithmic relationship between the strength of a stimulus and the response elicited. The work of Weber and Fechner led to the beginning of **experimental psychology**. The German physicist and physiologist **Hermann Ludwig Ferdinand von Helmholtz** (b. 1821; d. 1894) invented the ophthalmoscope to examine the interior of the eye.

HB8 Content Notes *(cont'd)*

In addition, he explained the workings of the cochlea and how sounds combine to produce a particular tone and timbre. Advances in the field of **neuroscience** have solved a number of problems related to the processing of information by the sense organs. Yet despite these accomplishments the manner in which the brain works to coordinate the information detected by the senses remains largely a mystery to be solved by future research.

In Lesson #1, students will identify the different types of sensory receptors of the skin.

In Lesson #2, students will dissect a sheep's eye to identify the parts of the eye.

In Lesson #3, students will identify the parts of the ear and the organ of balance.

In Lesson #4, students will test the taste receptors of the tongue.

ANSWERS TO THE HOMEWORK PROBLEMS

Students' essays will vary but should evidence the fact that information from the two restricted fields of vision being sent to the brain leads to the "perception" of a hole in the hand that does not exist.

ANSWERS TO THE END-OF-THE-WEEK REVIEW QUIZ

1. true	6. can	11. eye	16. ear	21. nose	26. eye
2. true	7. true	12. ear	17. skin	22. ear	
3. photons	8. sound	13. skin	18. eye	23. ear	
4. back	9. true	14. eye	19. skin	24. ear	
5. true	10. joints/muscles	15. eye	20. tongue	25. ear	

ESSAY: There are no molecules in outer space to "transfer" the mechanical energy necessary to activate the microphone.

HB8 Fact Sheet

THE SENSE ORGANS

CLASSWORK AGENDA FOR THE WEEK

(1)   Identify the different types of sensory receptors of the skin.
(2)   Dissect a sheep's eye to identify the parts of the eye.
(3)   Identify the parts of the ear and the organ of balance.
(4)   Test the taste receptors of the tongue.

Any change in the environment that affects the way an organism behaves is called a **stimulus** (e.g., the plural is "stimuli"). The human body is equipped with **sense organs** that detect environmental changes. Human beings can recognize a variety of stimuli such as **light** and **sound**, **odor** and **flavor**, **pressure**, **heat**, and **cold**. The sense organs that detect this information are the *eyes* and *ears*, *nose* and *tongue*, and *skin*. An organism's reaction to a change in the environment is called a **response**.

Light is detected by the **eyes**. Light energy is a form of **electromagnetic energy** given off by a light source in the form of "energy packets" called **photons**. Photons come in a variety of wavelengths and frequencies, some of which appear to us as **visible light** (e.g., the colors of the rainbow—red, orange, yellow, green, blue, indigo, and violet). Photons pass through the transparent front of the eye called the **cornea** into the eye through the **pupil**. The amount of light that passes into the eye is controlled by a ring of colored muscles called the **iris**. A **lens** behind the iris focuses light toward the back of the eye. A layer of cells called the **retina** at the back of the eye have chemicals that react to different frequencies of light. When these chemical reactions occur the retinal cells send signals to the brain via a cable of nerve fibers called the **optic nerve**. The brain translates the nerve signals into visual images. A healthy eye cannot see without the brain. The brain, however, is able to form visual images such as those which appear to us in dreams without the eyes.

Sound is detected by the **ears**. Sound energy is a form of **mechanical energy** resulting from the movement of atoms and molecules in gases such as air, liquids and solids. A disturbance in a gas, a liquid or solid, causes the atoms and molecules in the substance to move. The atoms and molecules shake back and forth at varying frequencies that move through the matter in waves. The waves enter the **external ear** or **pinna** and move into the **auditory canal**. At the end of the auditory canal the waves vibrate a thin wall of tissue called the **tympanic membrane** (e.g., ear drum). The vibration shakes three small bones called the **malleus** (e.g., hammer), **incus** (e.g., anvil), and **stapes** (e.g., stirrup) located in the **middle ear** on the opposite side of the tympanic membrane. The shaking stapes vibrates a liquid inside a "snail-shaped" organ in the **internal ear** called the **cochlea**. The inner walls of the coiled cochlea are lined with microscopic hairs that vibrate with the vibrating fluid. The hairs are connected to nerve fibers that send signals to the brain where the information is translated into sound.

Odors are detected by **olfactory cells** located in the **nasal mucous membrane** inside the nose. Chemicals in the air excite these cells to send messages to the **olfactory bulbs** inside the front of the skull on the underside of the brain. The sense of taste is largely a matter of telling the difference between different odors. Without the help of the nose a person could only tell if something were sweet, salty, bitter, or sour, because the top of the tongue—layered with taste buds—can only sense the presence of substances having those four qualities. That is the reason why a person with a "stuffy" cold can hardly taste the food that is eaten.

Pressure, heat, and cold are detected by specialized cells in the **dermis** (e.g., middle layer) **of the skin**. Two types of nerve endings called **Meissner** and **Pacinian corpuscles** send messages to the brain when light or heavy pressure is exerted against the skin. **Ruffini's end organs** are sensitive to the presence of heat; **Krause bulbs** are sensitive to the loss of heat (e.g., cold); and, **free nerve endings** in the skin and tissues of the internal organs send messages to the brain that are translated into the sensation of pain. Pressure endings found in the joints and muscles of the skeleton allow the brain to keep track of the position of the head, torso, arms and legs.

Homework Directions

Perform the following demonstration to show how the brain can be confused by visual stimuli. (1) Roll a piece of looseleaf paper lengthwise into a cylinder. (2) Hold the tube over your right eye. (3) Keep both eyes open and place the left hand against the tube about 10 centimeters from your face with the palm facing you. You will observe a hole in your hand! (4) Explain how the eyes and brain work together to create this illusion.

Assignment due: _____

_____   _____   ___/___/___
      Student's Signature   Parent's Signature   Date

THE SENSE ORGANS

Work Date: ____/____/____

LESSON OBJECTIVE

Students will identify the different types of sensory receptors of the skin.

Classroom Activities

On Your Mark!

Use the information in the Teacher's Classwork Agenda and Content Notes to give a brief lecture about the history of psychophysiology.

Get Set!

Assist students in labelling the diagram of the skin on Journal Sheet #1, indicating the function of each receptor. The sensory receptors from left to right in the illustration are as follows: Krause end bulbs sense cold, Ruffini end-organs sense warmth, free nerve endings sense pain, Meissner corpuscles sense light pressure, and Pacinian corpuscles sense heavy pressure.

Go!

Give students ample time to complete the activity described in Figure A on Journal Sheet #1. Students should report that the forearms and back are less sensitive than the forehead, fingers, and thumb. They should conclude that the pressure sensors in the former locations are spread farther apart than those in the latter locations.

Materials

tape, pencils

HB8 Journal Sheet #1

THE SENSE ORGANS

EPIDERMIS

DERMIS

HYPODERMIS

location touched	number of pencil points touching each location			
forehead				
back of forearm				
front of forearm				
tip of index finger				
tip of thumb				
middle or side of back				

FIGURE A

<u>Directions</u>: (1) Tape 2 pencils together with both points touching the table when the pencils rest vertically on the table. (2) Have a groupmate close his or her eyes. (3) Gently touch the different locations listed in the above table at random with a single point or double point. (4) Record with a number "1" or "2" the number of points you used. (5) Have your classmate report the number of points felt. (6) Put an "X" over each incorrect guess. (7) After comparing the results of touching the different regions, explain how the pressure receptors at each location are distibuted in the skin. Are they farther apart or closer together than the pencil points?

THE SENSE ORGANS

Work Date: ____/____/____

LESSON OBJECTIVE

Students will dissect a sheep's eye to identify the parts of the eye.

Classroom Activities

On Your Mark!

Prepare for this lesson by purchasing sheep eyes from a laboratory supply house.

Assist students in labelling the diagram of the eye shown on Journal Sheet #2. Beginning at "12 o'clock" the structures are as follows: the sclera is the hard outer covering of the eyeball; the **choroid** contains blood vessels that supply the eye with nutrients; the **retina** is the light sensitive layer of **rods** and **cones**; the fovea is the cone-rich focal point where images are focussed; the **macula** is the "blind spot" where nerves exit the eye; the **optic nerve** sends information to the brain; the **vitreous chamber** is filled with a jelly-like fluid that keeps the organs of the eye in place; the **lenticular muscles** change the shape of the lens; the **lens** bends light to bring it into focus on the fovea; the **iris muscles** control the amount of light that enters the eye; the **pupil** is a "hole" in the iris; the **cornea** is the transparent front of the eye. Write a phrase that helps to identify the function of each part of the eye and have students copy the information.

Get Set!

Perform the following demonstration to show students how they can prove that each eye has a "blind spot" that does not have light-sensitive cells. <u>Tell them to watch what you do first before you lead them through the steps one at a time</u>. (1) Draw a dark spot about 5 centimeters in diameter on the board. (2) Walk to the back of the classroom. (3) Cover your left eye with your left hand. (4) Extend your right arm out in front of you with your index finger pointing up, covering the dark spot on the board so that you cannot see it. (5) Slowly move the finger toward the left while keeping your open eye focussed on the finger! **Do not look back at the dot!** (6) When the finger gets about 20–30 centimeters from its starting point the dot on the board will disappear from your peripheral vision. Have the students repeat your instructions step-by-step as you give them. Afterward, have a student volunteer stand in the corner of the room so that everyone can use the same procedure to make the volunteer's head disappear!

Go!

Give students ample time to complete the activities described in Figure B and Figure C on Journal Sheet #2. After staring at the colored flag in Figure B chemicals responsible for the vision of particular colors become depleted, leaving the chemicals sensitive to other colors. Upon looking at the white paper, the "afterimage" of green is a red or pink. The afterimage of yellow is an aqua or blue. Circulate around the room during the dissection to make sure that students are correctly identifying the major organs of the sheep's eye (e.g., sclera, retina, vitreous humor, lens, iris, cornea, optic nerve).

Materials

sheep eyes (if available), dissecting kits, dissecting tray, paper towels, mirrors

HB8 JOURNAL SHEET #2

THE SENSE ORGANS

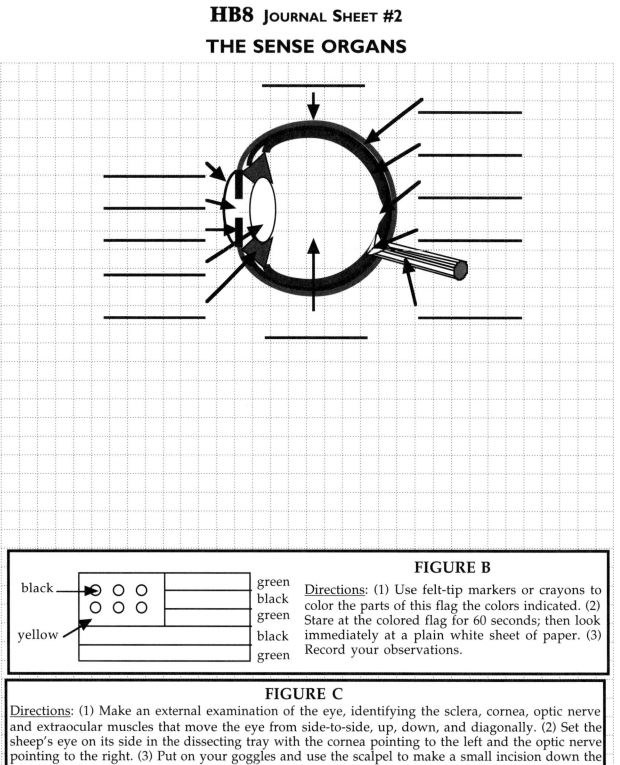

FIGURE B

black ──▶ ⊙ ○ ○
○ ○ ○

yellow ──▶

green
black
green
black
green

Directions: (1) Use felt-tip markers or crayons to color the parts of this flag the colors indicated. (2) Stare at the colored flag for 60 seconds; then look immediately at a plain white sheet of paper. (3) Record your observations.

FIGURE C

Directions: (1) Make an external examination of the eye, identifying the sclera, cornea, optic nerve and extraocular muscles that move the eye from side-to-side, up, down, and diagonally. (2) Set the sheep's eye on its side in the dissecting tray with the cornea pointing to the left and the optic nerve pointing to the right. (3) Put on your goggles and use the scalpel to make a small incision down the middle of the eye. As you make your incision be careful not to cut yourself! The sclera is tough tissue and some force is required to make the cut. Jelly-like vitreous humor will leak and may squirt from the eye as you make the cut. (4) Insert the sharp point of the scissors into the incision and cut around the eye to separate the front of the eye from the back of the eye. (5) Identify the vitreous humor, the lens, iris muscles, and retina.

GENERAL HEALTH AND SAFETY GUIDELINES
Wear goggles. Wash your hands with soap and water when you are finished handling the eye.

THE SENSE ORGANS

Work Date: ____/____/____

LESSON OBJECTIVE

Students will identify the parts of the ear and the organ of balance.

Classroom Activities

On Your Mark!

Assist students in labelling the diagram of the ear shown on Journal Sheet #3. Beginning at "12 o'clock" the structures are as follows: the **semicircular canals** tell the brain the position of the body when hairs in the three perpendicular loops are excited by changes in the position of the head; the **auditory nerve** sends information to the brain about the frequency of mechanical vibrations; the **cochlea** contains microscopic hairs that vibrate at particular frequencies; the **eustachian tube** leading to the pharynx (e.g., throat) allows air to pass into the middle ear preventing the eardrum from bursting as a result of unequal pressure on opposite sides of the membrane; the ossicles (e.g., bones) of the middle ear; the **tympanic membrane** (e.g., ear drum) that vibrates with the mechanical energy in the surrounding environment; the **auditory canal** whose lining is coated with a waxy substance to trap dust and dirt that can damage the ear drum; and the **pinna** that "catches" sound waves and focuses them into the auditory canal.

Get Set!

Explain that the human ear can register mechanical vibrations in the surrounding medium that are within the range of about 16 to 16,000 vibrations per second. The keys of a piano can emit frequencies from about 26 to 4,096 cycles per second. Other animals are adapted to register other frequencies.

Draw Illustration A on the board to explain how the semicircular canals help the brain to know the position of the head. The canals are placed at right angles to one another and filled with liquid. Like the cochlea, the tubes are lined with microscopic hairs that

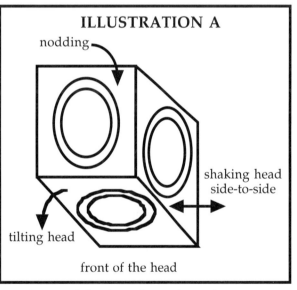

ILLUSTRATION A

nodding

shaking head side-to-side

tilting head

front of the head

vibrate in response to gravity. Movement in any of the three dimensions of space causes the hairs to "waver" sending messages to the brain about the position of the head.

Go!

Give students ample time to complete the activities described in Figure D on Journal Sheet #3.

Materials

metric rulers

HB8 JOURNAL SHEET #3

THE SENSE ORGANS

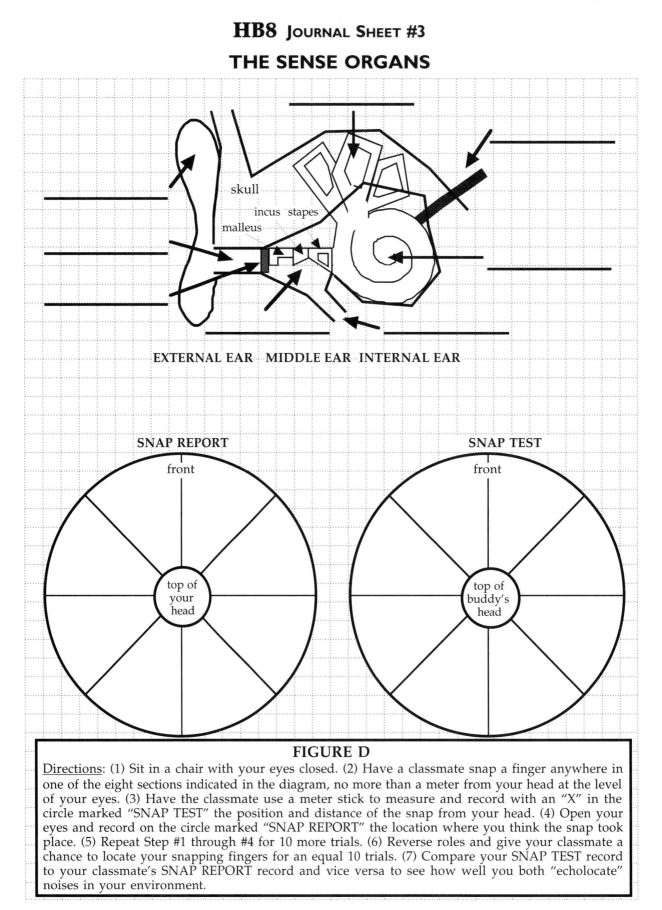

skull

incus stapes

malleus

EXTERNAL EAR   MIDDLE EAR   INTERNAL EAR

SNAP REPORT

front

top of
your
head

SNAP TEST

front

top of
buddy's
head

FIGURE D

Directions: (1) Sit in a chair with your eyes closed. (2) Have a classmate snap a finger anywhere in one of the eight sections indicated in the diagram, no more than a meter from your head at the level of your eyes. (3) Have the classmate use a meter stick to measure and record with an "X" in the circle marked "SNAP TEST" the position and distance of the snap from your head. (4) Open your eyes and record on the circle marked "SNAP REPORT" the location where you think the snap took place. (5) Repeat Step #1 through #4 for 10 more trials. (6) Reverse roles and give your classmate a chance to locate your snapping fingers for an equal 10 trials. (7) Compare your SNAP TEST record to your classmate's SNAP REPORT record and vice versa to see how well you both "echolocate" noises in your environment.

THE SENSE ORGANS

Work Date: ____/____/____

LESSON OBJECTIVE

Students will test the taste receptors of the tongue.

Classroom Activities

On Your Mark!

Prepare for class by chopping bits and pieces of apple and onion (e.g., cubic centimeter pieces) to demonstrate the incapacity of the tongue to recognize odors.

Begin the lesson with this classic demonstration using a responsible, emotionally stable student who is not allergic to apples or onions. Instruct the class to remain absolutely silent so that the volunteer can give an accurate reporting of their observations. Then, (1) have a blindfolded student hold their nostrils closed tightly. (2) Ask the student to report on the taste of the "apple" you will put into their mouth. (3) Use a toothpick to randomly feed the volunteer small chunks of apple and onion from a baggie. The student is likely to report that they can taste nothing. (4) Have the student let go of their nostrils and remove the blindfold. The will probably react with surprise at the onion smell permeating their mucous membranes.

Get Set!

Refer to the diagram on Journal Sheet #4 to identify the parts of the human **olfactory system**. Write the following terms on the board and have students copy your list and examples on their Journal Sheet, pointing out that the **nose** is the primary organ of "taste": camphoraceous (e.g., moth balls), ethereal (e.g., dry-cleaning fluid), floral (e.g., roses), musky (e.g., angelica root oil), peppermint (e.g., mint candy), pungent (e.g., vinegar), and putrid (e.g., rotting eggs). Explain that the tongue is only sensitive to bitter (e.g., soapy), sour (e.g, acidic), salty, and sweet.

Remind students that inhaling an unknown or foreign substance can cause dizziness, illness, or death!

Go!

Give students ample time complete the activities described in Figure E on Journal Sheet #4.

Materials

salt, sugar, lemons, water, clean and sterile 100 ml beakers, clean and sterile medicine droppers, apples, onions, blindfold

HB8 JOURNAL SHEET #4

THE SENSE ORGANS

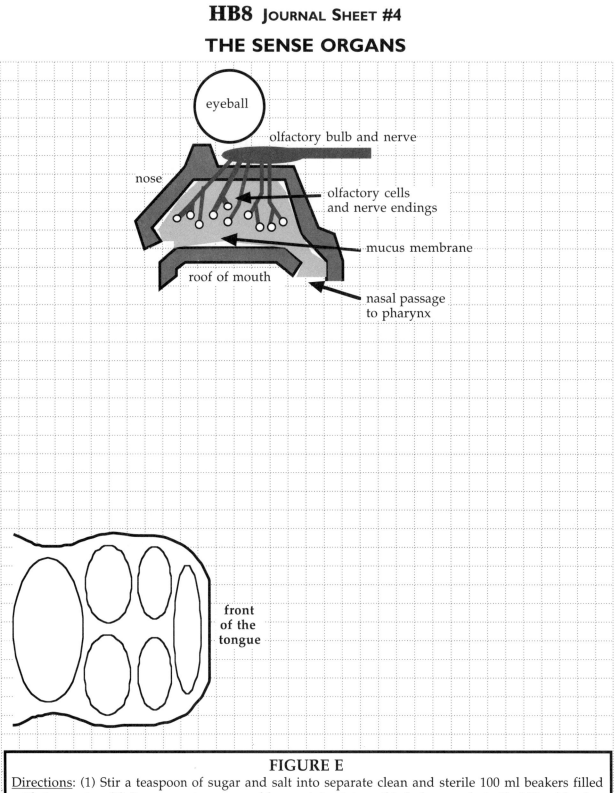

eyeball

olfactory bulb and nerve

nose

olfactory cells
and nerve endings

mucus membrane

roof of mouth

nasal passage
to pharynx

front
of the
tongue

FIGURE E

Directions: (1) Stir a teaspoon of sugar and salt into separate clean and sterile 100 ml beakers filled with tap water. (2) Squeeze a teaspoon of lemon juice into a third clean and sterile 100 ml beaker filled with tap water. (3) Have a classmate use a clean and sterile medicine dropper to administer one drop of the sugar solution to the four regions of the tongue indicated in the diagram. (4) Label the region where you tasted the sugar by writing the word "SUGAR". (5) Repeat Steps #3 and #4 for the salt and lemon juice solutions by writing the terms "SALT" and "SOUR", respectively.

HB8 Review Quiz

Directions: Keep your eyes on your own work.
Read all directions and questions carefully.
THINK BEFORE YOU ANSWER!
Watch your spelling, be neat, and do the best you can.

CLASSWORK   (~40): _____
HOMEWORK   (~20): _____
CURRENT EVENT   (~10): _____
TEST   (~30): _____

TOTAL   (~100): _____
(A ≥ 90, B ≥ 80, C ≥ 70, D ≥ 60, F < 60)

LETTER GRADE: _____

TEACHER'S COMMENTS: _____
_____

THE SENSE ORGANS

TRUE–FALSE FILL-IN: If the statement is true, write the word TRUE. If the statement is false, change the underlined word to make the statement true. *10 points*

_____ 1. Any change in the environment that affects the way an organism behaves is called a <u>stimulus</u>.

_____ 2. <u>Light</u> energy is a form of electromagnetic energy.

_____ 3. Tiny "energy packets" of light are called <u>protons</u>.

_____ 4. The layer of cells at the <u>front</u> of the eye has chemicals that react to different frequencies of light.

_____ 5. A healthy eye <u>cannot</u> form conscious visual images without the brain.

_____ 6. The brain <u>cannot</u> form visual images without the eyes.

_____ 7. <u>Sound</u> energy is a form of mechanical energy.

_____ 8. <u>Light</u> results from the movement of atoms and molecules in gases such as air, liquids and solids.

_____ 9. Most flavors are detected by specialized cells in the <u>nose</u>.

_____ 10. The brain knows the position of the head, torso, arms, and legs because it receives nerve signals from sensory endings in the <u>skin</u>.

ESSAY: Write a sentence to explain why an explosion in outer space would not be detected by a nearby microphone. *4 points*

_____

_____

_____

PROBLEM

Directions: Write the word "eye", "ear", "nose", "tongue", or "skin" next to each term to identify the organ to which each part belongs. *16 points*

_____ 11. cornea

_____ 12. malleus

_____ 13. corpuscle

_____ 14. retina

_____ 15. lens

_____ 16. tympanic membrane

_____ 17. Krause bulb

_____ 18. optic nerve

_____ 19. Ruffini organ

_____ 20. taste bud

_____ 21. olfactory cell

_____ 22. incus

_____ 23. stapes

_____ 24. cochlea

_____ 25. pinna

_____ 26. iris

THE NERVOUS SYSTEM

TEACHER'S CLASSWORK AGENDA AND CONTENT NOTES

Classwork Agenda for the Week

1. Students will create a graphic organizer that helps to identify the major divisions and functions of the parts of the nervous system.

2. Students will explain how nerve cells conduct nerve impulses and distinguish between spinal and autonomic reflexes.

3. Students will test the ability of the brain to process different kinds of sensory stimuli.

4. Students will illustrate the organs of the nervous system to be added to the human body chart project.

Content Notes for Lecture and Discussion

The teachings of **Aristotle** (b. 384 B.C.; d. 322 B.C.) and **Plato** (b. 427 B.C.; d. 347 B.C.)—adopted by the Church through the Middle Ages—held that the "immortal soul" initiated all higher mental functions and relegated those functions to the confines of the brain. The nerve fibers leading to the brain—identified in the dissections of the Greek physicians **Herophilus of Chalcedon** (c. 330 B.C.; c. 260 B.C.) and **Erasistratus** (c. 304 B.C.; c. 250 B.C.)—gave the immortal soul its window on the world. The French philosopher-mathematician **René Descartes** (b. 1596; d. 1650) saw the body as a machine whose function and actions could be explained by the same laws that governed the rest of the physical universe. However, Descartes still identified the "mind" as separate from matter and the forces governing motion by postulating that the impulse of thought came from God. Descartes's "mind-body dualism" not only protected his controversial views from the ire of the church but is an idea that persists today among philosophers in their debates over the origins and nature of consciousness.

Nearing the end of the 18th century, the mechanist view of the human body held sway over more metaphysical theories leading to attempts by many physicians and physiologists of the time to localize mental functions in different anatomical regions of the brain. The attempts culminated in the development of **phrenology** by German neuroanatomist **Franz Joseph Gall** (b. 1758; d. 1828) and **Johannes Spurzheim** (b. 1776; d. 1832). The phrenologists believed that highly developed cerebral functions would be reflected in more highly developed regions of the cerebral cortex as well as overlying cranial structures. According to their theory, an individual's mental abilities could be measured by analyzing the lumps and bumps on the skull. While the work of phrenologists fell inevitably into disrepute, the idea of "localization of brain function" has since been firmly established. In the 19th century, following the general acceptance of **the cell theory** proposed by German biologists **Theodor Schwann** (b. 1810; d. 1882) and **Matthias Jakob Schleiden** (b. 1804; d. 1881) in 1838, the detailed analysis of nervous tissue began. The Swiss physiologist **Rudolph Albert von Kölliker** (b. 1817; d. 1905) made the first notable descriptions of nerve cells under the microscope. In the 1880s, the Italian histologist **Camillo Golgi** (b. 1843; d. 1926) described the cerebral cortex as a network of neurons fused at the dendrites, a description that gave support to the then popular **reticular theory of the nervous system**. The work of Swiss scientists **William His** (b. 1831; d. 1904) and **August Forel** (b. 1848; d. 1931) contradicted the reticular theory. His's work was based on his numerous embryological studies while Forel studied the degeneration of nerve tissue following the destruction of nerve bundles. The patterns of degeneration in nerve fibers were stained and observed under the microscope using a variety of histological techniques still in use today. The Spanish cell biologist **Santiago Ramón y Cajal** (b. 1852; d. 1934) established the **neuronal theory of the nervous system**, a theory later used by the English neurophysiologist **Charles Robert Sherrington** (b. 1857; d. 1952) to develop the principles of **reflex action**. In 1963, the Australian physiologist **Sir John Carew Eccles** (b. 1903) shared the Nobel Prize with English physiologists **Alan Lloyd Hodgkin** (b. 1914) and **Andrew Fielding Huxley** (b. 1917) for describing the mechanism underlying the transmission of nerve impulses.

Neuroscientists of the middle and late 20th century have made great strides in elucidating the neuroanatomy and neurophysiology of the human nervous system. Attempts, however, to correlate nervous function with the many behaviors they appear to govern, in light of the sheer complexity of the system, have proved only marginally successful, leaving a number of exciting mysteries to be solved.

In Lesson #1, students will create a graphic organizer that helps to identify the major divisions and functions of the parts of the nervous system.

In Lesson #2, students will explain how nerve cells conduct nerve impulses and distinguish between spinal and autonomic reflexes.

In Lesson #3, students will test the ability of the brain to process different kinds of sensory stimuli.

In Lesson #4, students will illustrate the organs of the nervous system to be added to the human body chart project.

ANSWERS TO THE HOMEWORK PROBLEMS

Students' essays will vary but should describe the path of the initial visual stimulus to the eyes, then through the eyes to the diencephalon, to sensory cortex of the cerebrum, to motor cortex of the cerebrum, to the cerebellum that will insure coordinated body movements, to the brain stem controlling the acceleration of the heart and respiration rate, down to the spinal cord and peripheral nerves of the muscles and other organs of the body resulting in a "flight or fight" response.

ANSWERS TO THE END-OF-THE-WEEK REVIEW QUIZ

1. neurons	6. electrochemical	11. D
2. Ramón y Cajal	7. true	12. B
3. Glial cells	8. true	13. C
4. true	9. brain stem	14. A
5. true	10. cerebellum	15. E

HB9 Fact Sheet

THE NERVOUS SYSTEM

CLASSWORK AGENDA FOR THE WEEK

(1) Create a graphic organizer that helps to identify the major divisions and functions of the parts of the nervous system.

(2) Explain how nerve cells conduct nerve impulses and distinguish between spinal and autonomic reflexes.

(3) Test the ability of the brain to process different kinds of sensory stimuli.

(4) Illustrate the organs of the nervous system to be added to the human body chart project.

The survival of any organism depends upon its ability to sense and respond appropriately to environmental stimuli. Sense organs relay information to the brain which "makes sense" out of environmental change through a network of cells called nerve cells or **neurons**. According to recent estimates there are several hundred billion nerve cells in the human body. The brain alone contains over 100 billion nerve cells. Surrounding the neurons of the brain are supportive **glial cells**. Glial cells greatly out-number nerve cells. Scientists suspect that glial cells have other functions besides supporting nerve cells but are not sure what those functions are.

The Spanish cell biologist **Ramón y Cajal** (b. 1852; d. 1934) was the first to show that the nervous system is made of individual neurons. Each neuron has a **cell body** with a cell nucleus containing genetic material. Branching **dendrites** extend from the body of each nerve cell like the arms on a telephone pole. The function of dendrites is to receive signals from other nerve cells. A single "wirelike" **axon** shoots out from the body of every neuron sending signals to other nerve cells. There are axons in the human body that are more than a meter long, sending signals from your big toe nearly all the way to your brain.

Nerve cells transmit messages to one another by sending **electrochemical signals**. While a neuron is at rest, the intracellular medium of the cell is different from its extracellular medium. The intracellular medium is loaded with negatively charged **chloride ions**. The extracellular medium is loaded with positively charged **sodium ions**. The difference in concentration of these oppositely charged ions inside and outside the nerve cell creates a voltage across the cell membrane. This separation of ionic charges is similar to the separation of oppositely charged chemical "pastes" that create a voltage in a chemical battery. When specialized proteins embedded in the cell membrane are "stimulated" they alter the membrane slightly, allowing ions to flow freely across the membrane. As the ions flow across the membrane, the strength of the voltage across the membrane changes. This electrochemical change in voltage moves all the way to the end of the axon. At the end of the axon a **chemical transmitter** is released into a **synapse** (e.g., meaning "a space") between the axon's **terminal branches** and the dendrites of other nerve cells. The chemical transmitter "excites" the cell membrane of the next nerve cell to send the signal onward. Drugs can numb sensation and paralyze nerves by interfering with these electrochemical events. Drugs can stop a signal from moving along an axon or prevent chemical transmitters from doing their work at the synapse.

The *brain, spinal cord* and *peripheral nerves* make up the major divisions of **the nervous system**. The **brain** is composed of four major sections: the *cerebrum*, the *diencephalon, cerebellum,* and *brain stem*. The **cerebrum** covering the top of the brain is the site of conscious thought, sensory impressions and motor commands. The **diencephalon** found in the middle of the brain "filters" the sensory signals coming into the brain before they reach the cerebrum. When you are asleep, the diencephalon "decides" which stimuli are worthy of your attention and whether or not you need to wake up to tend to them. The diencephalon also controls the body's physiological equilibrium (e.g., homeostasis). It commands a gland at the base of the brain called the **pituitary gland** to release hormones that influence the functions of many body organs. The **cerebellum** at the back of the brain controls the smooth coordination of movements initiated in the cerebrum. The **brain stem** located at the bottom and back of the brain controls the body's **autonomic** (e.g., meaning "automatic") **functions** like heart and respiration rate, and the contraction of smooth muscles along the digestive tract. Protected by bony vertebrae (e.g., bones of the back), the **spinal cord** relays information between the brain and the tissues of the body. The spinal cord controls reflexes like the "knee jerk reflex" and "hot iron reflex." Spinal reflexes cause muscles of the body to react quickly to harmful stimuli in order to prevent the body from sustaining serious injury. The **peripheral nerves** branching out from the spinal cord are the "wires" that attach directly to all of the organs of the body.

Homework Directions

Write a paragraph and draw a diagram that gives a detailed description of how the nervous system would help you to react to the sudden appearance of a wild and hungry lion in the classroom. Begin your description with how your brain is made aware of the lion's presence and how your brain will help you to survive when the lion decides to make you its next meal.

Assignment due: _____

_____   _____   ___/___/___
Student's Signature   Parent's Signature   Date

THE NERVOUS SYSTEM

Work Date: ____/____/____

LESSON OBJECTIVE

Students will create a graphic organizer that helps to identify the major divisions and functions of the parts of the nervous system.

Classroom Activities

On Your Mark!

Prepare for this lesson by purchasing a sheep brain from a laboratory supply house if possible. Dissect the cerebrum from the diencephalon, cerebellum, and brain stem as you lecture on the function of each part.

Use the information in the Teacher's Classwork Agenda and Content Notes to give a brief lecture about the views of **Aristotle** (b. 384 B.C.; d. 322 B.C.), **Plato** (b. 427 B.C.; d. 347 B.C.), and **René Descartes** (b. 1596; d. 1650) culminating in Descartes's idea of "mind-body dualism." Point out that the generally accepted view of today's neuroscientists is that the "mind" is a product of the biological processes taking place in the nervous system. Mention the invalid works of German **phrenologists Franz Joseph Gall** (b. 1758; d. 1828) and **Johannes Spurzheim** (b. 1776; d. 1832) stressing that all scientific theories are subject to review and criticism and that scientific advances are achieved by replacing inadequate theories with better ones. Mention that although phrenology turned out to be a baseless discipline it succeeded in generating much neuroanatomical research.

Get Set!

Draw the illustration that appears on the Journal Sheet #1 and label the cerebrum, diencephalon, cerebellum, and brain stem, spinal cord, and peripheral nerves. Point out that this illustration represents a "cutaway" view of the nervous system (e.g., the system is sliced down the midline of the body).

Go!

Give students ample time to complete the activity described in Figure A on Journal Sheet #1. Circulate around the room to be sure that students are organizing the information in the Fact Sheet correctly in their graphic organizer. Quiz students orally on the major function of each part of the nervous system. The **cerebrum** is the site of conscious thought. The **diencephalon** "filters" information from the senses before it reaches the cerebrum. The **cerebellum** insures the coordination of skeletal muscles. The **brain stem** coordinates autonomic (e.g., meaning "automatic") functions such as heart and respiratory rate. The **spinal cord** governs automatic muscular reflexes in response to stimuli and is the "freeway" of sensory information to and from the torso and limbs. The peripheral nerves are the "information cables" that attach to all the organs of the body.

Materials

sheep brain (if available), dissection kit (if necessary), Journal Sheet #1

HB9 JOURNAL SHEET #1

THE NERVOUS SYSTEM

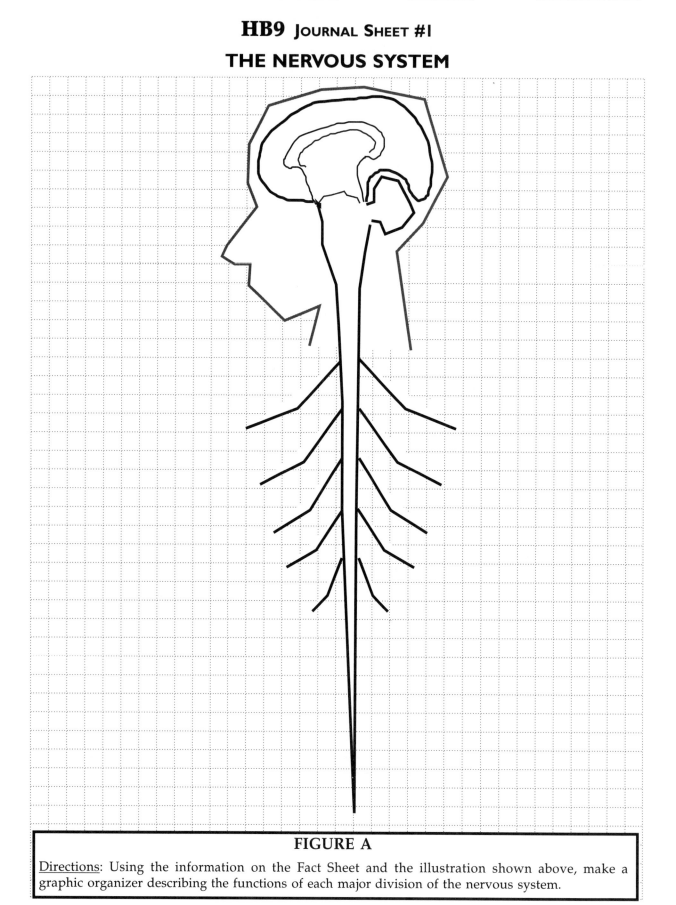

FIGURE A

<u>Directions</u>: Using the information on the Fact Sheet and the illustration shown above, make a graphic organizer describing the functions of each major division of the nervous system.

THE NERVOUS SYSTEM

Work Date: ____/____/____

LESSON OBJECTIVE

Students will explain how nerve cells conduct nerve impulses and distinguish between spinal and autonomic reflexes.

Classroom Activities

On Your Mark!

Begin with the following simple demonstration. (1) Set up a row of dominoes. (2) Tilt the first domino until it causes the others to fall in a fluid chain reaction. Explain that the dominoes represent the cell membrane of a nerve cell or **neuron**. A "disturbance" in the cell membrane causes a chain reaction of **electrochemical** events that flow down the length of the nerve cell causing a similar disturbance in the next nerve cell. Assist students in labelling the parts of the diagram appearing in Illustration A and on Journal Sheet #2.

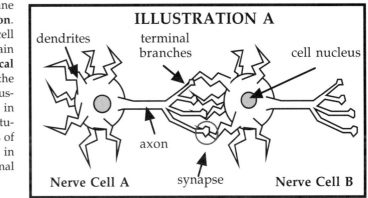

ILLUSTRATION A

dendrites • terminal branches • cell nucleus • axon • synapse

Nerve Cell A **Nerve Cell B**

Get Set!

Draw Illustration B on the board and have students copy your drawing on Journal Sheet #2. Give them a moment to read paragraph #3 on their Fact Sheet. Explain that the voltage set up across the cell membrane is much like the voltage set up between the isolated chemical pastes inside a battery. The membrane of a neuron is "sensitive to" **chemical transmitters** that change the shape of proteins embedded in the membrane. A disturbance in the membrane causes charged ions to flow across the membrane and reduce the voltage. The disturbance flows down the cell body and axon to the next cell, stimulating the release of the transmitters that will excite the next neuron.

ILLUSTRATION B

negatively charged intracellular medium • positively charged extracellular medium • ions • proteins

Go!

Give students ample time to complete the activities described in Figure B on Journal Sheet #2. Point out that the "knee jerk reflex" is controlled by the spinal cord and that the "pupillary reflex" is controlled by the brain.

Materials

pencils, 1-holed rubber stoppers, mirrors

HB9 JOURNAL SHEET #2

THE NERVOUS SYSTEM

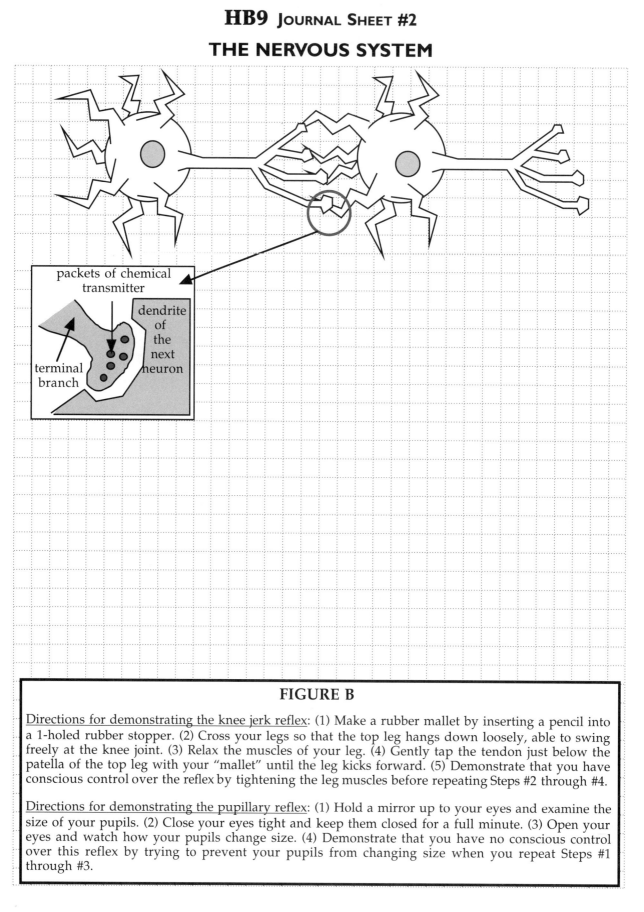

packets of chemical transmitter

dendrite of the next neuron

terminal branch

FIGURE B

<u>Directions for demonstrating the knee jerk reflex</u>: (1) Make a rubber mallet by inserting a pencil into a 1-holed rubber stopper. (2) Cross your legs so that the top leg hangs down loosely, able to swing freely at the knee joint. (3) Relax the muscles of your leg. (4) Gently tap the tendon just below the patella of the top leg with your "mallet" until the leg kicks forward. (5) Demonstrate that you have conscious control over the reflex by tightening the leg muscles before repeating Steps #2 through #4.

<u>Directions for demonstrating the pupillary reflex</u>: (1) Hold a mirror up to your eyes and examine the size of your pupils. (2) Close your eyes tight and keep them closed for a full minute. (3) Open your eyes and watch how your pupils change size. (4) Demonstrate that you have no conscious control over this reflex by trying to prevent your pupils from changing size when you repeat Steps #1 through #3.

THE NERVOUS SYSTEM

Work Date: ____/____/____

LESSON OBJECTIVE

Students will test the ability of the brain to process different kinds of sensory stimuli.

Classroom Activities

On Your Mark!

Begin with the following demonstration. (1) Have students roll a piece of loose-leaf paper into a tube. (2) Instruct them to hold the tube over their right eye. (3) Keeping both eyes open, they should place their open left hand against the tube with palm facing them. (4) Tell them to move the left hand back and forth until they see a "hole in their hand." Point out that the brain has to process a lot of information from all of the sense organs and frequently becomes "confused," although it does the best job it can at making sense of the external environment. "Seeing is *not* always believing." In this case, the restricted fields of view received by the retinas of each eye caused the brain to produce an illusion that was not a true representation of reality.

Get Set!

Discuss the other illusions investigated in Lesson #2 of the previous unit on *The Sense Organs*. Remind students that the processing of information from the sense organs by the brain requires time. Some sensory information takes longer to process than other types of sensory information.

Go!

Give students ample time to complete the activities described in Figure C and Figure D on Journal Sheet #3. Students may find the first activity extremely frustrating. They will find that coordinating eye and hand movements when given "reversed cues" from the mirror is extremely difficult. In the second activity they should find that visual information is usually processed faster than auditory information, which is generally processed faster than somatic (e.g., skin) information.

Materials

mirrors, rulers, Journal Sheet #3

HB9 JOURNAL SHEET #3

THE NERVOUS SYSTEM

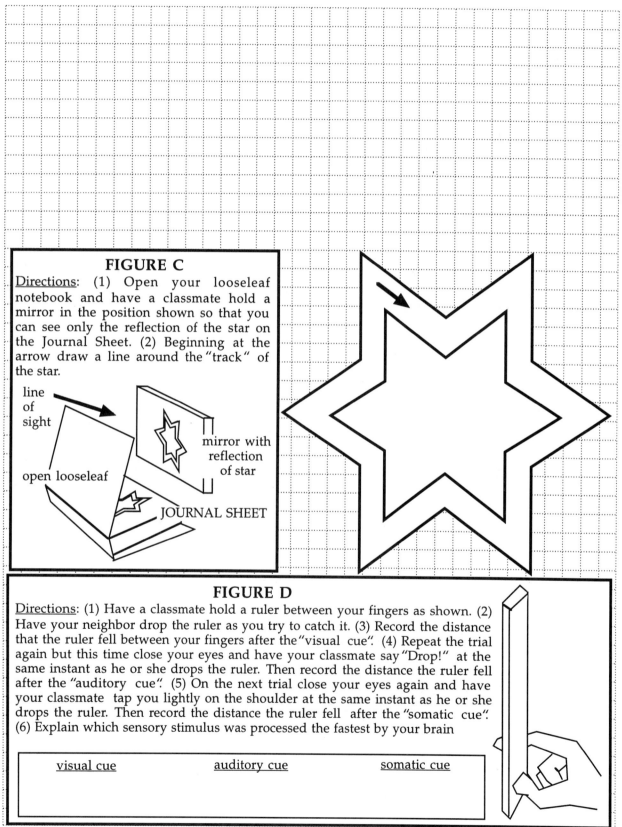

FIGURE C

<u>Directions</u>: (1) Open your looseleaf notebook and have a classmate hold a mirror in the position shown so that you can see only the reflection of the star on the Journal Sheet. (2) Beginning at the arrow draw a line around the "track" of the star.

line of sight

open looseleaf

mirror with reflection of star

JOURNAL SHEET

FIGURE D

<u>Directions</u>: (1) Have a classmate hold a ruler between your fingers as shown. (2) Have your neighbor drop the ruler as you try to catch it. (3) Record the distance that the ruler fell between your fingers after the "visual cue". (4) Repeat the trial again but this time close your eyes and have your classmate say "Drop!" at the same instant as he or she drops the ruler. Then record the distance the ruler fell after the "auditory cue". (5) On the next trial close your eyes again and have your classmate tap you lightly on the shoulder at the same instant as he or she drops the ruler. Then record the distance the ruler fell after the "somatic cue". (6) Explain which sensory stimulus was processed the fastest by your brain

<u>visual cue</u>	<u>auditory cue</u>	<u>somatic cue</u>

THE NERVOUS SYSTEM

Work Date: ____/____/____

LESSON OBJECTIVE

Students will illustrate the organs of the nervous system to be added to the human body chart project.

Classroom Activities

On Your Mark!

Display textbook illustrations of the major parts of the nervous system in addition to the illustration on Journal Sheet #1. Explain to students that they will continue working on their long-term project of the human body chart.

Get Set!

Distribute posters and art materials.

Go!

Give students ample time to complete the activity described in Figure E on Journal Sheet #4. As in previous lessons, discourage students from designing three-dimensional structures as their project will be difficult to store in the weeks ahead.

Materials

butcher paper, construction paper, scissors, crayon or felt-tip markers

HB9 JOURNAL SHEET #4

THE NERVOUS SYSTEM

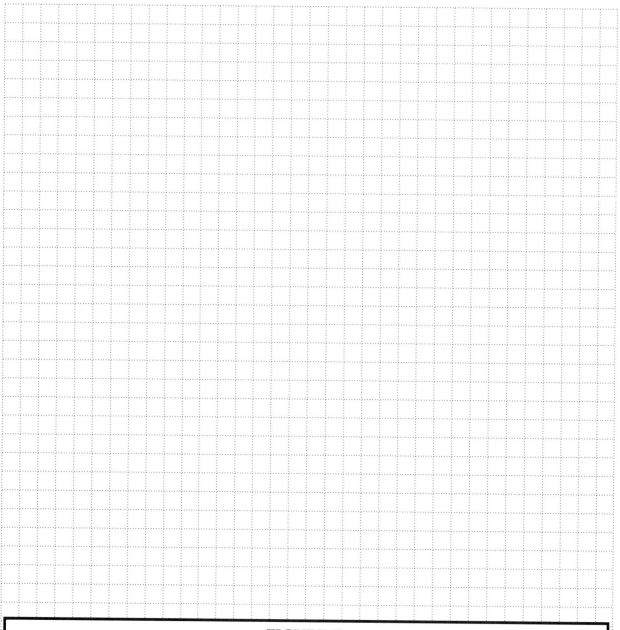

FIGURE E

<u>Directions</u>: (1) Continue working on your HUMAN BODY CHART. (2) Use the materials provided by your instructor to draw pictures of the individual structures of the nervous system. (3) You will need to lift out most of the organs to position the spinal cord against the vertebrae while overlapping the peripheral nerves that supply the many organs. You may decide to do a "cutaway" view of the skull on one side to show the brain inside the cranial cavity. (4) Use small sections of tape <u>no more than a centimeter in length</u> to secure the paper parts. DO NOT SECURE THEM PERMANENTLY! You will have to change their positions again to add the endocrine organs in the next unit. (5) Roll up the chart neatly and wrap it with a rubber band before securing it in the box provided by your instructor. (6) Use the remainder of this Journal Sheet to record any tasks you might need to accomplish at home to enhance the look of this project.

HB9 REVIEW QUIZ

Directions: Keep your eyes on your own work.
Read all directions and questions carefully.
THINK BEFORE YOU ANSWER!
Watch your spelling, be neat, and do the best you can.

CLASSWORK	(~40):	_____
HOMEWORK	(~20):	_____
CURRENT EVENT	(~10):	_____
TEST	(~30):	_____
TOTAL	(~100):	_____

(A ≥ 90, B ≥ 80, C ≥ 70, D ≥ 60, F < 60)

LETTER GRADE: _____

TEACHER'S COMMENTS: _____
_____

THE NERVOUS SYSTEM

TRUE–FALSE FILL-IN: If the statement is true, write the word TRUE. If the statement is false, change the underlined word to make the statement true. *20 points*

_____ 1. Nerve cells are also called <u>glial cells</u>.

_____ 2. The working units of the nervous system were discovered by <u>Einstein</u>.

_____ 3. <u>Neurons</u> support and outnumber nerve cells.

_____ 4. <u>Dendrites</u> receive information from other nerve cells.

_____ 5. <u>Axons</u> send information to other nerve cells.

_____ 6. Nerve cells transmit messages to one another by sending <u>electromagnetic</u> signals.

_____ 7. The <u>cerebrum</u> is the site of conscious thought.

_____ 8. The <u>diencephalon</u> "filters" sensory information from the body.

_____ 9. The <u>cerebellum</u> controls the beat of the heart and respiration rate.

_____ 10. The <u>brain stem</u> insures the coordinated movement of skeletal muscles.

PROBLEM

MATCHING: Study the diagram of the skin and muscle, spinal cord and brain shown below. The shaded areas represent damage to nerve cells in those areas resulting from a variety of possible injuries. Write the letter of the shaded area where damage would result in the set of symptoms described in sentences #11 through #15. *10 points*

_____ 11. Damage to this region would result in the loss of the spinal reflex but not interfere with the sensation or control of the muscle.

_____ 12. Damage to this region would result in the loss of sensation but not interfere with the spinal reflex or control of the muscle.

_____ 13. Damage to this region would result in complete numbness of the skin and total paralysis of the muscle.

_____ 14. Damage to this region would result in the loss of conscious control over the muscle but not interfere with the spinal reflex or sensation from the skin.

_____ 15. Damage to this region would result in the loss of conscious control over the muscle and loss of the spinal reflex but not interfere with sensation from the skin.

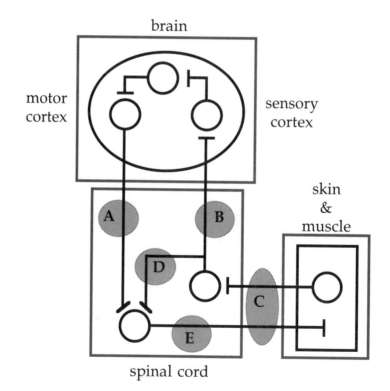

HORMONES AND THE ENDOCRINE SYSTEM

Teacher's Classwork Agenda and Content Notes

Classwork Agenda for the Week

1. Students will identify the organs of the endocrine system and the hormones secreted by each organ.

2. Students will explain how the brain influences the production of hormones via the pituitary or "master" gland.

3. Students will prepare and present a brief summary of the location and function of a particular endocrine organ.

4. Students will write a paragraph explaining the difference between "mobile" and "fixed-membrane" hormone receptors.

Content Notes for Lecture and Discussion

The term "hormone" is derived from the Greek word *hormaein* meaning "to excite or set in motion." The term was coined by English physiologists **Ernest Henry Starling** (b. 1866; d. 1927) and **William Maddock Bayliss** (b. 1860; d. 1924) in 1902 to describe a newly discovered compound: secretin. Secretin is produced in the walls of the small intestine and stimulates the release of digestive juices from the pancreas. Direct evidence of "action at a distance" by chemical substances produced by remote cells of the body fascinated biologists of the time and was the beginning of the science of **endocrinology**.

Endocrinologists of the 19th century correlated a variety of diseases with abnormalities of the endocrine organs. The Irish physician **Robert James Graves** (b. 1796; d. 1853) described symptoms resulting from the overactivity of the thyroid: a condition resulting in the swelling of the gland called goiter. English physician **Thomas Addison** (b. 1793; d. 1860) was the first to recognize symptoms resulting from deficiency of adrenal cortical function which resulted in weakness, abnormal skin secretions, weight loss, and low blood pressure. In 1894, the English physiologist **Edward Albert Sharpey-Schafer** (b. 1850; d. 1935) and his coworker **George Oliver** (b. 1841; d. 1915) discovered the functions of the adrenal medula in the production of the "flight or fight" hormone: adrenaline. The American neurophysiologist **Walter Bradford Cannon** (b. 1871; d. 1945) is best known for his clear description of the "flight or fight" response. When confronted with a threatening or anxiety-producing situation the adrenal medulla secretes adrenaline (e.g., also called epinephrine) directly into the bloodstream. The powerful hormone initiates a variety of responses in different body cells; it (1) causes the liver to release its reserves of carbohydrate for quick energy, (2) dilates blood vessels supplying blood to the heart, lungs, and skeletal muscles, (3) constricts blood vessels of the intestinal tract to slow down energy-consuming digestive functions, and (4) promotes quick blood-clotting in the event an injury should occur to the body. Prolonged stress and anxiety can have disastrous effects on a person's overall health. Preparing the body for action when no action can be taken can have serious side effects. **Fixed-membrane receptors** (e.g., specialized proteins embedded in the cell membrane) serve as the "switch" that turns on a particular cell's custom-made response (e.g., increased production of glucose). Other hormones such as the growth hormone (e.g., also called somatotropin)—first isolated in 1966, then synthesized by the Chinese-born American biologist **Cho Hao Li** (b. 1913)—may act by binding with free-floating receptors inside the cell to produce a **mobile receptor** that instigates action by DNA. The DNA molecule is "prompted" to increase its production of specialized proteins such as those that make up the structure of bone.

In Lesson #1, students will identify the organs of the endocrine system and the hormones secreted by each organ.

In Lesson #2, students will explain how the brain influences the production of hormones via the pituitary or "master" gland.

In Lesson #3, students will prepare and present a brief summary of the location and function of a particular endocrine organ.

In Lesson #4, students will write a paragraph explaining the difference between "mobile" and "fixed-membrane" hormone receptors.

ANSWERS TO THE HOMEWORK PROBLEMS

Students essays should reflect the understanding of the concept of "negative feedback." A rise in room temperature prompts the thermostat to "shut down" the heater. A high level of a particular hormone in the blood causes the responsible endocrine organ to "shut down" the production of that hormone.

ANSWERS TO THE END-OF-THE-WEEK REVIEW QUIZ

1. hormones	6. protein	11. G	16. A
2. nervous	7. true	12. D	17. F
3. diencephalon	8. true	13. B	
4. capillaries	9. true	14. E	
5. bloodstream	10. constant	15. C	

The answers to questions #18, #19, and #20 may include any of the following endocrine functions: (1) regulate the metabolism of essential nutrients, vitamins, and minerals, (2) respond to danger, (3) produce healthy offspring, or (4) grow.

HB10 FACT SHEET

HORMONES AND THE ENDOCRINE SYSTEM

CLASSWORK AGENDA FOR THE WEEK

(1)   Identify the organs of the endocrine system and the hormones secreted by each organ.
(2)   Explain how the brain influences the production of hormones via the pituitary or "master" gland.
(3)   Prepare and present a brief summary of the location and function of a particular endocrine organ.
(4)   Write a paragraph explaining the difference between "mobile" and "fixed-membrane" hormone receptors.

The metabolism of mammals is regulated by proteins called **hormones** that are produced by organs under the control of the nervous system. The organs that produce hormones are called *endocrine glands*. An **endocrine gland** is an organ that discharges or "secretes" hormones into the extracellular environment or directly into the bloodstream. Hormones influence the body's ability to (1) regulate essential nutrients, vitamins and minerals, (2) respond to danger, (3) produce healthy offspring, and (4) grow.

The major organs of the endocrine system are the **pituitary gland**, the **pineal gland**, the **thyroid gland**, the **parathyroid gland**, the **thymus gland**, the **adrenal glands**, and the glands of the male and female reproductive organs: the **testes** and **ovaries**.

The nervous system can control endocrine glands by sending nerve signals directly to a particular gland. Or it can send signals to a "master gland" called the *pituitary gland*. The pituitary gland is located in the diencephalon in a region of the brain called the **hypothalamus**. Nerve cells in the hypothalamus send signals to the pituitary gland which, in turn, produces hormones that influence the secretions of other endocrine glands. The pituitary gland located at the base of the brain is surrounded by capillaries that transport its hormonal secretions throughout the body.

Specialized hormones released into the bloodstream can influence the function of specific groups of cells or influence every cell to change their rates of metabolism. The ability of a hormone to affect the cells of the body depends upon the types of **protein receptors** present in individual cells. One type of hormone "teams up" with specific cell proteins to produce a "mobile unit" that influences the production of other proteins. This **mobile receptor** activates specific genes (e.g., DNA molecules) to produce specific proteins. A second type of hormone "locks" onto a specific protein receptor present in the cell membranes of most cells. The **fixed-membrane receptor** influences that cell to perform a specific function such as alter its rate of sugar metabolism.

Endocrine glands are sensitive to the presence of too much hormone. When the amount of a particular hormone rises to high levels, the gland that produces that hormone will "shut down" to prevent the cells it controls from "overreacting". This type of control is called **negative feedback**. The ability of glands to respond to negative feedback allows the body to achieve **homeostasis**: the maintenance of a constant internal environment.

Homework Directions

Write a paragraph that explains the similarities between the human endocrine system and the thermostat that controls the temperature of your home.

Assignment due: _____

_____   _____   ____/____/____
Student's Signature   Parent's Signature   Date

HB10 Lesson #1

HORMONES AND THE ENDOCRINE SYSTEM

Work Date: ____/____/____

LESSON OBJECTIVE

Students will identify the organs of the endocrine system and the hormones secreted by each organ.

Classroom Activities

On Your Mark!

Prepare for this lesson by putting together a "fake surprise test" containing questions that are virtually impossible for the students to answer. Before the lesson begins, check your grade roster for students with heart disease or asthma and brief these students on the "anxiety-producing" demonstration you are about to give the class.

Begin the lesson by announcing that in the next few minutes students will take a surprise exam that will weigh heavily in determining their final grade in the class. Be as stern and serious as you can be in explaining the importance of this exam. Distribute the exam—ignoring protests of how unfair you are—and give students 3–5 minutes to begin work on the "impossible test." Then stop the test, tell students to look up, and smile at them. Ask: "How many of you are experiencing an accelerated heart beat?" Point out the flushed and reddened faces around the room. Ask "How many of you are feeling queasy and upset? Not just mentally but physically?" As you collect the test—pointing out that their responses on the test will have absolutely no impact on their grade—explain that their emotional state was a natural response governed by their **nervous** and **endocrine system**.

Get Set!

Explain that the endocrine system is a system of organs distributed throughout the body that manufacture special proteins called **hormones** that control the metabolism and function of many tissues and organs. Refer students to the illustration on Journal Sheet #1 and help them to identify the location and major function of each endocrine organ. Beginning at the top the organs are as follows: **pineal gland**—involved in the production of **melatonin** that affects skin pigment and inhibits the function of female ovaries; **pituitary gland**—under nervous control of the **hypothalamus** in the brain, this "master gland" secretes a number of **stimulating hormones** that control the functions of all the other glands; **thyroid gland**—secretes **thyroxine** which controls overall metabolic rate; **parathyroid glands**—secrete **parathyroid hormone** which regulates calcium and phosphorus metabolism; **thymus gland**—secretes **thymosins** believed to assist the immune system in producing disease-fighting cells; the **adrenal cortex**—secretes a number of "**steroid-like**" hormones that control sugar and mineral metabolism and the development of some male secondary sexual characteristics; **adrenal medulla**—secretes **adrenaline** which produces the "flight or fight" response; **ovaries**—secrete **estrogen** which stimulates and maintains the development of female sexual characteristics; **testes**—secrete **testosterone** which stimulates and maintains the development of male sexual characteristics.

Go!

Give students ample time to complete the activity described in Figure A on Journal Sheet #1.

Materials

human body charts, butcher paper, construction paper, scissors, crayon or felt-tip markers

HB10 JOURNAL SHEET #1

HORMONES AND THE ENDOCRINE SYSTEM

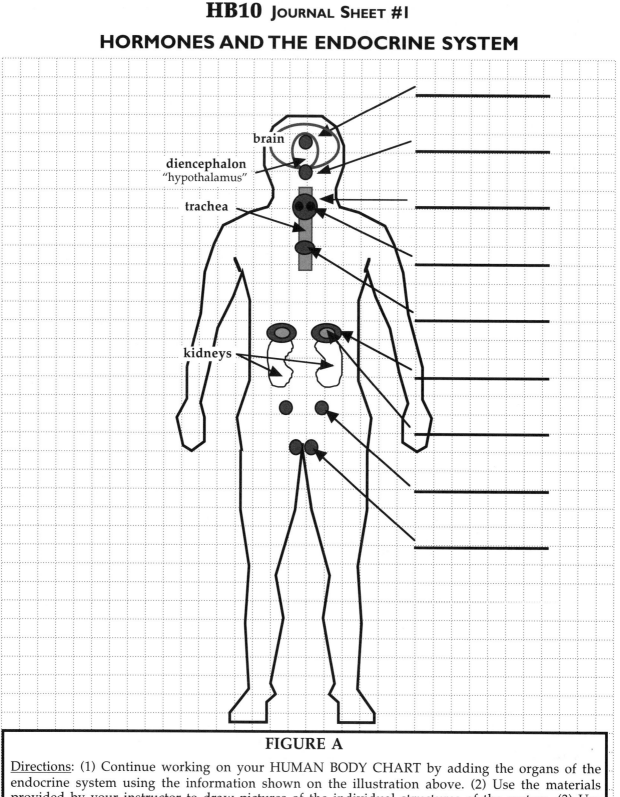

FIGURE A

<u>Directions</u>: (1) Continue working on your HUMAN BODY CHART by adding the organs of the endocrine system using the information shown on the illustration above. (2) Use the materials provided by your instructor to draw pictures of the individual structures of the system. (3) Use small sections of tape <u>no more than a centimeter in length</u> to secure the paper parts. DO NOT SECURE THEM PERMANENTLY! You will have to change their positions again to add several lymph glands which are part of the body's immune system. (4) Roll up the chart neatly and wrap it with a rubber band before securing it in the box provided by your instructor.

HB10 Lesson #2

HORMONES AND THE ENDOCRINE SYSTEM

Work Date: ____/____/____

LESSON OBJECTIVE

Students will explain how the brain influences the production of hormones via the pituitary or "master" gland.

Classroom Activities

On Your Mark!

Begin the lesson by giving a brief lecture on the history of **endocrinology** using the information in the Teacher's Classwork Agenda and Content Notes. If available, distribute pictures of the various hormonal disorders resulting from "hypo-" (e.g., reduced) and "hyper-" (e.g., increased) activity of the endocrine glands: hypothyroidism—**cretinism**; hyperthyroidism—**Grave's disease** or **goiter**; hypoparathyroidism—**muscular tremors, cramps**, and **convulsions**; hyperparathyroidism—**extraneous calcium deposits** and **weakening of bone**; hypofunction of adrenal cortex—**Addison's disease**; hypopituitaryism—**impaired growth** to produce a "midget"; hyperpituitaryism—**acromegaly** or overgrowth of bones and tissues to produce a "giant."

Get Set!

Draw Illustration A on the board and have students copy your drawing on Journal Sheet #2. Explain the anatomy of the **pituitary gland** and its connection to the **hypothalamus** of the **diencephalon**. Hormones of the **posterior lobe** of the pituitary include **oxytocin** to stimulate uterine contractions and milk production, and **vasopressin** to stimulate contraction of smooth muscles and kidney function. Hormones of the anterior lobe of the pituitary include **growth hormone, thyrotropin** to stimulate the thyroid, **adrenocorticotropin hormone** to stimulate the adrenal cortex, **follicle-stimulating hormone** to stimulate the growth of

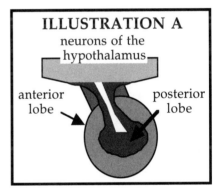

ILLUSTRATION A
neurons of the hypothalamus

anterior lobe   posterior lobe

ovaries in females and testes in males, **luteinizing hormone** to stimulate the release of estrogen from ovaries and testosterone from testes, **prolactin** to stimulate milk production, and **melanocyte-stimulating hormone** to mediate the breakdown of skin pigment.

Explain the concept of "negative feedback," a mechanism that controls the action of endocrine glands. Point out that a high level of a particular hormone in the bloodstream "shuts down" the production of that hormone by the endocrine organ responsible for its production. Negative feedback prevents a hormone's activity from becoming "hyperactivity." The failure of this mechanism is the cause of several endocrine organ disorders.

Go!

Give students ample time to complete the activity described in Figure B on Journal Sheet #2.

Materials

Journal Sheet #2

HB10 Journal Sheet #2

HORMONES AND THE ENDOCRINE SYSTEM

FIGURE B

<u>Directions</u>: (1) Brainstorm with your classmates to create a diagram that illustrates the "chain of command" at your school. (2) Put your school principal at the top of the diagram and illustrate how that "master controller" influences the behavior of others at your school. (3) Write a paragraph to explain why your principal can be compared to the pituitary gland.

HORMONES AND THE ENDOCRINE SYSTEM

Work Date: ____/____/____

LESSON OBJECTIVE

Students will prepare and present a brief summary of the location and function of a particular endocrine organ.

Classroom Activities

On Your Mark!

Prepare for this class by obtaining a short description of each endocrine organ from an encyclopedia or other text.

Get Set!

Distribute the resources to cooperative groups of students.

Go!

Give students ample time to prepare their slides and draw the micro-organisms in the spaces provided according to the directions in Figure C on Journal Sheet #3.

Materials

library/text resources

HB10 SMALL CAPS JOURNAL SHEET #3

HORMONES AND THE ENDOCRINE SYSTEM

| PITUITARY | PINEAL |

| THYROID | PARATHYROID |

| THYMUS | ADRENALS |

| OVARIES | TESTES |

FIGURE C

<u>Directions</u>: (1) Use the resources provided by your instructor to gather information about the endocrine organ assigned to you. (2) Spend 10 minutes brainstorming with your friends about how you will present your information to the class in 5 minutes. (3) Take notes on the other endocrine organs provided by your classmates during their brief presentation.

HORMONES AND THE ENDOCRINE SYSTEM

Work Date: ____/____/____

LESSON OBJECTIVE

Students will write a paragraph explaining the difference between "mobile" and "fixed-membrane" hormone receptors.

Classroom Activities

On Your Mark!

Review some of the functions of hormones mentioned in the previous lesson. Point out that some hormones change the metabolism of many cells while others have a specific action that influences only a few types of cells.

Get Set!

Refer students to the diagrams on Journal Sheet #4. Have students take notes as you list the action mechanisms of **Mobile** and **Fixed-Membrane** receptors.

Mobile Receptors

(1) hormone enters cell
(2) hormone combines with receptor
(3) mobile receptor enters cell nucleus
(4) receptor helps DNA make specific RNA for protein production
(5) specific RNA complete
(6) RNA exits nucleus into cytoplasm
(7) RNA synthesizes new protein

Fixed-Membrane Receptors

(1) hormone attaches to "fixed" receptor
(2) hormone activates receptor
(3) receptor deactivates "high energy" ATP molecule
(4) . . . to form "low energy" cyclic AMP
(5) cAMP activates specific "protein activator" (e.g., protein kinase)
(6) protein activator puts specific protein to work

Go!

Give students ample time to prepare their paragraph summarizing the difference between **Mobile** and **Fixed-Membrane** receptors. In addition to demonstrating their ability to take and apply their lecture notes, students' paragraphs should mention that the former action mechanism involves the interplay of genes (e.g., DNA) while the latter does not.

Materials

Journal Sheet #4

HB10 Journal Sheet #4

HORMONES AND THE ENDOCRINE SYSTEM

MOBILE RECEPTOR   FIXED-MEMBRANE RECEPTOR

FIGURE D

Directions: (1) Examine the action mechanisms described by your instructor to explain the function of MOBILE and FIXED-MEMBRANE HORMONE RECEPTORS. (2) Compose a paragraph to explain the difference between both action mechanisms and how they affect the behavior of "target cells" influenced by different hormones.

HB10 REVIEW QUIZ

Directions: Keep your eyes on your own work.
Read all directions and questions carefully.
THINK BEFORE YOU ANSWER!
Watch your spelling, be neat, and do the best you can.

CLASSWORK	(~40): _____
HOMEWORK	(~20): _____
CURRENT EVENT	(~10): _____
TEST	(~30): _____
TOTAL	(~100): _____

(A ≥ 90, B ≥ 80, C ≥ 70, D ≥ 60, F < 60)

LETTER GRADE: _____

TEACHER'S COMMENTS: _____

_____

HORMONES AND THE ENDOCRINE SYSTEM

TRUE–FALSE FILL-IN: If the statement is true, write the word TRUE. If the statement is false, change the underlined word to make the statement true. *20 points*

_____ 1. The metabolism of mammals is regulated by proteins called <u>transmitters</u>.

_____ 2. The <u>digestive</u> system can control endocrine glands by sending signals directly to a particular gland.

_____ 3. The pituitary gland is located in the <u>cerebellum</u> in a region of the brain called the hypothalamus.

_____ 4. The pituitary gland is surrounded by <u>glial cells</u> that transports its hormonal secretions throughout the body.

_____ 5. Specialized hormones released into the <u>nervous system</u> can influence the function of specific groups of cells or influence every cell to change their rates of metabolism.

_____ 6. The ability of a hormone to affect the cells of the body depends upon the types of <u>carbohydrate</u> receptors present in individual cells.

_____ 7. <u>Mobile</u> receptors activate specific genes to produce specific proteins.

_____ 8. <u>Fixed-membrane</u> receptors influence a cell to perform a specific function such as alter its rate of sugar metabolism.

_____ 9. When hormones rise to a high level in the bloodstream endocrine glands <u>decrease</u> the production of that hormone.

_____ 10. The ability of glands to respond to "negative feedback" allows the body to achieve homeostasis, the maintenance of a <u>variable</u> internal environment.

HB10 Review Quiz *(cont'd)*

MATCHING: Choose the letter of the phrase that best describes the effect of the hormone(s) produced by each endocrine gland. *7 points*

_____11. pineal

_____12. thyroid

_____13. parathyroid

_____14. thymus

_____15. adrenals

_____16. testes

_____17. ovaries

(A) produces male sexual characteristics

(B) controls the metabolism of bone minerals

(C) gets the body ready to "fight or flee"

(D) regulates overall metabolic rate

(E) helps the body to become immune to germs

(F) produces female sexual characteristics

(G) sensitive to light falling on the retina

ESSAY: Write a sentence describing three activities regulated by hormones that influence the body's ability to perform basic functions. *3 points*

18. _____

_____

_____

19. _____

_____

_____

20. _____

_____

_____

_____   _____   ___/___/___
Student's Signature   Parent's Signature   Date

REPRODUCTION
AND DEVELOPMENT

TEACHER'S CLASSWORK AGENDA AND CONTENT NOTES

Classwork Agenda for the Week

1. Students will identify the organs of the male and female reproductive systems and explain the process of gametogenesis.
2. Students will explain the major events that occur during fertilization and differentiation.
3. Students will identify the major stages of prenatal development.
4. Students will identify the major stages of postnatal development.

Content Notes for Lecture and Discussion

According to early scientists, the possession of sexual organs defined the members of a given species as either male or female and the "intermingling" of male and female fluids seemed to be a prerequisite for the production of offspring. In 1651, the English physician **William Harvey** (b. 1578; d. 1657)—who discovered the workings of the human circulatory system—published *On the Generation of Animals* in which he argued that the essential characteristics of offspring were carried in the "primordial ovum" of the female. His views were supported by the discovery of egg follicles in the ovaries of both animals and human females (e.g., cadavers). By the end of the 18th century, sexual reproduction was considered the major method of procreation for all organisms of the Animal Kingdom. The Swedish botanist **Carolus Linnaeus** (b. 1707; d. 1778) identified the sexual organs of plants (e.g., male anthers, female ovules) and described the cells they contained (e.g., pollen and seeds) as analogous to the reproductive cells of humans that had been identified as "spermatic animalcules" and "seedlings" by the Dutch microscopist **Anton von Leeuwenhoek** (b. 1632; d. 1723). Unlike von Leeuwenhoek, who argued that sperm carried the "preformed" human embryo that required the female womb merely for development, Linnaeus argued that both male and female sex cells contributed their characteristics to their offspring. However, it was not until the work of the German zoologist **Wilhelm August Oscar Hertwig** (b. 1849; d. 1922) that it was shown that fertilization involved the fusion of a single sperm and a single egg. At the start of the 20th century, the controversy surrounding the contributions made to a viable offspring by sperm and egg was resolved following the rediscovery of the works of Austrian monk **Gregor Johann Mendel** (b. 1822; d. 1884), the "father of modern genetics." The work of French physiologist **Charles Brown-Séquard** (b. 1817; d. 1894) and English physiologist **Edward Sharpey-Schaefer** (b. 1850; d. 1935) elucidated the roles of hormones in the development of secondary sex characteristics (e.g., genital hair, breasts, etc.). The work of German zoologist **Ernst Heinrich Philipp August Haekel** (b. 1834; d. 1919) showed that the developing embryo passes through a number of stages that oddly resemble the evolutionary transitions made by living organisms from ancestral reptilian to human form. His view that "ontogeny recapitulates phylogeny" ultimately proved false but stimulated much research in the area by laying a foundation for further embryological study.

The natural fertilization of an egg by a sperm leads to the division and differentiation of cells that produce a new organism. Modern cloning methods, however, involve the artificial stimulation of the egg and subsequent development of a fully functional organism. One method of cloning involves the fusion of nuclear material from one cell with that of an unfertilized egg whose nucleus has been removed. In 1996, scientists succeeded in bringing a healthy mammal—a sheep

HB11 Content Notes (cont'd)

named Dolly—into the world using this method. Dolly was the product of the fusion of a mammary gland cell and an enucleated egg cell. The fused cell was stimulated to divide with mild electric shocks and transferred in the morula stage to the uterus of a surrogate mother sheep.

In Lesson #1, students will identify the organs of the male and female reproductive systems and explain the process of gametogenesis.

In Lesson #2, students will explain the major events that occur during fertilization and differentiation.

In Lesson #3, students will identify the major stages of prenatal development.

In Lesson #4, students will identify the major stages of postnatal development.

ANSWERS TO THE HOMEWORK PROBLEMS

(1) Student essays should emphasize the role of the placenta in nourishing the embryo and removing the wastes that it produces. They should mention that any foods or drugs the mother imbibes will pass into the developing human's circulatory system and into its organs. Improper nourishment will directly affect the development of the different organ systems.

(2) Students should mention that throughout infancy, childhood, and adolescence, cells, tissues, and organs continue to develop. Drugs, tobacco, and alcohol all interfere with the healthy development of these body parts. Poorly developed or maldeveloped cells, tissues, and organs invariably lead to medical problems.

ANSWERS TO THE END-OF-THE-WEEK REVIEW QUIZ

1. true	6. sperm	11. B	16. E	21. J
2. reproductive	7. egg	12. C	17. M	22. K
3. true	8. true (e.g., 23 pairs)	13. A	18. H	23. L
4. gametes	9. true	14. F	19. G	
5. DNA	10. true	15. D	20. I	

__7__adult __5__child __2__embryo __3__fetus __1__zygote
__4__ infant __6__adolescent

HB11 FACT SHEET

REPRODUCTION AND DEVELOPMENT

CLASSWORK AGENDA FOR THE WEEK

(1) Identify the organs of the male and female reproductive systems and explain the process of gametogenesis.
(2) Explain the major events that occur during fertilization and differentiation.
(3) Identify the major stages of prenatal development.
(4) Identify the major stages of postnatal development.

Not all individuals of a species must reproduce for that species to survive. However, some individuals must raise healthy young until those young are mature enough to have offspring of their own. The **human reproductive** system produces the specialized cells that perpetuate the human race. These cells are called **gametes** and are made during a process of cell division called **gametogenesis**. The gametes of male and female parents contain all of the **species traits** and **individual traits** that make us members of the same human family with all our individual differences. The traits of human males and females are passed from one generation to the next in the **chromosomes** (e.g., genetic material or DNA) contained in gametes. The male sex cell—called a **sperm**—is united with a female sex cell—called an **egg**—during a process called **fertilization**. Each sperm and egg contains 23 chromosomes that carry the biological traits of each parent. A fertilized human egg contains a full 46 human chromosomes (e.g., 23 pairs).

The male reproductive system includes two **testes**. Testes produce sperm throughout the life of a human male and a hormone called **testosterone**. Testosterone influences the development of the male reproductive organs and "secondary male sexual characteristics" such as facial and genital hair, a low-pitched voice, and bulky muscles. Testes are found in an external pouch called the **scrotum**. The female reproductive system includes two internal **ovaries**. Ovaries produce eggs and a hormone called **estrogen**. **Estrogen** influences the development of the female reproductive organs, "secondary female sexual characteristics" such as genital hair and breasts, and regulates the onset of **menstruation**. Although females are born with a lifetime supply of eggs the **menstrual cycle** prepares eggs for fertilization on a periodic basis.

During the menstrual cycle, an egg is released from the **ovary** and passed into the **Fallopian tube** in a process called **ovulation**. The lining of the **uterus** thickens to get ready for the attachment of a fertilized egg. If fertilization does not take place, the egg and thickened lining along the wall of the uterus break down and pass out of the body. If sperm are present in the Fallopian tube leading to the uterus an egg may become fertilized.

A fertilized egg is called a **zygote**. This single-celled zygote divides again and again soon after fertilization forming a "ball-shaped" structure that becomes embedded in the wall of the uterus. During the first eight weeks of **gestation** the developing human is called an **embryo.** Surrounded by the **placenta**, a collection of protective and nourishing tissues, the embryo receives oxygen and nutrients from the mother's circulatory system. Carbon dioxide and waste products from the embryo are excreted into the mother's circulatory system and removed through her excretory system. The embryo is further protected by a layer of tissue called the **amniotic sac** which is filled with **amniotic fluid**. The **umbilical cord**, containing two arteries and a vein, connects the embryo to the placenta.

A human being takes approximately nine months to develop completely before it is ready to be born. But development does not stop after birth. All human beings, like other animals, continue to grow throughout their lives. Humans change from **infants** (0 to 2 years) to **children** (2 to 13 years), to **adolescents** (13 to 20 years), to **adults.** Late in adult life, women go through a physical change called **menopause.** After menopause ovulation no longer occurs.

Homework Directions

(1) In a paragraph of no less than fifty (50) words explain how the eating habits of a pregnant woman can affect her developing fetus.

(2) In a paragraph of no less than fifty (50) words explain how nonprescription drugs, tobacco, and alcohol can interfere with the physical and mental transitions from childhood to adolescence and adolescence to adulthood.

Assignment due: _____

_____   _____   ____/____/____
Student's Signature   Parent's Signature   Date

HB11 Lesson #1

REPRODUCTION AND DEVELOPMENT

Work Date: _____/_____/_____

LESSON OBJECTIVE

Students will identify the organs of the male and female reproductive systems and explain the process of gametogenesis.

Classroom Activities

On Your Mark!

Use the information in the Teacher's Classwork Agenda and Content Notes to give a brief lecture on some of the views held by early scientists regarding sex and reproduction.

Get Set!

Refer students to the illustrations of the **Male** and **Female Reproductive Organs** shown on Journal Sheet #1. Copy the illustrations on the board or use a transparency and overhead projector to facilitate student notetaking. Label the organs and briefly describe their major function. The organs of each system are listed from top to bottom as they appear on Journal Sheet #1.

Male Reproductive Organs
urinary bladder—stores urine
prostate—releases a fluid that
   activates sperm and prevents
   them from lumping together
seminal vesicle—produces fluid
   released by prostate
vas deferens—tube leading from
   testis to prostate
testis—produces sperm
   and testosterone
penis—leads urethra to the outside

Female Reproductive Organs
uterus—womb
Fallopian tube—leads to uterus
egg follicles—unfertilized eggs
ovary—stores eggs and produces
   estrogen
cervix—opening that leads from
   uterus, dilating during parturition
   to allow passage of newborn
vagina—opening to the outside
urinary bladder—appears behind the
   uterus

Briefly discuss the process of **gametogenesis**. In the testes and ovaries, sperm and eggs are produced and stored. Females are born with all of the eggs they will carry throughout life. Males produce sperm continually throughout life. Unlike regularly dividing cells (e.g., **mitosis**), gametes are reproduced from "primordial cells" called **primary spermatocytes** and **primary oocytes,** respectively, that do not duplicate their complement of chromosomes before they divide. Thus, the resulting cells carry half as many chromosomes as other body cells (e.g., **haploid** cells as opposed to **diploid** cells resulting from the division process called **meiosis**).

Go!

Give students ample time to complete the activity described in Figure A on Journal Sheet #1. Students will discover that the human population will double in the next 20 years at this rate of growth.

Materials

Journal Sheet #1

Name: _____ Period:_____ Date: ____/____/____

HB11 JOURNAL SHEET #1

REPRODUCTION AND DEVELOPMENT

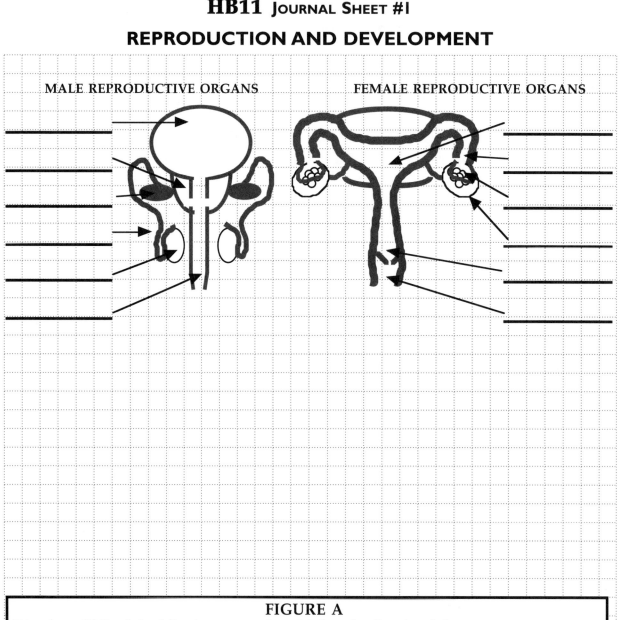

MALE REPRODUCTIVE ORGANS   FEMALE REPRODUCTIVE ORGANS

FIGURE A

Directions: (1) Read the following paragraph and follow the directions below.

Humans comprised a minor population of about 10 million members during their first 2 million years of existence on the planet. Less than 10,000 years ago, the number of humans began to increase at a faster rate. They developed agriculture and domesticated animals so there was little need to migrate in search of game. As a result, the human population experienced dramatic growth. By the end of the Roman Empire, the human population had reached 250 million and by the 16th and 17th centuries half a billion. In different parts of the world, at different times in human history, plagues have killed millions, reducing and controlling the growing population. However, the recent triumph of the medical sciences over many diseases on a worldwide scale has reduced the death rate among humans of all ages. As a result, the human population is growing by as much as 3.5% per year. Currently, the human population of the world is about 6 billion.

(2) Make a graph to show what the population of the world will be 2, 4, 6, 8, 10, 12, 14,16, 18, and 20 years from now if it continues to increase at the present rate. (3) Write a short paragraph describing any problems you think our species may encounter as a result of this population growth. (4) Make suggestions about how we might be able to avoid these problems.

HB11 Lesson #2

REPRODUCTION AND DEVELOPMENT

Work Date: ____/____/____

LESSON OBJECTIVE

Students will explain the major events that occur during fertilization and differentiation.

Classroom Activities

On Your Mark!

Begin the lesson with a brief explanation of the events that occur during fertilization. Fertilization of the human egg takes place inside the female's **Fallopian tube**. A single male sperm penetrates the surface of the egg, piercing a protective membrane surrounding the egg called the **zona pellucida**. Penetration of the zona pellucida and the release of enzymes from the sperm "seals" the egg cell membrane, making it resistant to invasion by additional sperm. The fertilized egg containing 23 pairs of chromosomes (e.g., 23 single chromosomes from each parent) begins to divide. By the third day of pregnancy the bundle of eggs enters and binds to the wall of the mother's uterus and within 1–2 weeks, is receiving nourishment from the capillaries of the mother's uterine wall (cf. "blastocyst" in Lesson #3). There, the cells of the developing embryo continue to multiply and differentiate for another 36 weeks (e.g., 9 months).

Get Set!

Explain that one of the most challenging problems of **developmental biology**—also called **embryology**—is to discover how different sections of the DNA molecule are "turned on and off" in different cells to make groups of cells different from one another so that the various tissues and organs of the human body can be developed. By the third week this process of **differentiation** leads to the development of three distinguishable layers of cells that will eventually comprise the different organ systems of the body. List the tissues and organs on the board that will originate in each of the three **germ layers** and have students draw and label the structures in the appropriate "fetal diagrams" on Journal Sheet #3. From left to right on Journal Sheet #3 the germ layers are as follows:

Ectoderm	Mesoderm	Endoderm
skin and hair	skeletal bones	esophagus
nails and teeth	skeletal muscles	stomach
brain	heart	small intestine
teeth	arteries and veins	large intestine
spinal cord	outer lining of lungs	liver and gall bladder
peripheral nerves	kidneys	pancreas
sensory organs		inner lining of lungs
pituitary gland		most endocrine glands

Go!

Give students ample time to complete the activity described in Figure B on Journal Sheet #2.

Materials

Journal Sheet #2

HB11 JOURNAL SHEET #2

REPRODUCTION AND DEVELOPMENT

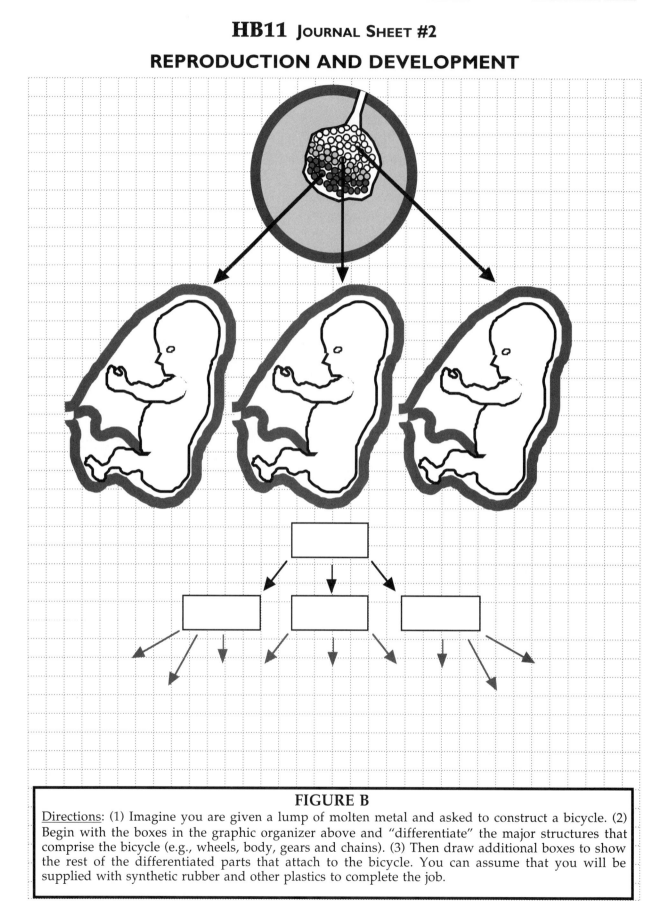

FIGURE B

Directions: (1) Imagine you are given a lump of molten metal and asked to construct a bicycle. (2) Begin with the boxes in the graphic organizer above and "differentiate" the major structures that comprise the bicycle (e.g., wheels, body, gears and chains). (3) Then draw additional boxes to show the rest of the differentiated parts that attach to the bicycle. You can assume that you will be supplied with synthetic rubber and other plastics to complete the job.

HB11 Lesson #3

REPRODUCTION AND DEVELOPMENT

Work Date: _____/_____/_____

LESSON OBJECTIVE

Students will identify the major stages of prenatal development.

Classroom Activities

On Your Mark!

Review the concept of differentiation and some of the strategies that students used to change the lump of molten metal into a bicycle. Explain that the process they used could be divided into "stages" that could be identified by defining some of the major events that took place during each stage. During **prenatal** (e.g., meaning "before birth") **development** a new human being also develops in stages.

Get Set!

Define the major stages of development illustrated on Journal Sheet #3 and have students carefully copy your notes as you describe each stage. You may draw the illustration on the board or use a transparency and overhead projector to facilitate student notetaking. Beginning at upper left and proceeding across and down the Journal Sheet the prenatal stages are illustrated as follows:

Stage	Major Events
fertilization	A single male sperm among thousands punctures the cell membrane of the female egg and the membrane "seals" against further invasion. The genetic material (e.g., chromosomes) of the parents are combined in the nucleus of the egg. The fertilized egg becomes embedded in the wall of the mother's uterus.
two-cell stage	The egg divides to form two identical cells. Should these cells separate and develop independently, identical twins will be born. Fraternal twins develop from separately fertilized eggs.
morula	The morula results from the repeated division of cells.
blastocyst	Containing about 1,000 cells, the cells of the blastocyst become aligned along an outer sphere of cells called the **trophoblast.** This structure will become the placenta. The fluid-filled **blastoceol** will become the amniotic sac.
embryonic disc	The **inner cell mass** of the blastocyst differentiates into the three germinal layers that will become the organ systems of the embryo.
embryo	The four-week-old embryo is about 5 mm in length. The umbilical cord is firmly attached to the wall of the placenta where the embryo's capillaries intermingle with those of the mother's circulatory system. Nutrients filter from the mother to the embryo as embryonic wastes pass into the mother's circulation.
fetus	The first bones are formed at the end of the eighth to tenth week marking the start of the fetal period. The developing fetus gestates for another 28 weeks, its bones remaining soft for **parturition** (e.g., birth).

Go!

Give students ample time to complete the activity described in Figure C on Journal Sheet #3.

Materials

Journal Sheet #3

HB11 JOURNAL SHEET #3

REPRODUCTION AND DEVELOPMENT

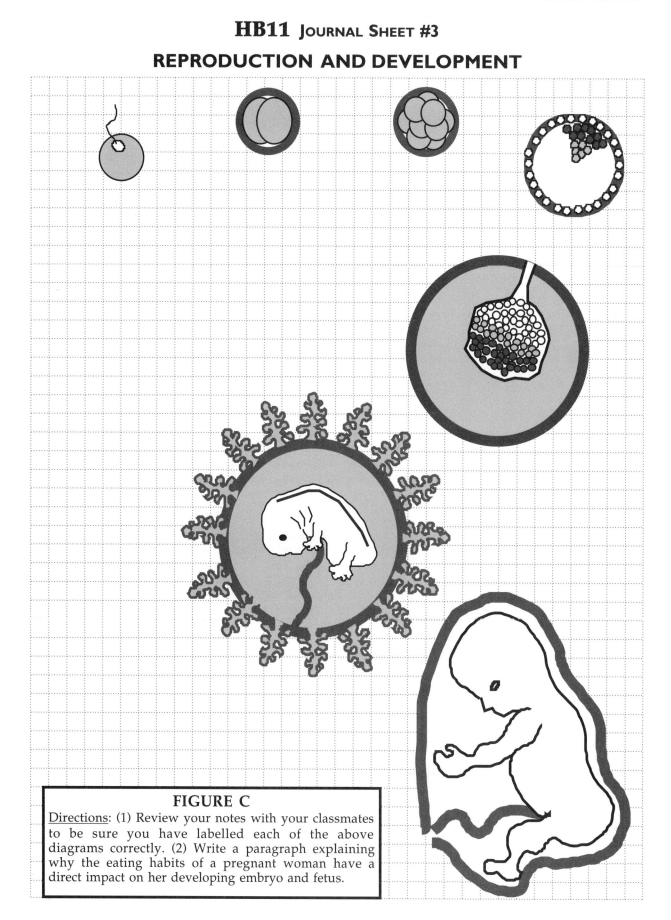

FIGURE C

Directions: (1) Review your notes with your classmates to be sure you have labelled each of the above diagrams correctly. (2) Write a paragraph explaining why the eating habits of a pregnant woman have a direct impact on her developing embryo and fetus.

HB11 Lesson #4

REPRODUCTION AND DEVELOPMENT

Work Date: ____/____/____

LESSON OBJECTIVE

Students will identify the major stages of postnatal development.

Classroom Activities

On Your Mark!

Prepare for class by compiling 10–20 pictures of infants, children, adolescents, adults and elders.

Write the stages of **postnatal** (e.g., meaning "after birth") **development** on the board: **infancy** (e.g., 0 to 2 years), **childhood** (e.g., 2 to 12 years), **adolescence** (e.g., 13 to 18 years), and **adulthood**. Distribute the pictures at the start of class and lead a discussion that compares and contrasts the distinctive physical features of each group. List those features below each category and have students copy your list.

Get Set!

As the discussion proceeds point out the following major events that occur during each stage. During infancy, visual acuity, recognition skills, and muscular coordination begin to develop. An infant recognizes its parents and siblings and enters the "toddler" phase. During childhood, social skills (e.g., interaction with peers) and language develop. Puberty (e.g., the development of secondary sex characteristics) marks the onset of adolescence. The completed development of the reproductive systems is the beginning of adulthood. At about 50 years of age females experience a "change of life" called **menopause** marked by the cessation of the menstrual cycle. Although males do not experience any such change both elder males and females begin to lose bone and muscle mass, and in some cases sensory and mental faculties (e.g., eyesight, hearing, and memory), although a well-balanced diet and exercise program can help to maintain good health in later life.

Go!

Give students ample time to complete the activity described in Figure D on Journal Sheet #4.

Materials

rulers, Journal Sheet #3

HB11 JOURNAL SHEET #4

REPRODUCTION AND DEVELOPMENT

minus 6 months   minus 3 months   birth to 1 year   2 to 5 years   6 to 13 years   14 to adult

FIGURE D

Directions: (1) Use a ruler to compare the size of the head to the size of the entire body (e.g., head included) at each stage of development from 6 months prior to birth to adulthood. (2) Write a paragraph describing the rate of growth of the head and body from the fetal stage through infancy, infancy through childhood, childhood through adolescence, and adolescence through adulthood.

HB11 REVIEW QUIZ

Directions: Keep your eyes on your own work.
Read all directions and questions carefully.
THINK BEFORE YOU ANSWER!
Watch your spelling, be neat, and do the best you can.

CLASSWORK	(~40): _____
HOMEWORK	(~20): _____
CURRENT EVENT	(~10): _____
TEST	(~30): _____
TOTAL	(~100): _____

(A ≥ 90, B ≥ 80, C ≥ 70, D ≥ 60, F < 60)

LETTER GRADE: _____

TEACHER'S COMMENTS: _____
_____

REPRODUCTION AND DEVELOPMENT

TRUE–FALSE FILL-IN: If the statement is true, write the word TRUE. If the statement is false, change the underlined word to make the statement true. *10 points*

_____ 1. <u>Not all</u> individuals of a species must reproduce for a species to survive.

_____ 2. The human <u>endocrine</u> system produces specialized cells that perpetuate the human race.

_____ 3. Reproductive cells are called <u>gametes</u>.

_____ 4. The haploid <u>nerve cells</u> of human parents contain all of the species traits and individual traits that make us human.

_____ 5. Human traits are passed from one generation to the next in chromosomes made of <u>ATP</u>.

_____ 6. The male sex cell is called a(n) <u>egg</u>.

_____ 7. The female sex cell is called a(n) <u>sperm</u>.

_____ 8. A healthy fertilized human egg contains <u>46</u> chromosomes.

_____ 9. <u>Testes</u> are male reproductive organs.

_____ 10. <u>Ovaries</u> are female reproductive organs.

STAGES OF DEVELOPMENT: Put the number 1, 2, 3, 4, 5, 6, or 7 in the blank next to each of the following stages of human development to show the order in which they occur. *7 points*

_____ adult _____ child _____ embryo _____ fetus _____ zygote

_____ infant _____ adolescent

HB11 Review Quiz *(cont'd)*

MATCHING: Choose the letter or the phrase that best describes the term at left. *13 points*

_____	11.	testis	(A)	hormone produces male sexual characteristics
_____	12.	scrotum	(B)	male reproductive organ
_____	13.	testosterone	(C)	external pouch protects male reproductive organs
_____	14.	estrogen	(D)	route of egg to womb
_____	15.	Fallopian Tube	(E)	womb of developing organism
_____	16.	uterus	(F)	hormone produces female sexual characteristics
_____	17.	ovary	(G)	provides nutrients and removes waste for fetus
_____	18.	menstruation	(H)	unfertilized egg excreted
_____	19.	placenta	(I)	period of development
_____	20.	gestation	(J)	parents' biological traits are joined
_____	21.	fertilization	(K)	sex cells are produced
_____	22.	gametogenesis	(L)	filled with fluid to protect developing organism
_____	23.	amniotic sac	(M)	female reproductive organ

IMMUNITY AND DISEASE

Teacher's Classwork Agenda and Content Notes

Classwork Agenda for the Week

1. Students will list and describe microorganisms that cause infectious diseases.

2. Students will describe the body's major lines of defense against disease.

3. Students will explain the meaning of active and passive immunity and how the body responds to a virus.

4. Students will complete the Human Body Chart by adding the organs of the lymphatic system.

Content Notes for Lecture and Discussion

Hippocrates (b. 460 B.C.; d. 377 B.C.) believed that epidemic outbreaks of infectious diseases were rooted in the disruption of the earth's atmosphere. Noting that epidemics were usually associated with poor weather conditions and local disasters (e.g., earthquakes and volcanic eruptions)—leading to sickening "exhalations" from poisoned or stagnating pools of water that accelerated putrification of plant and animal matter—Hippocrates's **miasmatic theory** remained the most widely accepted theory of disease until the late 19th century.

The observation of the Dutch microscopist **Anton van Leeuwenhoek** (b 1632; d. 1723) led to the belief by many epidemiologists that **microbes** could be the cause of disease, although there was little direct evidence to support that view. The English physician **Edward Jenner** (b. 1749; d. 1823) succeeded in finding an effective vaccine against smallpox in 1796 but could not explain how his treatment worked. In the middle of the 19th century, the English physician **John Snow** (b. 1813; d. 1858) published *On the Mode of Communication of Cholera* in which he proposed that the agent of transmission that had spread cholera to epidemic proportions throughout London was in the contaminated water of a local well. He could not, however, isolate the agent. In 1840, the German anatomist and histologist **Jacob Henle** (b. 1809; d. 1885) published his *Pathological Investigations* in which he argued that living organisms were responsible for diseases in man, animals, and plants. He noted that living things alone were capable of reproduction and that progressively morbid infectious diseases must have a similar organic cause. He proposed a series of "filtration" methods to isolate the microbes responsible for ill health. The German bacteriologist **Heinrich Hermann Robert Koch** (b. 1843; d. 1910) fulfilled that dream less than forty years later. Koch and his associates developed techniques for the isolation and culturing of bacteria so that they could be used to replicate diseases in laboratory animals. In 1860, the French chemist and microbiologist **Louis Pasteur** (b. 1822; d. 1895) discovered that fermentation of sugars was dependent upon the action of microorganisms (e.g., anaerobic bacteria and yeasts) and that these "germs" could be killed by heat. **Pasteurization**—a method of heating the fermenting mixture gently to 50°C—is used today as the primary method of killing yeasts used in the manufacture of beers, wines, and dairy products. Pasteur published his **germ theory** in 1865, inspiring the English surgeon **Joseph Lister** (b. 1827; d. 1912) to perform the first antiseptic operation in 1867. In 1891, the German bacteriologist **Paul Ehrlich** (b. 1854; d. 1915) developed the first techniques in **chemotherapy** using synthetic drugs to kill infectious organisms. In the 1880s, the Dutch bacteriologist **Martinus Willem Beijerinck** (b. 1851; d. 1931) found the causative agent responsible for the mottling and destruction of tobacco leaves which he determined to be several magnitudes smaller than any known bacteria. He called the germ a **virus**, meaning "poison" (e.g., tobacco mosaic virus).

HB12 Content Notes *(cont'd)*

The science of **immunology** is fairly new, having progressed since the middle of the 20th century with the science of **molecular biology**. In 1938, the Swedish chemist **Arne Wilhelm Kaurin Tiselius** (b. 1902; d. 1971) used his newly invented electrophoresis technique to isolate a number of animal proteins, among them a variety of elusive alpha-, beta-, and gammaglobulin antibodies. Of increasing interest to modern immunologists are the **autoimmune diseases** (e.g., rheumatoid arthritis and AIDS) that defy easy analysis. The immune system gone awry, attacking its own body tissues as it would a foreign invader, is the most challenging group of diseases to face the medical research laboratories of the world.

In Lesson #1, students will list and describe microorganisms that cause infectious diseases.

In Lesson #2, students will describe the body's major lines of defense against disease.

In Lesson #3, students will explain the meaning of active and passive immunity and how the body responds to a virus.

In Lesson #4, students will complete the Human Body Chart by adding the organs of the lymphatic system.

ANSWERS TO THE HOMEWORK PROBLEMS

Students' essays should summarize the understanding of active immunity.

ANSWERS TO THE END-OF-THE-WEEK REVIEW QUIZ

1. germs
2. true
3. true
4. true
5. second

6. first
7. true
8. interferon
9. true
10. vaccine

Students' answers to essay statements #11 through #15 will vary but should demonstrate their understanding of how infectious diseases are transmitted. They should mention that germs can be spread by touching, sneezing, coughing, or coming into contact with another person's bodily fluids (e.g., saliva on a shared drinking glass). They can suggest a variety of ways to avoid the spread of germs by these acts.

HB12 FACT SHEET

IMMUNITY AND DISEASE

CLASSWORK AGENDA FOR THE WEEK

(1) List and describe microorganisms that cause infectious diseases.
(2) Describe the body's major lines of defense against disease.
(3) Explain the meaning of active and passive immunity and how the body responds to a virus.
(4) Complete the Human Body Chart by adding the organs of the lymphatic system.

The human body is vulnerable to attack by a variety of foreign organisms we call "germs." The term refers to any number of microscopic organisms such as **bacteria**, **viruses**, **protists**, and **fungi**. A person carrying germs can infect others with those germs. Germs can be spread by touching, sneezing, coughing, or coming into contact with another person's bodily fluids (e.g., saliva on a shared drinking glass). Scientists were not always aware of the existence of germs. The **germ theory** was first proposed by the French chemist and microbiologist **Louis Pasteur** (b. 1822; d. 1895). Pasteur's student **Joseph Lister** (b. 1827; d. 1912) performed the first "antiseptic" surgery in 1867. Earlier surgeons did not recognize the importance of sterilizing their surgical equipment or washing their hands before performing an operation. The German bacteriologist **H. H. Robert Koch** (b. 1843; d. 1910) devised the first methods for isolating, culturing, and studying germs that cause **infectious diseases**.

The body has three lines of defense against disease: (1) *mucous membranes* and *skin*, (2) the *inflammatory response*, and (3) the *immune response*.

The first line of defense includes the **mucous membranes** of the respiratory tract and the **skin**. Mucous membranes of the nose and respiratory tract trap dust and dirt that carry microscopic germs. "Hairlike" **cilia** embedded in the membranes gently "sweep" the foreign material out of the nose and mouth. The skin serves as a barrier that protects the internal organs from invasion by foreign substances called **antigens**.

When the skin is broken the body's second line of defense goes into action: the **inflammatory response**. When invading microorganisms attack body cells the body increases the blood supply to the affected area. **Blood platelets** clot the blood and seal the injury. **White blood cells** attack the antigens and destroy them. The protein interferon present in the bloodstream and extracellular fluid "interferes" with the reproduction of viruses that get into the wound.

If the invasion of germs is successful, then the body's third line of defense, the **immune response**, goes to work. The immune response is controlled by two systems: the **lymphatic** and **immune systems**. The lymphatic system is one of interconnected lymph nodes and "accessory" organs: **spleen**, **thymus**, **tonsils**, and **adenoids**. The vessels and nodes of the lymphatic system filter foreign substances and cell wastes from blood and extracellular fluids. Lymph nodes also store **lymphocytes**, the most plentiful type of white blood cell produced in the bones. Specialized white blood cells called **T-cells** alert other special cells called **B-cells** to produce **antibodies**. Antibody molecules are large protein strands that surround and bind to viruses, bacteria, and other foreign invaders. When a specific group of invaders is immobilized, white blood cells can gather, attack, and destroy them. Antibodies can remain in the bloodstream for a long time making the body resistant to future invasion by the same germs. This resistance is called **immunity**.

Immunity is the resistance to a disease-carrying organism or harmful substance. There are two types of immunity: *active* immunity and *passive* immunity. **Active immunity** results when a person's own immune system responds to the presence of an antigen by producing antibodies. The immune system is "activated" every day by germs entering the body. The immune system can also respond to a "vaccine." A **vaccine** is a laboratory-prepared form of a virus that instigates the production of antibodies against a particular disease. A vaccine is usually made of a "dead" or "inactivated" form of the germ. **Passive immunity** results from the direct transfer of antibodies from one source to another. For example, a pregnant mother can transfer her antibodies to her developing offspring.

In normal cases the immune system can recognize and destroy invaders without hurting the body's healthy cells. Sometimes, however, the body's own defenses behave abnormally and start attacking the body's own tissues. Physicians call this condition an **autoimmune disease**. Rheumatoid arthritis and lupus are autoimmune diseases.

Homework Directions

Interview your parents to find out if you have had any of the following diseases: chicken pox, measles, mumps. Then write a paragraph to explain why you don't get these same diseases over and over again.

Assignment due: _____

_____ _____ ___/___/___
Student's Signature   Parent's Signature   Date

IMMUNITY AND DISEASE

Work Date: ____/____/____

LESSON OBJECTIVE

Students will list and describe microorganisms that cause infectious diseases.

Classroom Activities

On Your Mark!

Use the information in the Teacher's Classwork Agenda and Content Notes to give a brief lecture on the history of our understanding of infectious diseases. Explain that early scientists believed that insect pests and microorganisms were produced by decaying nonliving matter in a process called "spontaneous generation." They believed that fly larva grew from rotting meat and bacteria, yeast, and mold were the product of spoiling broth. Draw Illustration A on the board and explain the work of Italian physician **Francesco Redi** (b. 1626; d. 1697) and French microbiologist **Louis Pasteur** (b. 1822; d. 1895) in demonstrating the falsity of "spontaneous generation." Redi placed raw meat in 3 containers, left one uncovered (A), a second covered one with gauze (B), and a third (C) covered with parchment. Maggots were produced in the first container. Fly eggs were found on the gauze but no maggots developed in the second

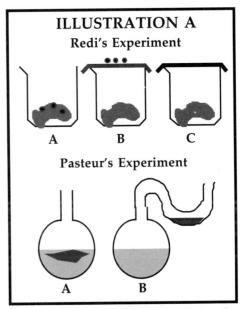

ILLUSTRATION A
Redi's Experiment

A   B   C

Pasteur's Experiment

A   B

container. Neither eggs nor maggots were found in the third container. Redi concluded that fly larva came from fly eggs and were not generated "spontaneously." Pasteur showed that bacteria eventually developed in broth that was boiled (e.g., sterilized) and allowed to cool in container "A" but not in container "B" which was fitted with an S-shaped mouth. He showed that the airborne bacteria became trapped in the film lining the curve of the tube. This demonstration not only showed the falsity of spontaneous generation but also demonstrated how easily bacteria could be spread through the air.

Get Set!

Refer students to the illustrations on Journal Sheet #1. Copy the illustrations on the board or use a transparency and overhead projector to assist students in comparing and contrasting the size and structure of these microorganisms.

Go!

Give students ample time to complete the activity described in Figure A on Journal Sheet #1.

Materials

Journal Sheet #1

HB12 JOURNAL SHEET #1

IMMUNITY AND DISEASE

VIRUSES	PROTISTS	BACTERIA

helical

icosahedral

bacteriophage

10 - 100 nm

ameba

0.05 - 0.5mm

1 - 10 μm

bacillus

spirochete

diplococcus

staphylococcus

streptococcus

SOME DISEASE-CAUSING MICROBES

VIRUSES   common cold, chicken pox, influenza, mumps, polio, rabies, small pox, yellow fever, HIV

PROTISTS   amoebic dysentery, malaria, sleeping sickness

BACTERIA   cholera, pneumonia, scarlet fever, tetanus, tuberculosis, typhoid fever

FUNGI   ringworm, athlete's foot

FIGURE A

Directions: Perform the necessary math calculations to solve the problems.

(A) If every virus-infected cell produced 10 new viruses in 24 hours, how many virus-infected cells would there be after one week?

(B) If a person sneezed only once per day, expelling 10 airborne viruses with each sneeze, and 10 other people inhaled 1 virus each and began sneezing at the same rate, how many people would be infected after one week?

HB12 Lesson #2

IMMUNITY AND DISEASE

Work Date: ____/____/____

LESSON OBJECTIVE

Students will describe the body's major lines of defense against disease.

Classroom Activities

On Your Mark!

Refer students to the illustration on Journal Sheet #2. Copy the illustration on the board or use a transparency and overhead projector to assist students in identifying the major organs responsible for defending the body against infectious diseases and other harmful substances.

Get Set!

Point out that the **mucous membranes** and **cilia** of the respiratory tract as well as the **skin** constitute the body's first line of defense. Identify the **heart** and **circulatory system** as the route by which **platelets**, **white blood cells** (e.g., lymphocytes), **interferon**, and **antibodies** are distributed throughout the body. Discuss the role of the body's second line of defense, the **inflammatory response**, in getting the body's disease-fighting resources to where they are needed. Identify the organs of the body's third line of defense: the **lymphatic** and **immune systems**. Identify the organs indicated in the illustration. From top to bottom they are as follows: **tonsils, thymus gland, spleen, thoracic duct,** and **bone marrow**. Point out how the glands of the lymphatic system are connected by an array of **lymph vessels** and **lymph nodes** that store disease-fighting cells until they are needed. Point out that while lymphocytes are formed in the bones, some of those cells develop to maturity in the thymus gland. Mention that the thoracic duct and two major ducts located at the right and left subclavian veins (e.g., vessels leading from the arms back to the heart) are the major ducts that flush liquid lymph back into the bloodstream. Muscular action of the legs and abdomen forces lymph drawn from the extracellular fluids up to those ducts from the lower parts of the body.

Go!

Give students ample time to complete the activity described in Figure B on Journal Sheet #2. Circulate around the room to make sure that students are taking the information provided from your lecture and those in the Fact Sheet to accurately summarize the body's three lines of defense in their graphic organizer.

Materials

Journal Sheet #2

HB12 JOURNAL SHEET #2

IMMUNITY AND DISEASE

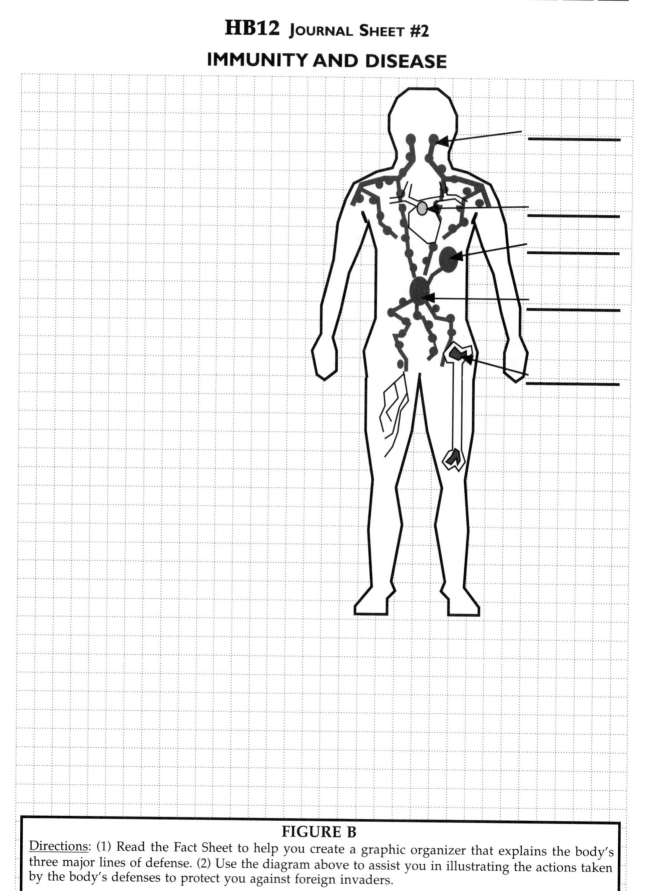

FIGURE B

<u>Directions</u>: (1) Read the Fact Sheet to help you create a graphic organizer that explains the body's three major lines of defense. (2) Use the diagram above to assist you in illustrating the actions taken by the body's defenses to protect you against foreign invaders.

IMMUNITY AND DISEASE

Work Date: _____/_____/_____

LESSON OBJECTIVE

Students will explain the meaning of active and passive immunity and how the body responds to a virus.

Classroom Activities

On Your Mark!

Begin the lesson by comparing the human body to a country. Explain that the immune system employs an "army" of cellular and molecular defenders much like a country employs an army of intelligence and military officers to defend itself against foreign enemies. Compare the microbes that cause infectious diseases to world terrorists threatening to disrupt the peaceful business of free people.

Get Set!

Refer students to the illustration on Journal Sheet #3. Copy the illustration on the board or use a transparency and overhead projector to assist students in identifying the strategy used by the body's third line of defense, the immune system, to fight invading germs. (1) Large **macrophages** (e.g., lymphocytes/white blood cells) attack and devour members of an invading group of viruses. (2) The macrophages dismember the captured viruses and send information about their structure to specialized white blood cells called **T-cells**. (3) The T-cells alert **helper T-cells**. (4) The **helper T-cells** instruct **B-cells** to manufacture specialized proteins that will recognize the invaders. (5) The B-cells manufacture these **antibodies** and release them into the bloodstream. (6) The antibodies attack and immobilize the remaining viruses until they can be destroyed by more macrophages. Remaining on guard for varying lengths of time, the antibodies recognize future invaders when they appear.

Have students read paragraph #6 of their Fact Sheet; then instruct them to write a quick definition of active and passive immunity. **Active immunity** involves the body's own action in manufacturing antibodies against infectious germs. **Passive immunity** is the transfer of "ready-made" antibodies from one person to another.

Go!

Give students ample time to complete the activity described in Figure C on Journal Sheet #3. Give students time to share their stories.

Materials

Journal Sheet #3

HB12 JOURNAL SHEET #3

IMMUNITY AND DISEASE

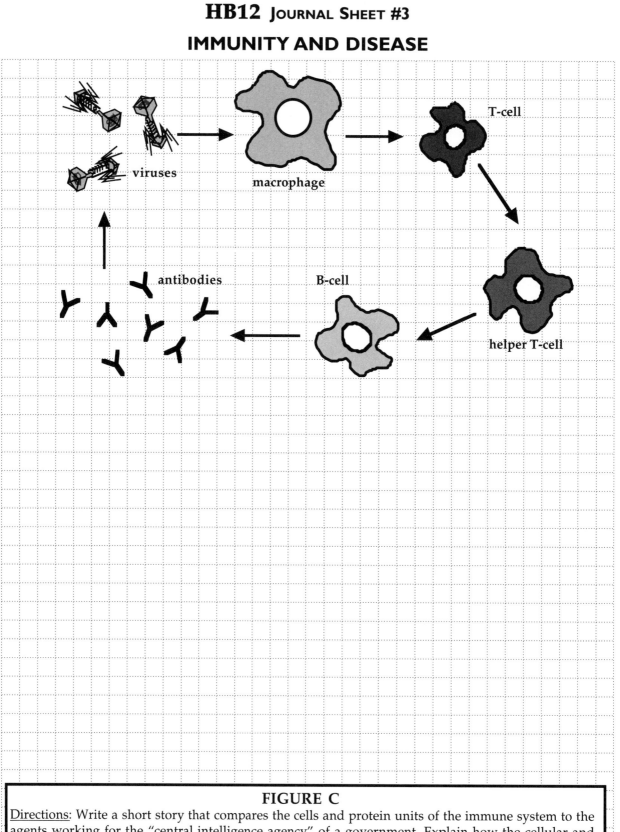

FIGURE C
<u>Directions</u>: Write a short story that compares the cells and protein units of the immune system to the agents working for the "central intelligence agency" of a government. Explain how the cellular and molecular "agents" work together to identify and destroy a virus attacking an organ (e.g., a foreign terrorist plotting to destroy a national monument).

IMMUNITY AND DISEASE

Work Date: ____/____/____

LESSON OBJECTIVE

Students will complete the Human Body Chart by adding the organs of the lymphatic system.

Classroom Activities

On Your Mark!

Refer students to the illustration on Journal Sheet #2. Explain that students will complete their Human Body Chart by adding the organs of the lymphatic system.

Get Set!

Distribute posters and art materials.

Go!

Give students ample time to complete the activity described in Figure D on Journal Sheet #4. Instruct them to use glue to permanently attach the organs of the body. Advise them to attach organs so that they can be "folded back" to view underlying structure.

Materials

glue, butcher paper, construction paper, scissors, crayon or felt-tip markers

HB12 JOURNAL SHEET #4

IMMUNITY AND DISEASE

FIGURE D

Directions: (1) Complete your HUMAN BODY CHART by adding the organs of the lymphatic system, using the information shown on the illustration on Journal Sheet #2. (2) Use the materials provided by your instructor to draw pictures of the individual structures of the system. (3) Use glue to permanently secure the paper parts. ATTACH ALL ORGANS SO THAT THEY CAN BE 'FOLDED BACK' TO VIEW UNDERLYING STRUCTURES. (4) Lay your finished chart in a cool place to give the glue plenty of time to dry.

HB12 Review Quiz

Directions: Keep your eyes on your own work.
Read all directions and questions carefully.
THINK BEFORE YOU ANSWER!
Watch your spelling, be neat, and do the best you can.

CLASSWORK   (~40): _____
HOMEWORK   (~20): _____
CURRENT EVENT   (~10): _____
TEST   (~30): _____

TOTAL   (~100): _____
(A ≥ 90, B ≥ 80, C ≥ 70, D ≥ 60, F < 60)

LETTER GRADE: _____

TEACHER'S COMMENTS: _____
_____

IMMUNITY AND DISEASE

TRUE–FALSE FILL-IN: If the statement is true, write the word TRUE. If the statement is false, change the underlined word to make the statement true. *20 points*

_____ 1. The human body is vulnerable to attack by bacteria, viruses, protists, and fungi that together are commonly called <u>mold</u>.

_____ 2. The germ theory was first proposed by <u>Louis Pasteur</u>.

_____ 3. <u>Joseph Lister</u> performed the first "antiseptic" surgery in 1867.

_____ 4. <u>Robert Koch</u> devised the first methods for isolating, culturing, and studying germs that cause infectious diseases.

_____ 5. The body's <u>first</u> line of defense against disease includes the inflammatory response.

_____ 6. The body's <u>second</u> line of defense against disease includes the mucous membranes of the respiratory tract and the skin.

_____ 7. The body's <u>third</u> line of defense against disease includes the lymphatic and immune systems.

_____ 8. The protein <u>hemoglobin</u> present in the bloodstream and extracellular fluid "interferes" with the reproduction of viruses that get into the wound.

_____ 9. <u>Immunity</u> is the resistance to a disease-carrying organism or harmful substance.

_____ 10. A(n) <u>antibody</u> is a laboratory-prepared form of a virus that helps the body to build an immunity to a particular antigen.

HB12 Review Quiz *(cont'd)*

ESSAY: Make a list of at least five (5) precautions you can take to avoid spreading a common cold virus among the members of your family. *10 points*

11. _____

_____

12. _____

_____

13. _____

_____

14. _____

_____

15. _____

_____

FROG DISSECTION

Teacher's Classwork Agenda and Content Notes

Classwork Agenda for the Week

1. Students will perform an external examination of the frog to identify its physical adaptations.

2. Students will begin the dissection of a frog to compare the arrangement of internal organs to that of a human being.

3. Students will continue the dissection of a frog to compare the arrangement of internal organs to that of a human being.

4. Students will contrast the structure and arrangement of organs in the frog to those of a human being.

Content Notes for Lecture and Discussion

Throughout history since the time of **Aristotle** (b. 384 B.C.; d. 322 B.C.), the study of **anatomy** has been the study of **comparative anatomy**. In order to arrange animals in the "chain of being," Aristotle dissected many animal species noting their structural similarities and differences and classifying them accordingly. Following the work of English naturalist **Charles Robert Darwin** (b. 1809; d. 1882) and his publication, *The Origin of Species*, the logical biological foundation for the study of comparative anatomy was established. Human dissection for the purpose of advancing the medical arts began with the Greek physicians **Herophilus of Chalcedon** (c. 330 B.C.; c. 260 B.C.) and **Erasistratus** (c. 304 B.C.; c. 250 B.C.) who left the most complete record of their work for future examination. The Greek physician **Galen** (b. 129; d. 200) adopted the "humourology" of **Hippocrates** (b. 460 B.C.; d. 377 B.C.) and related the great physician's work to the study of anatomy. The work of Galen dominated the Dark and Middle Ages until the artists and scientists of the Renaissance, led principally by the gifted Italian **Leonardo da Vinci** (b. 1452; d. 1519), began a new and thoroughly scientific study of anatomy. In 1543, the Belgian physician **Andreas Vesalius**, (b. 1514; d. 1564) published *On the Structure of the Human Body*, containing the best illustrated descriptions of the human body made to that date. The book laid the foundation for more detailed anatomical study. However, Vesalius's work—published in the same year as the works of the revolutionary astronomer **Nikolaus Copernicus** (b. 1473; d. 1543)—aroused such bitter controversy that Vesalius abandoned the field.

The dissection of a frog has been a standard educational strategy for teaching basic anatomy for more than a century. The convenient size and relative simplicity of the common little amphibian lends itself easily to the inquisitive eye of the beginning biology student.

In Lesson #1, students will perform an external examination of the frog to identify its physical adaptations.

In Lesson #2, students will begin the dissection of a frog to compare the arrangement of internal organs to that of a human being.

In Lesson #3, students will continue the dissection of a frog to compare the arrangement of internal organs to that of a human being.

In Lesson #4, students will contrast the structure and arrangement of organs in the frog to those of a human being.

HB13 Content Notes *(cont'd)*

ANSWERS TO THE HOMEWORK PROBLEMS

Students' Journal Sheets should clearly identify the major organs observed during their dissection of the frog.

ANSWERS TO THE END-OF-THE-WEEK REVIEW QUIZ

Students should be able to draw and label the following organs of the digestive system: the esophagus, the stomach, the small and large intestine, the cloaca, the liver, gall bladder, and pancreas.

Students should be able to draw and label the following organs of the circulatory and respiratory systems: the heart (e.g., two atria and the frog's single ventricle), lungs, and pulmonary arteries and pulmonary veins.

HB13 FACT SHEET

FROG DISSECTION

CLASSWORK AGENDA FOR THE WEEK

(1)   Perform an external examination of the frog to identify its physical adaptations.
(2)   Begin the dissection of a frog to compare the arrangement of internal organs to that of a human being.
(3)   Continue the dissection of a frog to compare the arrangement of internal organs to that of a human being.
(4)   Contrast the structure and arrangement of organs in the frog to those of a human being.

A frog is a **vertebrate** belonging to the class **amphibia**. A human being is a vertebrate belonging to the class **mammalia**. Both animals are adapted to life on land and have the same basic biological needs (e.g., air, food, and water); frogs, however, spend much of their time in water. Frogs and humans share similarities in anatomical structure that can be readily observed by *dissection*. **Dissection** is a method used to carefully separate the parts of an organism to determine the function of organs and their relationship to one another. One of the earliest recorded dissections was performed by the Italian-Greek physician **Alcmaeon of Crotona** (c. 500 B.C.). Alcmaeon dissected the eyes of animals and human cadavers to discover "the pathway of light to the brain." The Italian artist, inventor, and anatomist **Leonardo da Vinci** (b. 1452; d. 1519) performed many dissections on human cadavers to discover the function of different organs. He was one of the first investigators to discover that it is the function of muscles "to pull and not to push". Every student of medicine must make a successful dissection of a human cadaver to demonstrate their understanding of the relationship between the organs of the human body.

A frog's **external anatomy** gives clear indications of how its species has adapted for life on land and in the water. A frog's skin is smooth and in life is covered with a thin layer of mucus that allows it to glide easily through the water. The skin is colored to camouflage the frog, protecting it against attack by predators. The hind legs of the frog are adapted for leaping and swimming. Its feet are webbed for propelling it quickly through the water. The frog does not have external pinna for capturing sound waves. Its tympanic membranes (e.g., eardrums) are located on the sides of its head to detect small vibrations in water or air. The frog has a single opening to excrete both solid and liquid wastes. It has no external genital (e.g., sex) organs. The frog's eye is covered with an eyelid and an underlying nictitating membrane used to protect the eye underwater. The frog's tongue is attached at the front of its lower jaw and in life can extend out of its mouth to almost the full length of its body.

The **internal anatomy** of a frog is very similar in structure and function to that of a human being. A frog has the same organ systems as all other vertebrates: **skeletal, muscular, digestive, excretory, circulatory, respiratory, nervous, endocrine, immune,** and **reproductive systems**. The excretory and reproductive systems of the frog are the most noticeably different from those of mammals. The waste products of a frog's metabolism are deposited in a single pouch called the cloaca leading to the anus. The reproductive cells (e.g., the eggs of a female and the sperm of a male) are also deposited in the cloaca where they are expelled from the frog's body. Frogs reproduce in the water by the method of **external fertilization**. A female frog lays her eggs at the bottom of a pond. At the same time, a male frog sprays the submerged eggs with sperm. The fertilized frog eggs that are not devoured by predators divide and grow into tadpoles that eventually become adult frogs through **metamorphosis**.

Homework Directions

Use the notes you made in class during your examination of the frog to complete your drawings on the appropriate Journal Sheet. Color the organs for easy identification. Label each organ and briefly describe its function.

Assignment due: _____

_____   _____   ____/____/____
Student's Signature   Parent's Signature   Date

FROG DISSECTION

Work Date: ____/____/____

LESSON OBJECTIVE

Students will perform an external examination of the frog to identify its physical adaptations.

Classroom Activities

On Your Mark!

Prepare for this lesson by purchasing preserved grassfrogs from a laboratory supply house.

Begin the lesson by reviewing standard health and safety guidelines regarding the respectful treatment of preserved animal specimens and the proper use of dissecting equipment.

Get Set!

Give a brief lecture on the history of **dissection** as a method of inquiry into the anatomical and functional characteristics of organs and organ systems using the information in the Teacher's Classwork Agenda and Content Notes. List the common anatomical characteristics of all animals in **phylum chordata vertebrata** (e.g., fish, amphibians, reptiles, birds, and mammals). Point out that all these animals have the same organ systems: <u>skeletal</u>, <u>muscular</u>, <u>digestive</u>, <u>excretory</u>, <u>circulatory</u>, <u>respiratory</u>, <u>nervous</u>, <u>endocrine</u>, <u>immune</u>, and <u>reproductive systems</u>. **Comparative anatomists** use this fact to study animals of other classes in an attempt to learn more about the anatomical and functional characteristics of human organs and organ systems.

Go!

Before beginning the external examination of the frog, instruct students to read the directions completely, one step at a time. Depending upon the academic and skill level of your students, you may wish to read the directions aloud one at a time. You may also want to have the entire class perform the same step together as you circulate around the classroom making sure that the instructions are being followed. Give students ample time to complete the dissection activities described in Figure A on Journal Sheet #1. Have students refer to the second paragraph of their Fact Sheet, making the observations mentioned.

Materials

preserved frogs, dissection kits and trays, paper towels, zipper baggies, ethyl alcohol, antibacterial soap and water

HB13 JOURNAL SHEET #1

FROG DISSECTION

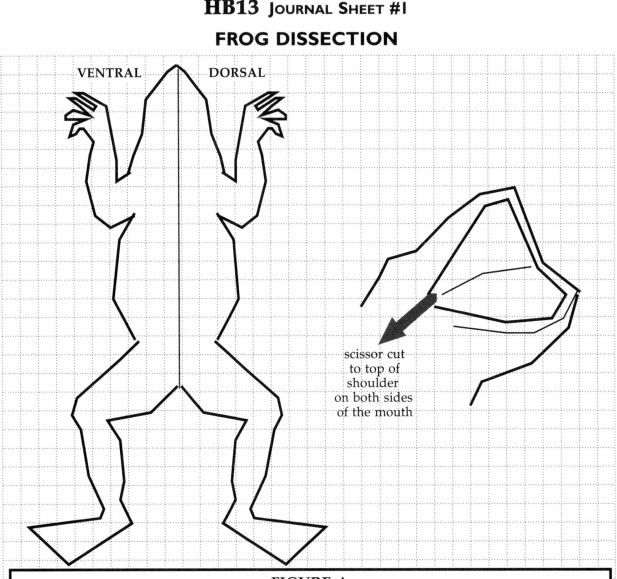

VENTRAL   DORSAL

scissor cut
to top of
shoulder
on both sides
of the mouth

FIGURE A

<u>Directions</u>: (1) Thoroughly rinse and dry the preserved frog given to you by your instructor. (2) Place the frog on its back on a paper towel in the dissecting tray. (3) Examine and record your observations of the frog's **ventral** (e.g., abdominal) side. Record its color, texture, and obvious markings. (4) Turn the frog over and examine its **dorsal** (e.g., back) side. Record its color, texture, and obvious markings. (5) Find the circular tympanic membranes on the sides of the frog's head and draw their position. (6) Find the frog's eyes and nostrils and draw their position. (7) Examine the frog's hands and feet and note how they differ from human hands and feet. (8) Find the frog's anus between its legs. (9) Lift the frog and use the blunt end of a scissor to pry open the frog's mouth. (10) Open the scissor and insert one scissor blade into the animal's mouth along the side of the jaw as shown above. (11) Carefully cut back through the bone to the top of the frog's shoulder. (12) Pry open the mouth, examine and draw the position of the tongue and how it attaches to the inside of the mouth. (13) Gently feel and draw the frog's teeth. (14) Identify and draw the frog's vomarine teeth: the two tiny bumps on the roof of its mouth. (15) Locate and draw the glottis leading to the frog's lungs and stomach at the back of its throat. (16) Rinse the frog with water and place it into a zipper baggie. Add 20 ml of alcohol to the baggie in order to reduce the reproduction of bacteria. (17) Store the frog overnight in a refrigerator. (18) Discard used paper towels and any loose biological tissue as instructed by your teacher. (19) Thoroughly wash your hands and used dissection equipment with soap and hot water.

FROG DISSECTION

Work Date: _____/_____/_____

LESSON OBJECTIVE

Students will begin the dissection of a frog to compare the arrangement of internal organs to that of a human being.

Classroom Activities

On Your Mark!

Begin the lesson by reviewing standard health and safety guidelines regarding the respectful treatment of preserved animal specimens and the proper use of dissecting equipment.

Get Set!

Briefly review the functions of the skin, the skeletal system, the muscular system, the digestive system, the circulatory system, and the respiratory system. Point out that although a frog spends much of its life in water it is adapted to life on land and must take in oxygen through the lungs in order to survive. Have students read the third paragraph of their Fact Sheet and briefly discuss the differences between the excretory and respiratory systems of amphibians and mammals.

Go!

Before beginning the internal examination of the frog, instruct students to read the directions completely, one step at a time. Depending upon the academic and skill level of your students, you may wish to read the directions aloud one at a time. You may also want to have the entire class perform the same step together as you circulate around the classroom making sure that the instructions are being followed. Give students ample time to complete the dissection activities described in Figure B on Journal Sheet #2.

Materials

preserved frogs, dissection kits and trays, paper towels, zipper baggies, ethyl alcohol, antibacterial soap and water

HB13 JOURNAL SHEET #2

FROG DISSECTION

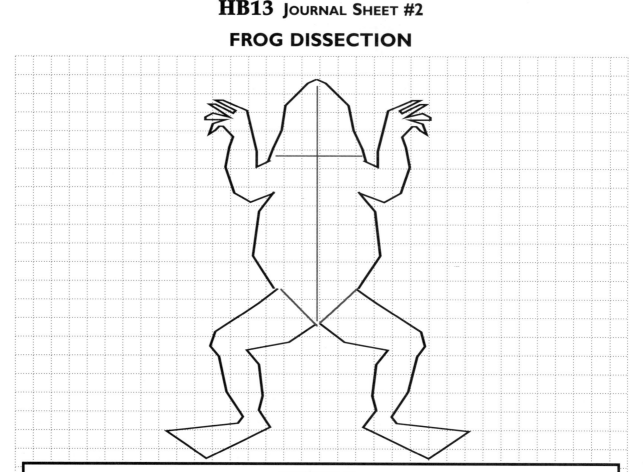

FIGURE B

READ EACH STEP COMPLETELY BEFORE EXECUTING THE DISSECTION

Directions: (1) Remove your frog from the zipper baggie. Thoroughly rinse and dry the frog and place it on its back on a paper towel in the dissecting tray. (2) Stretch and extend the frog's limbs and insert a T-pin at an angle through each wrist and ankle to secure the frog to the tray. You should be able to lift and invert the tray without the frog coming loose. (3) Use a tweezer to lift the skin between the frog's legs and use a scissor to make a shallow cut along the midline of the frog's body to the tip of its lower jaw. Avoid puncturing the underlying layer of abdominal muscles. Cut the skin perpendicular to the midline cut at shoulder level and make another pair of cuts from the midline across the top of each leg. (4) Use the tweezer to gently peel back the skin flaps and use two more T-pins to pin back the flaps. (5) Use a tweezer to lift the muscle between the frog's legs and use a scissor to make a shallow cut through the layer of muscles along the midline of the frog's body to the sternum. Avoid puncturing the underlying organs. When you reach the sternum you will need to exert pressure to cut through the ribs. Keep the scissor at a shallow angle to avoid damaging the underlying heart and lungs. Continue the cut to the tip of its lower jaw. Then cut the muscle layer perpendicular to the midline cut at shoulder level and make another pair of cuts from the midline across the top of each leg. (6) Use two more T-pins to pin back the muscle flaps. (7) Use a tweezer and scalpel to gently cut away and remove the yellowish "fat bodies" found between the internal organs. Place these tissues to the side of your dissecting tray. (8) If your specimen is a female, you will need to use the same procedure to remove the dark pouches of loosely bound "eggs". (9) Use a blunt probe to lift and identify the frog's heart and lungs, liver and gall bladder, esophagus, stomach, small and large intestines, urinary bladder and cloaca. Draw the position of each organ. (10) Carefully remove the T-pins. (11) Rinse the frog with water and place it into a zipper baggie. Add 20 ml of alcohol to the baggie to reduce the reproduction of bacteria. (12) Store the frog overnight in a refrigerator. (13) Discard used paper towels and any loose biological tissue as instructed by your teacher. (14) Thoroughly wash your hands and used dissection equipment with soap and hot water.

FROG DISSECTION

Work Date: ____/____/____

LESSON OBJECTIVE

Students will continue the dissection of a frog to compare the arrangement of internal organs to that of a human being.

Classroom Activities

On Your Mark!

Begin the lesson by reviewing standard health and safety guidelines regarding the respectful treatment of preserved animal specimens and the proper use of dissecting equipment.

Get Set!

Briefly review the functions of the excretory and the reproductive systems of the frog mentioned in paragraph #3 of the Fact Sheet. Review the function of the nervous system.

Go!

Before continuing the internal examination of the frog, instruct students to read the directions completely, one step at a time. Depending upon the academic and skill level of your students, you may wish to read the directions aloud one at a time. You may also want to have the entire class perform the same step together as you circulate around the classroom making sure that the instructions are being followed. Give students ample time to complete the dissection activities described in Figure C on Journal Sheet #3.

Advanced students may have time to conduct a dissection of the skull to expose the brain. This can be achieved by securing the frog—ventral side down—to the dissecting tray with T-pins and scraping away the skin between the eyes. The tiny brain (e.g., about the size of two grains of rice) is located under the bone between the eyes and tympanic membranes. A cautious, deliberate scraping of the bones of the skull with a scalpel toward the frog's snout will remove the bone, fragment by tiny fragment. Caution students to avoid uncontrolled slips of the scalpel. While scraping, the scalpel can become lodged between fragments of sliced bone and slip easily across the slippery surface of the skull, causing injury to the surgeon, mutilation of the specimen, or both.

Materials

preserved frogs, dissection kits and trays, paper towels, zipper baggies, ethyl alcohol, antibacterial soap and water

HB13 JOURNAL SHEET #3

FROG DISSECTION

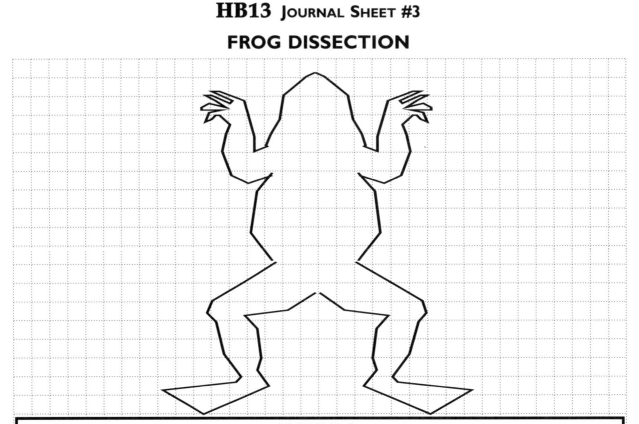

FIGURE C

READ EACH STEP COMPLETELY BEFORE EXECUTING THE DISSECTION

<u>Directions</u>: (1) Remove your frog from the zipper baggie. Thoroughly rinse and dry the frog and place it on its back on a paper towel in the dissecting tray. Use T-pins to secure the frog in the same position it was in when you completed the previous examination. (2) Use a tweezer to lift the brownish liver to identify where each liver lobe attaches to the body. Use a scissor or scalpel to cut through the attachments and carefully remove the lobes and gall bladder one organ at a time. Place these tissues to the side of your dissecting tray. (3) Examine the heart and its attachment to the lungs by a complex of pulmonary arteries and veins. Use a tweezer and scissor to remove the transparent pericardial sac of thin tissue surrounding the heart. Lift the heart and cut it away from the lungs. Use a scalpel to cut the heart open and examine its chambers. Remove the lungs in the same fashion. (4) Lift the stomach and identify the attached underlying grayish-white pancreas. Use a tweezer to hold the stomach in place. Make a cut along the length of the stomach with a scissor or scalpel to expose the contents of the frog's stomach. The tiny bugs and leaves you remove from the stomach were the frog's last meal. Examine these specimens to determine the nature of the frog's diet. (5) Use a probe to explore the upper and lower ends of the frog's digestive tract. Carefully snip through the clear connective tissue, keeping the small intestine together. Stretch out the intestine and examine its length. (6) Use a scissor to cut through the esophagus at its most forward point at the back of the mouth. After identifying the urinary bladder attached to the cloaca, cut through the end of the digestive tract where it attaches to the anus and remove the entire system. (7) Examine the purplish kidneys at the back of the cavity. A male frog will have small yellowish or pinkish testis attached to each kidney. Note the large blood vessels running along the midline on the inside of the frog's back. Draw the position of these organs. (8) Remove the kidneys using a scissor and scalpel. (9) Locate several yellowish spinal nerves protruding from the vertebrae of the backbone. Use a tweezer, scissor, and scalpel to follow the nerves into one of the frog's legs by carefully dissecting away the surrounding bundles of thick, leg muscle tissue. Nerves can usually be found running close to the length of the long bones. Draw the position of the nerves. (10) Wrap the remains of the frog and all loose biological tissue in a paper towel and place it in a zipper baggie. (11) Discard refuse materials as instructed by your teacher. (12) Thoroughly wash your hands and used dissection equipment with soap and hot water.

FROG DISSECTION

Work Date: ____/____/____

LESSON OBJECTIVE

Students will contrast the structure and arrangement of organs in the frog to those of a human being.

Classroom Activities

On Your Mark!

Display the Human Body Charts constructed in previous weeks.

Get Set!

Briefly review the notion that the human body is a collection of cells, tissues, organs, and organ systems all integrated for the purpose of providing us with the tools we require to satisfy our basic biological needs.

Go!

Give students ample time to complete the activity described in Figure D on Journal Sheet #4. Instruct them to use the "dorsal" and "ventral" sides of each diagram to draw deep body (e.g., kidneys) and superficial (e.g., intestines) organs, respectively.

Materials

human body chart projects, Journal Sheets #2 and #3

HB13 JOURNAL SHEET #4

FROG DISSECTION

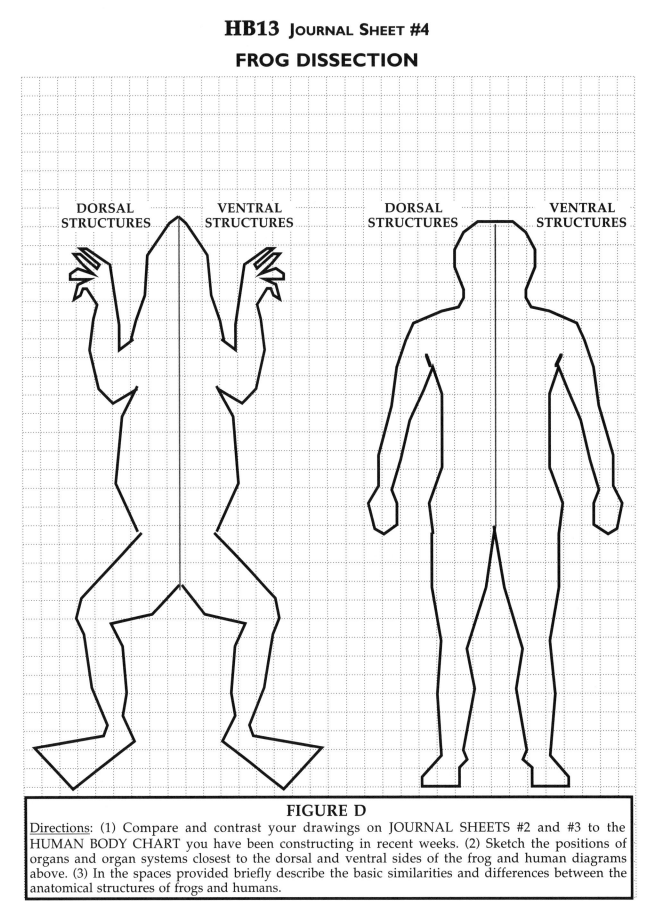

DORSAL STRUCTURES   VENTRAL STRUCTURES   DORSAL STRUCTURES   VENTRAL STRUCTURES

FIGURE D

Directions: (1) Compare and contrast your drawings on JOURNAL SHEETS #2 and #3 to the HUMAN BODY CHART you have been constructing in recent weeks. (2) Sketch the positions of organs and organ systems closest to the dorsal and ventral sides of the frog and human diagrams above. (3) In the spaces provided briefly describe the basic similarities and differences between the anatomical structures of frogs and humans.

Name: _____   **Period:** _____   **Date:** ____/____/____

HB13 Review Quiz

Directions: Keep your eyes on your own work.
Read all directions and questions carefully.
THINK BEFORE YOU ANSWER!
Watch your spelling, be neat, and do the best you can.

TEACHER'S COMMENTS: _____

_____

FROG DISSECTION

ORGAN SYSTEM IDENTIFICATION: Draw and label the major organs of each organ system of the frog shown below. *20 points*

DIGESTIVE SYSTEM   CIRCULATORY AND
                                                       RESPIRATORY SYSTEMS

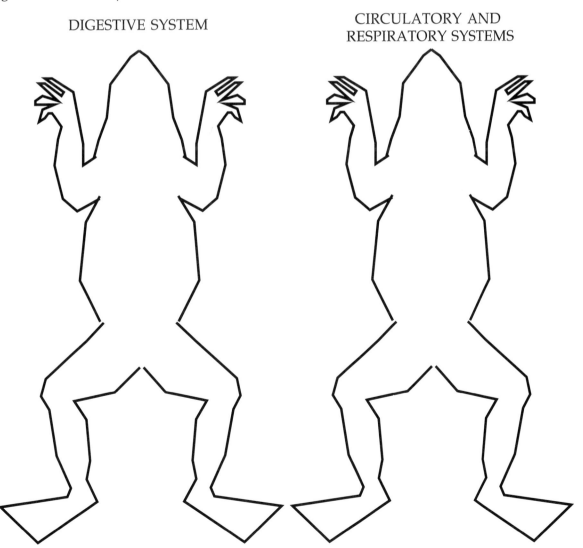

ESSAY: Describe the major differences between the excretory system of the frog and the excretory system of the human being. *5 points*

_____

_____

_____

_____

_____

_____

ESSAY: Describe the major differences between the reproductive system of the frog and the reproductive system of the human being. *5 points*

_____

_____

_____

_____

_____

_____

_____   _____   ___/___/___

Student's Signature   Parent's Signature   Date

HUMAN ANCESTORS

Teacher's Classwork Agenda and Content Notes

Classwork Agenda for the Week

1. Students will compare and contrast the human hand with the hands of other primates.
2. Students will compare and contrast the pelvis and leg bones of primate bipeds and quadrupeds.
3. Students will compare and contrast the human skull with the skulls of other primates.
4. Students will examine the lines of descent that lead to humans and other living primates.

Content Notes for Lecture and Discussion

Humans are members of the mammalian order Primates. The oldest fossils of our primate ancestors, stemming from the small and sometimes arboreal mammalian Insectivores, are found in rocks about 70 million years old buried along with the bones of dinosaurs. Following the disappearance of the dinosaurs, preprimate families such as **Plesiadapis** and **Smilodectes** flourished and diversified mostly as "squirrel-like" animals adapted to life in the trees. However, "true" primates resembling modern lemurs or tarsiers did not appear until about 45 million years ago. Unlike their preprimate ancestors these small creatures had characteristics common to all modern primates: a short-muzzled skull, well-developed binocular vision, and long fingers and toes with nails in place of claws.

The first evidence of "monkey-like" primates appears at about 40 million years ago. **Propliopithecus**—the most probable ancestor of **Proconsul** discovered by **Mary Douglas Leakey** (b. 1913; d. 1996) in 1948 on Rusinga Island, Lake Victoria, East Africa—was about the size of a cat. The more typical "monkey-like" primates (e.g., **Pliopthecus** and **Ramapithecus**) appeared about 22 million years ago. Throughout the millions of years that followed, the East African plains of the sub-Sahara were inhabited by a variety of primates with monkey-like attributes: long limbs and bodies, and apelike teeth and jaws.

Proconsul and its descendants lived in the woodlands of Namibia and migrated north and east to Europe and China. About 12 million years ago, **Oreopithecus**—with its long arms and barrel chest—inhabited the swampy islands of the Mediterranean. Recent studies stemming from newly developed techniques in molecular genetics show that humans have a close evolutionary relationship to the great apes of Africa (e.g., gorillas and chimpanzees) suggesting that both primate lines evolved from a common ancestor. However, fossilized "ape-like" creatures older than 6 million years, such as Ramapithecus, are now believed to have predated the split between modern humans and modern great apes which may have occurred as late as 1 to 5 million years ago.

The first prehominid genus is that of **Australopithecus** discovered by the English paleontologist **Raymond Arthur Dart** (b. 1893; d. 1988) in 1924. Its closest relative **Ardipithecus** occupied regions of East Africa about 4.5 to 1 million years ago. Despite the similarity in size to a chimpanzee Australopithecine specimens dating from 3 to 3.5 million years old are still classified as hominid, sharing anatomical characteristics with humans that allow for bipedalism and the use of simple tools. Some sites yielding Australopithecine fossils have produced stone tools that may have been used by these prehominids; but it is more likely that these creatures were no more adept at tool use than modern chimpanzees.

The first real evidence of behavior that separates the genus **Homo** from other primates is the regular use of simple stone choppers and flakes of rock dated at about 2.5 million years ago. The choppers are often found along with the bones of medium to large prey, making it likely that the tools were used to butcher the animal carcasses. More recent evidence of tool usage dates from about 2 million years ago at finds of the prehominid **Homo Erectus**. In Africa and western Asia, Homo erectus used tools such as the hand ax and a sharp, double-edged stone implement similar to a knife. Homo erectus may have also discovered fire for keeping warm and cooking.

About 400,000 years ago, the first heavy-browed, large-brained specimens of "archaic Homo sapiens" began to fossilize in Africa, Europe, and East Asia. As human populations migrated to a wider variety of habitats, more technologically advanced tools appeared in the frigid, glacial environments of western Asia and Europe. Among the new toolmakers was **Homo sapiens neanderthalensis**, an archaic Homo population that flourished between 180,000 and 35,000 years ago. Neanderthals were hardly apes. They were fully human, creating tools for cutting meat, scraping hides, and woodwork. Neanderthals buried their dead with "tools and trinkets" suggesting an aptitude for symbolic and even religious thought.

Recent studies in molecular genetics suggest that members of the entire human race are descended from a few thousand members of a single population that knew Africa as their homeland several million years ago.

In Lesson #1, students will compare and contrast the human hand with the hands of other primates.

In Lesson #2, students will compare and contrast the pelvis and leg bones of primate bipeds and quadrupeds.

In Lesson #3, students will compare and contrast the human skull with the skulls of other primates.

In Lesson #4, students will examine the lines of descent that lead to humans and other living primates.

ANSWERS TO THE HOMEWORK PROBLEMS

Students' essays should express the notion that the earliest evidence of human origins would need to be found in East Africa with more recent generations found in varying geographical locations, making evident a definite pattern of migration from the ancestral "birthplace."

ANSWERS TO THE END-OF-THE-WEEK REVIEW QUIZ

1. Charles Darwin	6. true
2. natural selection	7. true
3. hereditary	8. true
4. true	9. true
5. true	10. younger

ESSAY: Answers will vary but should express the main points summarized below.

11. The pelvis and bones of the feet can support the weight of the erect posture of the body.

12. The pelvis and bones of the feet cannot support the weight of the erect posture of the body.

13. The thumb is long and attached to strong muscles that can pull the thumb across the open palm.

14. The thumb is short and attaches to small muscles that cannot pull the thumb across the open palm.

15. The skull is large and can store a large brain that can handle the complexity of language.

16. The skull is small and stores a relatively small brain that cannot handle the complexity of language.

STAGES OF EVOLUTION

__4__ humans   __3__ prehominids

__2__ primates   __1__ mammals

Name: _____   **Period:** _____   **Date:** ____/____/____

HB14 Fact Sheet

HUMAN ANCESTORS

CLASSWORK AGENDA FOR THE WEEK

(1) Compare and contrast the human hand with the hands of other primates.
(2) Compare and contrast the pelvis and leg bones of primate bipeds and quadrupeds.
(3) Compare and contrast the human skull with the skulls of other primates.
(4) Examine the lines of descent that lead to humans and other living primates.

The mystery of human origins has fascinated scientists since the middle of the 19th century. In 1859, the English naturalist **Charles Robert Darwin** (b. 1809; d. 1882) published a book entitled *The Origin of Species* in which he explained how life on our planet might have become so diverse. He based his ideas on the evidence he collected on a five-year-long journey to the **Galápagos Islands** off the coast of South America. There he studied the adaptations made by plants and animals to the pressures of their natural environment. Darwin's conclusions became known as the **theory of evolution by means of natural selection**, a theory that soon became the cornerstone of modern biology and medicine. The term **evolution** means "change" but in biology it has a more specific meaning. To a biologist, evolution refers to the changes that take place in the **hereditary features** of a population such as the human population from one generation to the next. Before Darwin's discovery, scientists were already aware that many species alive in past ages are no longer alive today. After the publication of Darwin's book, scientists predicted that fossils of human ancestors would be discovered before long.

In 1891, the Dutch paleontologist **Eugéne Dubois** (b. 1858; d. 1940) discovered the fossilized remains of a "manlike" creature along the Solo River on the island of Java, Indonesia. His discovery became commonly known as **Java man**. The skull of Java man is much smaller than a human skull and its jaw resembles that of an ape more than of a human; but the structure of its leg bones indicates that the creature walked upright on two feet. It was a **biped** (e.g., meaning "two-legged") unlike other primates such as apes and chimpanzees who are **quadrupeds** (e.g., meaning "four-legged"). Paleontologists gave Java man the scientific name *Pithecanthropus erectus* which means "erect-postured apeman." But the species was later renamed to reflect its closer resemblance to humans (e.g., named *Homo sapiens* meaning "wise man"). Today, Java man is named *Homo erectus*.

By the 1920s, several major discoveries were made in China (e.g., Peking man) and Africa (e.g., South African ape). Peking man turned out to be another specimen of *Homo erectus* and the South African ape discovered by the English paleontologist **Raymond Arthur Dart** (b. 1893; d. 1988) turned out to be a much earlier species. Dart named his discovery *Australopithecus*. While Peking man occupied the caves near what is now the capitol city of China from about 400,000 to 600,000 years ago, species of *Australopithecus* roamed the African savannahs more than 3 million years ago.

Since the 1950s, paleontologists under the leadership of **Louis Seymour Bazett Leakey** (b. 1903; d. 1972) and his wife **Mary Douglas Leakey** (b. 1913; d. 1996) have uncovered the remains of dozens of early **hominid** (e.g., meaning "humanlike") specimens in the Olduvai Gorge in Tanzania, East Africa, which is believed to be the "birthplace" of humankind. Among the most recent finds made in Africa are a number of nearly complete skeletons estimated to be more than 3 million years old, and footprints in the plains at Laetoli, East Africa, estimated to be more than 3.7 million years old.

The anatomical characteristics shared by modern humans and our prehominid ancestors are decidedly different from those of other primates such as gorillas and chimpanzees. Humans can (1) walk erect, their hands and forelimbs free from the task of locomotion. (2) The arrangement of our thumb and other fingers of the hand have enabled us to use tools and weapons to defend us against more physically powerful animals. And, (3) our larger skulls provide room for a larger brain commanding speech, language, and complex social interaction.

Homework Directions

Write a paragraph describing the type of fossil evidence that would need to be found to support the idea that the savannahs of Tanzania, East Africa, are the "birthplace" of humankind.

Assignment due: _____

_____   _____   ____/____/____

HUMAN ANCESTORS

Work Date: ____/____/____

LESSON OBJECTIVE

Students will compare and contrast the human hand with the hands of other primates.

Classroom Activities

On Your Mark!

Prepare for this lesson by obtaining a model of a human skeleton and 10–20 magazine pictures of primates (e.g., tree shrews, tarsiers, lemurs, spider monkeys, chimpanzees, gorillas, and humans) including close-ups of their forelimbs and hands.

Give a brief lecture on the evolution of the Primate order using the information in the student Fact Sheet and the Teacher's Classwork Agenda and Content Notes.

Get Set!

Refer students to the illustration on Journal Sheet #1 depicting the possible movements of the human hand (e.g., divergence, convergence, prehensility, and opposability). Explain that humans are able to grasp a bar or tool with the thumb wrapping around the tool in the opposite direction as the other fingers of the hand while other primates, including chimpanzees and gorillas, are incapable of performing this simple act (e.g., opposability). Demonstrate this action using a bar or other tool (e.g., a hammer). Mimic the way a chimpanzee or gorilla would grasp a hammer with either all of the fingers wrapping in one direction or by weakly grasping the tool between the tips of the index finger and "stubby" thumb. Refer to the diagrams of the hands of each primate and point out that the thumb of a gorilla is shorter and positioned at a more shallow angle with respect to the other fingers of the hand than the thumb of a human. Have students note the large carpal bone called the trapezius under the meta-carpal of the thumb. This bone is less pronounced in other primates.

Go!

Give students ample time to complete the activity described in Figure A on Journal Sheet #1. Circulate around explaining that other primates are capable of varying degrees of divergence, convergence, and prehensility but only humans possess true opposability.

Materials

model of a human skeleton, 10–20 magazine pictures of primates (e.g., tree shrews, tarsiers, lemurs, spider monkeys, chimpanzees, gorillas, and humans) including close-ups of their forelimbs and hands, simple tools (e.g., hammer, screwdriver, etc.)

HB14 JOURNAL SHEET #I

HUMAN ANCESTORS

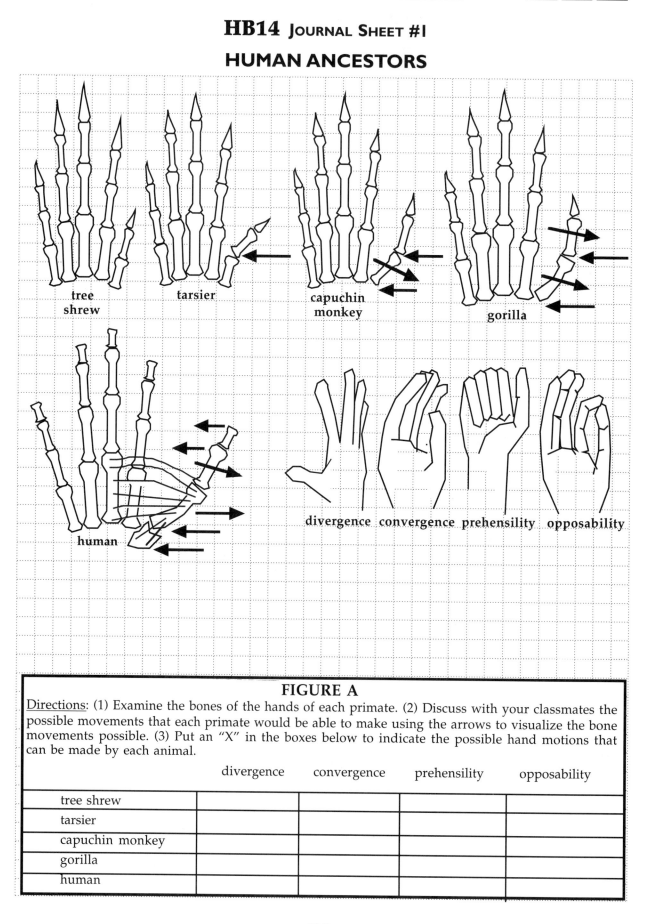

FIGURE A

Directions: (1) Examine the bones of the hands of each primate. (2) Discuss with your classmates the possible movements that each primate would be able to make using the arrows to visualize the bone movements possible. (3) Put an "X" in the boxes below to indicate the possible hand motions that can be made by each animal.

	divergence	convergence	prehensility	opposability
tree shrew				
tarsier				
capuchin monkey				
gorilla				
human				

HUMAN ANCESTORS

Work Date: ____/____/____

LESSON OBJECTIVE

Students will compare and contrast the pelvis and leg bones of primate bipeds and quadrupeds.

Classroom Activities

On Your Mark!

Prepare for this lesson by obtaining a model of a human skeleton and 10–20 magazine pictures of African great apes (e.g., chimpanzees and gorillas).

Begin the lesson by having students perform the activity described in Figure B on Journal Sheet #2. They will discover that girls have an easier time performing this task than boys. Explain that a woman's pelvis is set slightly wider and flatter than a male's pelvis which changes the body's center of gravity ever so slightly. This minute difference between the female's and male's center of gravity prevents the male from performing this task as easily as the female of the species.

Get Set!

Distribute the magazine pictures of great apes and humans. Refer students to the illustrations on Journal Sheet #2 depicting the pelvis and leg bones of the gorilla and human. Remind students of the problems one can have standing erect with even a slight change in the body's center of gravity. Point out the flat, forward tilt of the gorilla's pelvis and its bulky femur and tibia. Explain that despite the strength of this combination of bones, all African great apes are "four-legged" primates. They are **quadrupeds** that must rest on their knuckles to support their great bulk during locomotion. Have students discuss and list the major differences between the shapes and positions of the gorilla's pelvis and leg bones compared to those of a human.

Go!

Give students ample time to complete the activity described in Figure C on Journal Sheet #2.

Materials

model of a human skeleton, 10–20 magazine pictures of African great apes (e.g., chimpanzees and gorillas), chairs

HB14 JOURNAL SHEET #2

HUMAN ANCESTORS

GORILLA   HUMAN

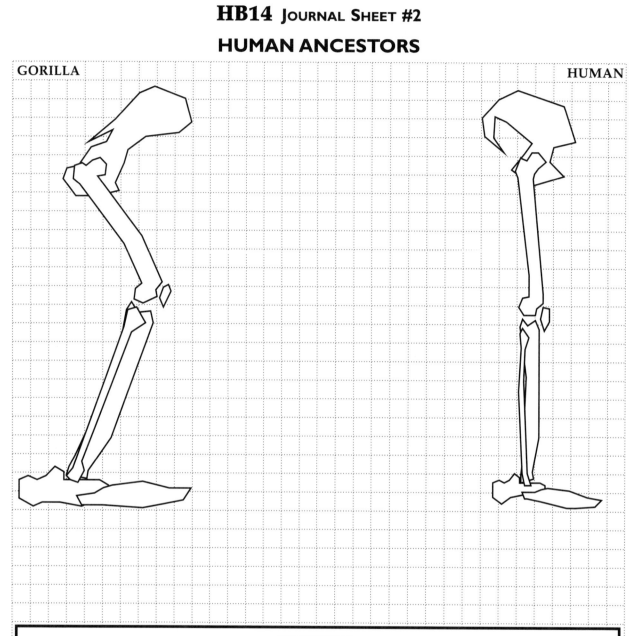

FIGURE B

<u>Directions</u>: (1) Stand with your toes against a wall. (2) Place the toes of your right foot directly behind the heel of the left foot, then move the left foot back alongside your right foot. (3) Take one more step back in exactly the same manner. (4) Have a classmate place a chair against the wall in front of you. (5) Bend over slowly and carefully place the top of your head against the wall so that your body is at about a 45° angle with your legs. (6) Grab the seat of the chair and lift it to your chest. (7) Try to stand up. (8) Record your observations of girls attempting this task as opposed to boys.

FIGURE C

<u>Directions</u>: (1) Examine the pelvic and leg bones of the gorilla and human shown above. (2) Examine the pictures of the gorilla and human provided by your instructor. (3) Considering the shape and bulk of the gorilla's torso (e.g., upper body) and powerful shoulders and arms compared to those of a human, consider the difficulties a gorilla would have trying to stand erect for a considerable period of time. Consider the difficulties a gorilla would have running swiftly to avoid a tiger that is chasing it across flat open ground. (4) Write a paragraph summarizing your conclusions.

HUMAN ANCESTORS

Work Date: _____/_____/_____

LESSON OBJECTIVE

Students will compare and contrast the human skull with the skulls of other primates.

Classroom Activities

On Your Mark!

Prepare for this lesson by obtaining a model of a human skull and 10–20 magazine pictures of prehominids (e.g., Australopithecus, Homo erectus, Homo sapiens neanderthalensis, etc.).

Point out that our genus of hominids, *Homosapiens*, is among the largest of the hominids, standing several feet taller than the more diminutive Australopithecines. Yet despite their size, early prehominids like Australopithecus survived the harsh environment of the dry African savannah, defending themselves against much stronger, faster animals like the saber-toothed tiger.

Get Set!

Point out that Homo erectus used tools, had fire, and probably the crude beginnings of a language. Discuss the advantages of being able to communicate, using spoken words, as opposed to facial expressions or posture as do other animals (e.g., big cats and canines). With a sophisticated language families of early humans could make plans, coordinate the hunt, and relate their daily experiences. They could learn from one another's mistakes. Explain that a large brain is probably a prerequisite for the use of a complex language.

Go!

Give students ample time to complete the activity described in Figure D on Journal Sheet #3.

Materials

model of a human skull, 10–20 magazine pictures of prehominids (e.g., Australopithecus, Homo erectus, Homo sapiens neanderthalensis, etc.), metric rulers

HB14 JOURNAL SHEET #3

HUMAN ANCESTORS

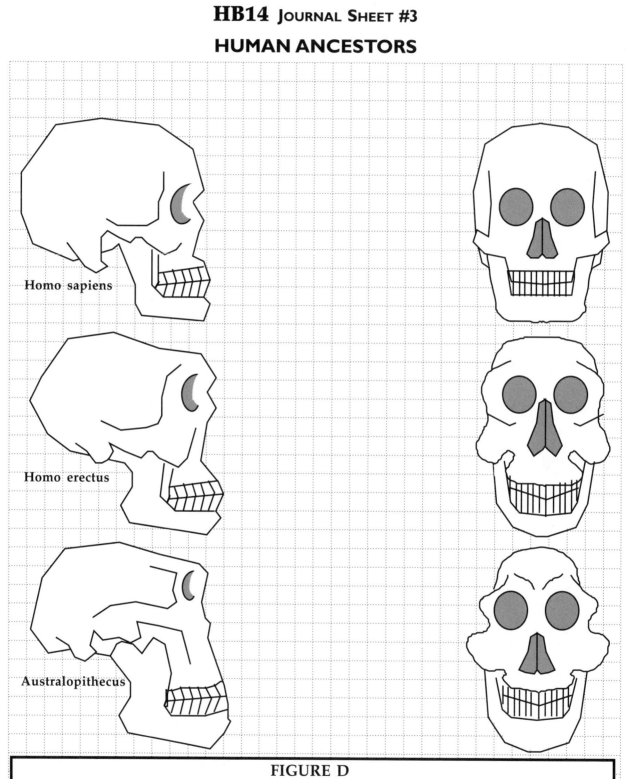

FIGURE D

Directions: (1) Examine the prehominid and human skulls shown above. (2) Use a ruler and measure to the nearest millimeter the approximate length (e.g., from the back of the skull to behind the eyes), width (e.g., from the left to right side at the widest point of the cranium), and depth (e.g., from the highest point on the skull to the top of the cheekbone) of each cranium (e.g., brain case). (3) Compare the relative sizes of each prehominid brain case as a percentage of the human brain case. (4) Write a paragraph summarizing the other differences between the skulls of these three primates.

HUMAN ANCESTORS

Work Date: ____/____/____

LESSON OBJECTIVE

Students will examine the lines of descent that lead to humans and other living primates.

Classroom Activities

On Your Mark!

Prepare for this lesson by obtaining information from library/text/Internet resources about the scores of primates that exist in the geological record as well as those alive today.

Begin the lesson by referring students to the illustration on Journal Sheet #4 and ask them to write in the spaces provided the names of the prehominid and other primates mentioned in class this week, doing their best to place the extinct forms in their correct place on the broken timeline. Explain that the "branches" of this "tree of evolution" are purposely separated, because it is impossible to say whether or not any one species is the direct descendant of another. It is correct to say—based on the theory of evolution by means of natural selection—that both humans and apes must have had a common ancestor. However, it is incorrect to say that humankind evolved from apes.

Get Set!

Distribute the references and have students examine the variety of primates shown in the references. Explain that primates are the order of mammals that includes monkeys, apes, humans, and similar forms. There are more than 200 living species of primates in the world today, grouped into more than 50 genera with about 100 extinct genera that can be found in the fossil record. Primates come in all sizes and have evolved a host of adaptive structures (e.g., tails), strategies, and habits that have assisted them in their survival.

Go!

Give students ample time to complete the activity described in Figure E on Journal Sheet #4.

Materials

library/text/Internet resources about primates both alive and extinct

HB14 Journal Sheet #4

HUMAN ANCESTORS

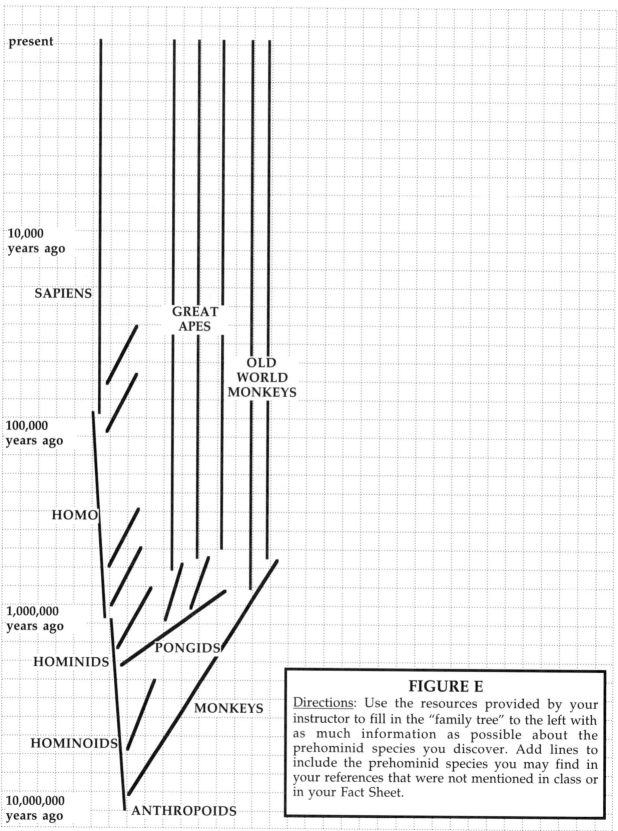

present

10,000
years ago

SAPIENS

GREAT
APES

OLD
WORLD
MONKEYS

100,000
years ago

HOMO

1,000,000
years ago

PONGIDS

HOMINIDS

MONKEYS

HOMINOIDS

10,000,000
years ago   ANTHROPOIDS

FIGURE E

<u>Directions</u>: Use the resources provided by your instructor to fill in the "family tree" to the left with as much information as possible about the prehominid species you discover. Add lines to include the prehominid species you may find in your references that were not mentioned in class or in your Fact Sheet.

HB14 Review Quiz

Directions: Keep your eyes on your own work.
Read all directions and questions carefully.
THINK BEFORE YOU ANSWER!
Watch your spelling, be neat, and do the best you can.

CLASSWORK   (~40): _____
HOMEWORK   (~20): _____
CURRENT EVENT   (~10): _____
TEST   (~30): _____

TOTAL   (~100): _____
(A ≥ 90, B ≥ 80, C ≥ 70, D ≥ 60, F < 60)

LETTER GRADE: _____

TEACHER'S COMMENTS: _____
_____

HUMAN ANCESTORS

TRUE–FALL FILL-IN: If the statement is true, write the word TRUE. If the statement is false, change the underlined word to make the statement true. *20 points*

_____ 1. The mystery of human origins has fascinated scientists since the publication of *The Origin of Species* by <u>Louis Pasteur.</u>

_____ 2. The theory of evolution by means of <u>chance</u> is based on studies of adaptations made by plants and animals to the pressures of their natural environment.

_____ 3. To a biologist, the term evolution refers to the changes that take place in the <u>cultural</u> features of a population such as the human population from one generation to the next.

_____ 4. In 1891, the Dutch paleontologist Eugéne Dubois discovered the fossilized remains of a "manlike" creature that became popularly known as <u>Java man.</u>

_____ 5. The skull of *Homo erectus* is much <u>smaller</u> than a *Homo sapiens*.

_____ 6. Australopithecus was a <u>biped.</u>

_____ 7. Great apes and chimpanzees are <u>quadrupeds.</u>

_____ 8. Peking man turned out to be a specimen of <u>Homo erectus.</u>

_____ 9. The first "manlike" ape was discovered in South Africa by <u>Raymond Arthur Dart.</u>

_____ 10. Fossils of *Homo erectus* are <u>older</u> than fossils of *Australopithecus*.

HB14 Review Quiz (cont'd)

ESSAY: Write a brief sentence or phrase mentioning the skeletal characteristics of each group of animals that results in the described observation. *6 points*

11. Prehominids and humans can walk erect, their hands and forelimbs free from the task of locomotion. _____

_____

12. Great apes cannot walk erect and must use their hands and forelimbs for locomotion.

_____

_____

13. Prehominids and humans can cross their thumbs over their open palms, making it possible to grasp and use tools. _____

_____

14. Great apes cannot cross their thumbs over their open palms, making it impossible for them to grasp and use tools. _____

_____

15. Humans use speech and complex language to communicate. _____

_____

16. Great apes do not use speech and complex language to communicate. _____

_____

STAGES OF EVOLUTION: Put the number 1, 2, 3, or 4 in the blank next to each group of animals to show the order in which they first appear in the fossil record. *4 points*

_____ humans   _____ prehominids

_____ primates   _____ mammals

_____   _____   / ___ / ___
Student's Signature   Parent's Signature   Date

INTRODUCTION
TO PSYCHOLOGY

Teacher's Classwork Agenda and Content Notes

Classwork Agenda for the Week

1. Students will examine how the brain processes different visual stimuli.
2. Students will explain the difference between linear and parallel processing of information.
3. Students will describe techniques that can be used to change behavior and improve memory.
4. Students will list and define medical conditions associated with abnormal behavior.

Content Notes for Lecture and Discussion

The term **psychology** derives from the Greek word *psyche* meaning "soul." The description and analysis of human nature, the relationship of body to mind and mind to soul, were of as much interest to the ancients as they are to modern scientists and philosophers.

At the start of the 17th century, mechanists of the tradition of **Sir Isaac Newton** (b. 1642; d. 1727) argued that the mind was a product of material interactions, which welcomed the physiologists to begin their study of it based on the laws of the natural sciences. The German anatomist and physiologist **Ernst Heinrich Weber** (b. 1795; d. 1878) carried the experimental methods he used in the study of physiology over to the study of psychology. He derived **Weber's Law** which states that a "just noticeable difference between the magnitudes of two stimuli is a constant ratio of their total magnitude." The German psychologist **Gustav Theodor Fechner** (b. 1801; d. 1887) picked up where Weber left off, deriving **Fechner's Law** which provided a precise mathematical formalism to the study of sensations. By the 1850s, psychologists were applying experimental research to the study of mental processes, thereby beginning the modern discipline of **experimental psychology**. The **structuralist school** of German psychologist **Wilhelm Wundt** (b. 1832; d. 1920) used the method of introspection to study states of consciousness, sensation, and emotion. Inspired by **Charles Robert Darwin**'s (b. 1809; d. 1882) theory of evolution, the functionalist school of American psychologist **William James** (b. 1842; d. 1910) combined objective experiments with introspection to discover how the mind had evolved out of adaptive necessity. By the end of the 19th century, **James Broadus Watson** (b. 1878; d. 1958) had evoked the principle of the **conditioned reflex** discovered by **Ivan Petrovich Pavlov** (b. 1849; d. 1936) to reject the study of "mental faculties" and opt for a pure analysis of observable performance to explain the nature of behavior. The contributions of Watson's **behaviorist school** was popularized by the American psychologist **B. F. Skinner** (b. 1904; d. 1990).

The ancient study of severe mental disorder was founded in a framework of magical-religious philosophy, possession by demons, or the infection of the body's humours. By the 18th century, more secular explanations of **psychosis**, based on the work of natural philosophers, earned command of the study. Terms used to describe abnormal mental states such as "delerium," "dementia," and "melancholia" came to identify states having a functional or organic cause. By the end of the 19th century, the German psychiatrist **Emil Kraepelin** (b. 1856; d. 1926) had divided the major forms of psychosis into two main categories: dementia praecox (e.g., schizophrenia) and manic-depression (e.g., melancholia). The fields of psychology and psychiatry in the latter part of the 20th century have become more closely associated with the field of **neuroscience**, the study of the nervous system. The elucidation of many of the brain's functions has yielded tools for the general treatment of many behavioral and personality disorders. **Chemotherapy** and **hormone**

therapy have proven somewhat successful in reducing—but not totally eliminating—the incidence of anomalous behaviors in patients suffering these abnormalities.

In Lesson #1, students will examine how the brain processes different visual stimuli.

In Lesson #2, students will explain the difference between linear and parallel processing of information.

In Lesson #3, students will describe techniques that can be used to change behavior and improve memory.

In Lesson #4, students will list and define medical conditions associated with abnormal behavior.

ANSWERS TO THE HOMEWORK PROBLEMS

Students' strategies will vary but should demonstrate their understanding and reasonable application of positive reinforcers in an effort to change their behavior.

ANSWERS TO THE END-OF-THE-WEEK REVIEW QUIZ

1. behavior	6. can	11. D
2. true	7. cannot	12. E
3. nature	8. true	13. B
4. nurture	9. true	14. C
5. true	10. true	15. A

Students' essays will vary but should demonstrate their understanding and reasonable application of positive reinforcers in an effort to change their behavior.

HB15 Fact Sheet

INTRODUCTION TO PSYCHOLOGY

CLASSWORK AGENDA FOR THE WEEK

(1) Examine how the brain processes different visual stimuli.
(2) Explain the difference between linear and parallel processing of information.
(3) Describe techniques that can be used to change behavior and improve memory.
(4) List and define medical conditions associated with abnormal behavior.

Psychology is the study of behavior. For centuries, psychologists have been interested in trying to find out why animals and people behave the way they do. Since behavior involves "sensing and responding" to the environment, psychologists have done a considerable amount of research on the senses and nervous system. The nervous system controls how living things perceive, sense, and respond to their environment. As a result of this research scientists have found that animals with a relatively simple nervous system (e.g., an earthworm or mollusk) have a limited set of behaviors. The behavior of many simple animals is almost purely "reflexive." Animals such as humans with a large complex brain perform a wide variety of "social behaviors" and can complete extremely complex tasks such as hunt or do algebra homework.

Psychologists have always debated whether the behavior of animals and people is the result "genetic programming" or "social programming." This debate is called the **nature versus nurture** debate. The term "nature" refers to the fact that our nervous system is the product of our genes and chromosomes, arranged in the DNA molecules that give us our hereditary characteristics. The term "nurture" refers to the influence of our environment. Nurture is the influence, assistance, support and care we get from our parents, family, friends, and society. Most psychologists believe that the way a person behaves depends on both of these factors and not exclusively on one or the other. A person may inherit the "tendency to develop" a particular set of abnormal behaviors (e.g., become an alcoholic); but it may be possible to teach that person to avoid or change some behaviors. The widely accepted view is that our environment plays a more important role in shaping the adults we become. Our genes may "command us" to find the food we need to survive; but we can "learn" to hunt for our food or grow it. In addition, we can pass that information on to our offspring using complex language. Our DNA builds a nervous system that can learn. The things we learn depend to a large extent on our experience.

The brain does not process information perfectly. A computer uses **linear processing** to complete the tasks it is given and can work faster and with sometimes greater precision than a human brain. A computer executes simple electronic commands one step at a time, each step determining precisely what the next will be. When a computer makes a mistake it is usually the result of a power failure or the defective hardware or software programs that tell the computer what to do. The human brain "sifts" through a lot of information all at once using **parallel processing** methods. The brain makes "conscious" and "subconscious" choices about the steps it will take to get a job done.

Learned behaviors are usually the result of **reinforcement**. A **reinforcer** is anything that increases the frequency of a behavior. Food can be used as a "primary reinforcer" to increase the frequency of a behavior. A mouse in a maze, for example, will learn to escape the maze more quickly than other mice (e.g., control groups) if it is given a "treat" for making the correct decisions about which way to turn in the maze. The theory that explains behavior as a series of actions developed using "reward and punishment" is called **behaviorism**. The American psychologist **John Broadus Watson** (b. 1878; d. 1958) is considered the "father of behaviorism." Watson based much of his work on the research of Russian physiologist **Ivan Petrovich Pavlov** (b. 1849; d.1936). Pavlov discovered **conditioned reflexes** in animals. He succeeded in making dogs salivate at the sound of a bell that had been rung immediately prior to the animals' dinner time. Eventually, the dogs began to "associate" the bell with food and began to salivate whenever it rang whether or not they were fed immediately afterward. Another American psychologist **B. F. Skinner** (b. 1904; d. 1990) popularized the theory of behaviorism. Today, psychologists use "behaviorist" techniques to help people break undesirable habits and increase the frequency of desired behaviors.

Abnormal psychology is the study of abnormal behaviors. Psychologists study and try to help people who exhibit abnormal behavior. However, the cause of most behavior disorders is largely a mystery. Complex behavior disorders—sometimes called **psychosis** or personality disorders—prevent a person from interacting successfully with other people and the environment. Two of the more common behavior disorders that can be relieved but not cured with the help of **psychotherapy** and prescription drugs are **manic-depression** and **schizophrenia**.

Homework Directions

Choose an undesirable habit you would like to break (e.g., biting your nails) and a behavior you would like to increase (e.g., read more). Write a thorough "reinforcement plan" that you could use to help you break the bad habit and increase the frequency of the desired behavior. Remember that "punishment" does not work as well as positive reinforcement. Think of ways to positively reinforce yourself for reducing the frequency of the undesirable behavior while increasing the frequency of the desired one.

Assignment due: _____

_____	_____	___/___/___
Student's Signature	Parent's Signature	Date

INTRODUCTION TO PSYCHOLOGY

Work Date: ____/____/____

LESSON OBJECTIVE

Students will examine how the brain processes different visual stimuli.

Classroom Activities

On Your Mark!

Begin the lesson by reviewing the "skin sensitivity demonstration," the "blind spot demonstration," and the "color afterimage demonstration" performed in *Unit 8: The Sense Organs*. Ask students if their senses and brain always report accurately on the state of the environment. The answer is obviously "no" considering the results of those demonstrations.

Get Set!

Define **psychology** as the study of behavior. Give a brief lecture on the history of psychology using the information on the student Fact Sheet and the Teacher's Classwork Agenda and Content Notes. Refer students to the illustrations on Journal Sheet #1 and explain that **experimental psychologists** use these and other types of illusions to try and figure out how the brain processes sensory information.

Go!

Give students ample time to complete the activity described in Figure A on Journal Sheet #1. Circulate around to make sure students are being honest with themselves about reporting exactly "what they see" and not "what they think or expect" the correct answer to be for each illusion.

Materials

metric ruler, Journal Sheet #1

HB15 JOURNAL SHEET #1

INTRODUCTION TO PSYCHOLOGY

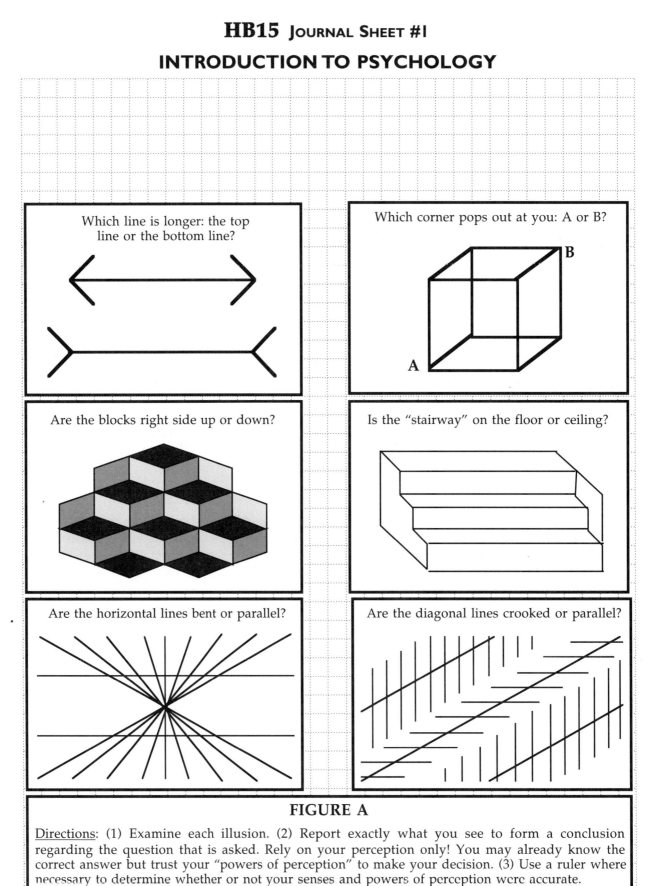

Which line is longer: the top line or the bottom line?

Which corner pops out at you: A or B?

Are the blocks right side up or down?

Is the "stairway" on the floor or ceiling?

Are the horizontal lines bent or parallel?

Are the diagonal lines crooked or parallel?

FIGURE A

<u>Directions:</u> (1) Examine each illusion. (2) Report exactly what you see to form a conclusion regarding the question that is asked. Rely on your perception only! You may already know the correct answer but trust your "powers of perception" to make your decision. (3) Use a ruler where necessary to determine whether or not your senses and powers of perception were accurate.

INTRODUCTION TO PSYCHOLOGY

Work Date: ___/___/___

LESSON OBJECTIVE

Students will explain the difference between linear and parallel processing of information.

Classroom Activities

On Your Mark!

Have students solve a simple math problem on a calculator. Then have them perform the same calculation using their own math skills, paper and a pencil. Briefly discuss the advantages of using a calculator (e.g., it's faster and less likely to make an error once the command to execute the operation is given).

Get Set!

Ask students the following question: Could the calculator have decided on its own which mathematical operation (e.g., addition, subtraction, multiplication, or division) to use had they not pressed the proper commands? Obviously, the computer does not have a "mind" of its own. Even the most sophisticated computers must be programmed with an "algorithm" or "set of rules" to solve a simple math problem. The reason for this is that computers solve problems using a method called "linear processing." Define **linear processing** as the step-by-step execution of commands, one command at a time, where each command determines the next step to be completed. Explain that the human brain must handle a lot of information all at once, then compare and contrast those sets of information before arriving at a course of action or even determining if a course of action is necessary. Remind students of the "problem" their brain had in deciphering the visual input presented in Lesson #1 of this unit and in Lesson #4 of *Unit 8: The Sense Organs.* Unlike a computer, the human nervous system processes different sets of information at once using a method called parallel processing. Define **parallel processing** as the simultaneous processing of separate sets of information while making continual comparisons and contrasts between the sets. Point out that computer scientists are hard at work trying to give computers the ability to process information in this way.

Go!

Give students ample time to complete the activity described in Figure B on Journal Sheet #2. Circulate around the room making sure that students are considering the level of complexity inherent in each question. Some of the questions lack an "operative" command that could be used to write an algorithm for a computer. Others involve the simultaneous consideration of lots of different facts that must be "weighed" against one another before a course of action is taken.

Materials

Journal Sheet #2

HB15 Journal Sheet #2

INTRODUCTION TO PSYCHOLOGY

FIGURE B

<u>Directions</u>: (1) Read each of the questions below. (2) Discuss with your groupmates whether or not a contemporary computer could be programmed to answer each question using linear processing. If your answer is "yes" define the "operative terms" that could be transformed into step-by-step instructions the computer could follow. If your answer is "no" explain the "sets of information" the human mind would have to simultaneously consider before answering that question.

(1) What is the product of five and nine?
(2) Which present should I get for my mother?
(3) Is it right to cheat on a test?
(4) If it rains should we use an umbrella?
(5) What is the capitol of Wisconsin?
(6) How many homeruns did Mark McGuire hit in 1998?
(7) How many stars are in this photograph of the night sky?
(8) What does the word "easy" mean?

INTRODUCTION TO PSYCHOLOGY

Work Date: ____/____/____

LESSON OBJECTIVE

Students will describe techniques that can be used to change behavior and improve memory.

Classroom Activities

On Your Mark!

Begin by reviewing the work of Russian physiologist **Ivan Petrovich Pavlov** (b. 1849; d. 1936). Pavlov trained his dogs to respond by salivating to the sound of a bell that had been "linked" with food. After several trials in which the bell was presented along with the food, the dogs began to salivate at the sound of the bell even though food was not presented. Pavlov called this new "association" a **conditioned reflex**.

Get Set!

Give students a moment to read paragraph #4 on their Fact Sheet; then briefly discuss the work of American behaviorists **John Broadus Watson** (b. 1878; d. 1958) and **B. F. Skinner** (b. 1904; d. 1990). Both psychologists succeeded in changing the behavior of animals and humans by associating a **positive reinforcer**—defined as anything that increases the frequency of a particular behavior—with a given behavior. Point out that basic needs like food, water, and air are **primary reinforcers** that can quickly change behavior in a powerful way. Most anyone will do almost anything for food when they are starving. Money is a **secondary reinforcer** because it allows us to satisfy our basic needs in a variety of ways. Explain that **punishment** is effective in changing behavior although it is much less powerful than positive reinforcement. Ask students to make a list of things they would consider positive reinforcers for them. Ask them to brainstorm with one another and come up with a positive reinforcer that might cause you—their instructor—to change your behavior (e.g., give less homework). Perhaps cooperating, focussing, and learning everything they need to know in class would work as your positive reinforcer and increase the frequency with which you assign less homework!

Go!

Give students ample time to complete the activity described in Figure C on Journal Sheet #3. Students will probably discover that those who used the *Memory Help Guidelines* did better on the "word test." Explain that the technique used was that of a **mnemonic device**. The word "mnemon" means "memory." The brain is "skilled" at recalling images that are out of the ordinary since it has evolved to quickly recognize "change."

Materials

Journal Sheet #3

HB15 JOURNAL SHEET #3

INTRODUCTION TO PSYCHOLOGY

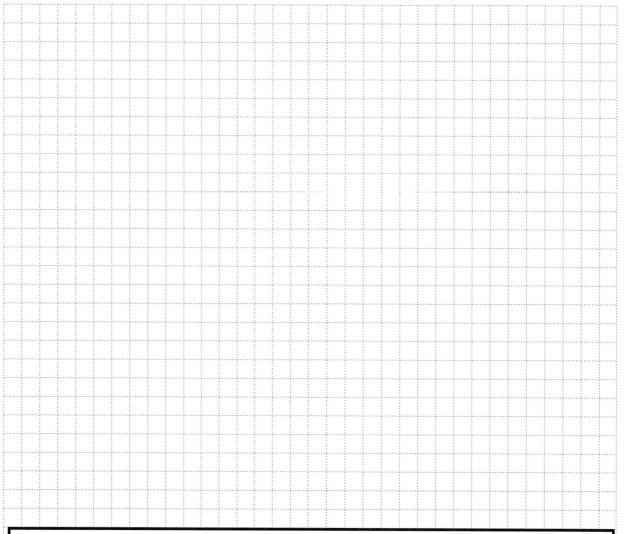

FIGURE C

<u>Directions</u>: (1) Write the numbers #1 through #10 above. (2) Next to each number write the name of a familiar object (e.g., airplane, banana, elephant, etc.). (3) Divide your classmates into two groups. One group will attempt to memorize the list of objects—in order—using the MEMORY HELP GUIDELINES. The other group will attempt to memorize the list of objects—in order—without using the guidelines. (4) As you read your list of objects to your classmates give them a full ten seconds to "commit each object to memory". (5) Test their memory by reading off numbers at random to see if they can match the correct object to its number. (6) Which group of students performed better on the test? Write a paragraph explaining the results.

MEMORY HELP GUIDELINES

1. Memorize the following list of rhyming "number-words": one = gun; two = shoe; three = tree; four = door; five = dive; six = sticks; seven = heaven; eight = gate; nine = wine; ten = hen.
2. In the ten seconds you are given to memorize your friend's list of familiar objects (e.g., airplane, banana, elephant, etc.) visualize each object with its rhyming "number-word" in a funny imaginary scene. For example, if your classmate says "Number six is elephant," imagine an elephant with "sticks" in its ears or up its trunk. The funnier the image the easier it will be to recall that "Number six is elephant".

INTRODUCTION TO PSYCHOLOGY

Work Date: ____/____/____

LESSON OBJECTIVE

Students will list and define medical conditions associated with abnormal behavior.

Classroom Activities

On Your Mark!

Give students a moment to read paragraph #5 on their Fact Sheet. Give a brief review of how the ancients viewed mental illness using the Teacher's Classwork Agenda and Content Notes. Define the word **psychosis** as an abnormal set of behaviors marked by a clear misinterpretation of reality. A psychotic person may "hallucinate," seeing things or hearing voices that do not exist. Point out that drugs can also induce "psychotic behaviors."

Get Set!

Use the information in the Teacher's Classwork Agenda and Content Notes to give a brief summation of the modern psychologist's view of severe mental disorder. Some mental disorders, such as mental retardation and Alzheimer's disease, may be the result of brain damage. Others, such as **schizophrenia** (e.g., dementia or split-personality) and **manic-depressive disorders** (e.g., alternating elation and melancholy), may involve a genetic defect. Abnormal behavior can also result from environmental factors such as **trauma** (e.g., a stressful and horrifying event). Experiencing a traumatic event can set up a series of abnormal responses that can be triggered by any number of future stimuli.

The study of mental disorders is called **psychopathology**. Treatments might include psychoanalysis, chemotherapy, or hormonal therapy. Behavior modification (e.g., behaviorist techniques) can also be used to ease symptoms of the disorders by changing habitual behaviors. Only extreme forms of mental illness that render persons incapable of caring for themselves or dangerous to others require institutionalization.

Go!

Give students ample time to complete the activity described in Figure D on Journal Sheet #4. Circulate around the room making sure that students are seriously considering the actions of the person described in the short story. Point out that the subject's behavior may not be psychotic at all. The protagonist might be a poor fisherman in a poor country, happy about his daily fishing catch. The student observer may be on vacation in a foreign land and not on a bus in an affluent city.

Materials

Journal Sheet #3

HB15 JOURNAL SHEET #4

INTRODUCTION TO PSYCHOLOGY

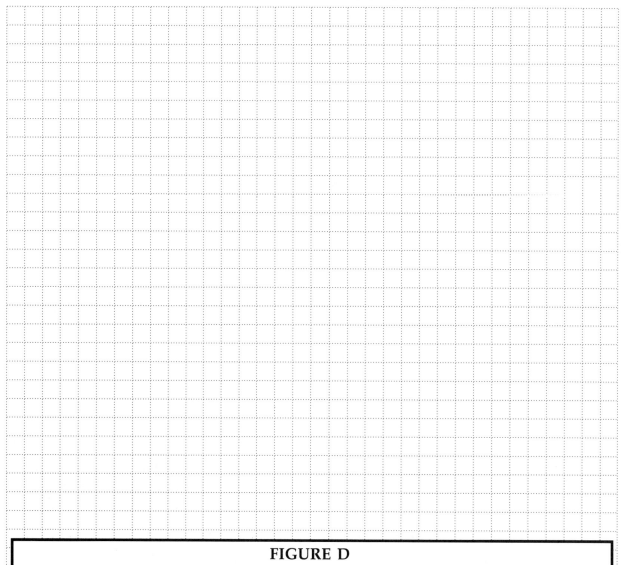

FIGURE D

<u>Directions</u>: (1) Read the short story presented below. (2) Consider the behavior of the person described in the story and brainstorm with your classmates for several minutes, analyzing that behavior. (3) Write a paragraph that summarizes the person's mental condition.

You are on a bus. The bus stops at a bus stop near a beach. You look out the window and observe the following.

A man holding a basket in torn, soiled clothing walks toward the bus from the beach. He is singing in a language you cannot understand. Every few steps he leaps into the air, clicks the heels of his bare feet, and twirls happily in a circle. As the man approaches the bus he waves his hand over the basket, then across his face, and screams at the top of his lungs. Then he smiles, leaps, clicks, and twirls before boarding the bus. The bus driver shakes his head at the man as he reaches into the basket and pulls out a smelly fish. He lays the stinking fish at the feet of the bus driver. The bus driver frowns but motions for the man to sit down, apparently wishing to avoid a scene. The man smiles and sings happily to himself for the entire ride until you get off the bus at your stop.

HB15 Review Quiz

Directions: Keep your eyes on your own work.
Read all directions and questions carefully.
THINK BEFORE YOU ANSWER!
Watch your spelling, be neat, and do the best you can.

CLASSWORK   (~40): _____
HOMEWORK   (~20): _____
CURRENT EVENT   (~10): _____
TEST   (~30): _____

TOTAL   (~100): _____
(A ≥ 90, B ≥ 80, C ≥ 70, D ≥ 60, F < 60)

LETTER GRADE: _____

TEACHER'S COMMENTS: _____
_____

INTRODUCTION TO PSYCHOLOGY

TRUE–FALSE FILL-IN: If the statement is true, write the word TRUE. If the statement is false, change the underlined word to make the statement true. *20 points*

_____ 1. Psychology is the study of <u>bad habits</u>.

_____ 2. The <u>nervous</u> system controls how living things perceive, sense, and respond to their environment.

_____ 3. Psychologists say that "genetic programming" is under the influence of <u>nurture</u>.

_____ 4. Psychologists say that "social programming" is under the influence of <u>nature</u>.

_____ 5. While most psychologists believe that the way a person behaves depends on both of their hereditary characteristics and their environment, the widely accepted view is that <u>nurture</u> plays a more important role in shaping the adults we become.

_____ 6. Most behaviors <u>cannot</u> be changed.

_____ 7. The brain <u>can</u> process information perfectly.

_____ 8. A computer uses <u>linear</u> processing to complete the tasks it is given.

_____ 9. The human brain "sifts" through information all at once using <u>parallel</u> processing methods.

_____ 10. A reinforcer is anything that <u>increases</u> the frequency of a behavior.

HB15 Review Quiz *(cont'd)*

MATCHING: Choose the letter of the phrase that best describes the term at left. *5 points*

_____ 11. behaviorism

_____ 12. conditioned reflex

_____ 13. primary reinforcer

_____ 14. psychosis

_____ 15. psychotherapy

(A)   treatment used in abnormal psychology

(B)   increases the frequency of a behavior

(C)   indicated by frequent abnormal behavior

(D)   behavior learned using reward and punishment

(E)   immediate response to a rewarding stimulus

ESSAY: Write a brief paragraph describing the methods you would use to successfully teach another person (e.g., your little brother or sister) to stay out of your room and keep away from your belongings. *5 points*

_____

_____

_____

_____

_____

_____

APPENDIX

NAME: _____ **PERIOD:** _____ **DATE:** ___ / ___ / ___

<u>Keep this Grade Roster in the Science Section of your notebook</u>

Date	Journal Points	Homework Points	Current Events Points	Quiz Points	Total Points	Letter Grade	Initials

How to Calculate Your Grade Point Average

Your Report Card grades in this class will be awarded to you according to your grade point average or GPA. You can calculate your GPA whenever you like to find out exactly how you are doing in this class.

First, award each of your weekly grades the following credits: each A is worth 4 credits; each B is worth 3 credits; each C is worth 2 credits; each D is worth 1 credit; and each F is worth 0.

Add your total credits earned. Then, divide by the number of packets listed on your Grade Roster and round the decimal result to the nearest tenths place. Your overall Letter Grade is assigned according to the following GPA values:

A+ ≥ 4.0	A ≥ 3.7	A– ≥ 3.4
B+ ≥ 3.1	B ≥ 2.8	B– ≥ 2.5
C+ ≥ 2.2	C ≥ 1.9	C– ≥ 1.6
D+ ≥ 1.3	D ≥ 1.0	D– ≥ 0.7
	F < 0.7	

FOR EXAMPLE:

John has completed five weeks of school and entered his grades from five packets on his Grade Roster. His grades are as follows: first week, A; second week, B; third week, C; fourth week, C; and fifth week, D.

John awards himself the correct amount of credit for each of his grades.

A	earns	4 credits
B	earns	3 credits
C	earns	2 credits
C	earns	2 credits
D	earns	1 credit
Total	earned is	12 credits

John divides his total credits earned by 5 (the number of packets on his Grade Roster).

<u>12 divided by 5 equals 2.4</u>

John's grade point average, or GPA, is 2.4. Referring to the grades shown above, John knows that he has a C+ in Science thus far, because 2.4 is greater than 2.2 (C+) but less than 2.5 (B–).

Name: _____ **Period:**_____ **Date:** ____/____/____

Extra Journal Sheet

Fact Sheet Title: _____ **Lesson #** _____

Using Current Events to Integrate Science Instruction Across Content Areas

Science does not take place in a vacuum. Scientists, like other professionals, are influenced by the economic and political realities of their time. In addition, the ideological and technological advances made by science can influence the economic and political structure of society—for better or worse. It is therefore essential that students have an awareness of the day-to-day science being done at laboratories around the world, important work being reported by an international news media.

Most State Departments of Education, make **CURRENT EVENTS** a regular part of their state science frameworks. Science instructors can use newspaper, magazine, and television reports to keep their students informed about the advances and controversies stemming from research in the many scientific disciplines. Teachers can also use current events to integrate science instruction across the curriculum.

Set aside a class period to show students how to prepare a **science** or **technology** current event. They can do this on a single sheet of standard looseleaf. You may require pupils to read all or part of a science/technology article depending on their reading level. Have them practice summarizing the lead and one or more paragraphs of the article *in their own words*. Advise them to keep a **thesaurus** on hand or to use the dictionary/thesaurus stored in their personal computer at home. Tell students to find *synonyms* they can use to replace most of the vocabulary words used by the article's author. This activity will help them to expand their vocabulary and improve grammar skills. Show students how to properly trim and paste the article's title and first few paragraphs on the front of a standard piece of looseleaf. They should write their summary on the opposite side of the page so that the article is visible to their classmates when they present their findings orally to the class. Allow students to make a report that summarizes a newsworthy item they may have heard on television. The latter report should be accompanied by the signature of a parent/guardian to insure the accuracy of the information being presented.

Students' skills at public speaking are sure to improve if they are given an opportunity to share their current event. Current events can be shared after the end-of-the-unit REVIEW QUIZ or whenever the clock permits at the end of a lesson that has been completed in a timely fashion. You can select students at random to make their presentations by drawing lots or ask for volunteers who might be especially excited about their article. Take time to discuss the ramifications of the article and avoid the temptation to express your personal views or bias. Remain objective and give students the opportunity to express their views and opinions. Encourage them to base their views on fact, not superstition or prejudice. Should the presentation turn into a debate, set aside a few minutes later in the week, giving students time to prepare what they would like to say. Model courtesy and respect for all points of view and emphasize the proper use of the English language in all modes of presentation, both written and oral.

TECHNIQUES AND TIPS FOR LABORATORY DISSECTIONS

There are few laboratory activities that excite student interest more than dissection. Although this resource provides instructions for the dissection of a limited few organisms, teachers are encouraged to replace or supplement any convenient lesson or lessons with the appropriate dissection.

Students need to be informed that the art of dissection is as precise as it is ancient. Its purpose is to carefully disjoin the identifiable organs of a specimen in order to (1) determine its anatomical (e.g., structural) relation to other organs and (2) to deduce its function if possible. Dissection is a painstaking separation of a specimen's anatomical structures, not a butchering process. Dissection tools are specifically designed for this purpose.

Prior to every dissection lab, students should be made aware of common sense health guidelines and the proper use of the tools.

Common Sense Health Guidelines

All preserved animal specimens should be washed in soap and water and rinsed thoroughly before dissection begins. Students should wear goggles, plastic surgical gloves, and an apron during dissection and cleanup. An eyewash consisting of clean tap water in a squeeze bottle should be placed at convenient locations around the laboratory and used immediately to rinse foreign organic substances splashed in the eyes. Students should take turns performing a dissection so that only one person at a time is handling sharp tools. The instructor should be informed immediately of any accidents. All gloves, broken tools, and biological materials should be discarded according to district biohazard guidelines. Aprons and goggles should be thoroughly rinsed with soap and water and dried. All surgical instruments should be sterilized under pressure in a steam-pressure cooker or autoclave. At the very least, instruments should be washed in dish soap and boiling hot water in an automatic dishwasher before being returned to storage in a secured cabinet. Students should wash their hands up to the middle of their forearms with antiseptic soap at the conclusion of the dissection period.

Use of Dissection Tools

paper towels	Paper towels are used to line the bottom of the dissection tray and for clean up.
dissection tray	The specimen should be placed in a metal or hard plastic tray having a synthetic rubber or wax bottom.
T-pins	Use T-pins (e.g., insect pins) to secure the specimen in the dissection tray. Pins are normally placed with the "T" pointed at an angle away from the specimen, the point piercing the flesh of the specimen and secured in the rubber or wax tray bottom. Pins can be removed and repositioned during dissection.
dissection needle	A dissection needle is used for probing or temporarily securing a flap of tissue.
plastic probe	A plastic probe is used to push aside organs or layers of tissue in order to temporarily examine underlying structures.
scissors	Scissors are used to cut away tissue in order to remove organs or expose underlying structures. The direction of a scissor cut should be horizontal to the underlying organs in an effort to avoid puncturing them.
scalpel	A scalpel is used to slice through tissue to expose underlying structures. Care should be taken to estimate the thickness of the tissue being cut in order to avoid damaging underlying structures. All cuts are straight cuts. Avoid "angle cuts" and do not change the direction of a cut as it is being made because the blade can slip or break. Connective tissue can be removed from between structures with a gentle sideways scraping action of the blade (e.g., perpendicular to the sharp edge of the blade).

forceps	Forceps are used to grasp organs and tissues in order to prepare them for pinning, cutting, or probing.
eyedropper	An eyedropper can be filled with water to keep tissues moist.
centimeter ruler	A centimeter ruler can be used to measure the sizes of structures for purposes of comparison.

BIO-DATA
CARDS

BIO-DATA CARD

THOMAS ADDISON
(born, 1793; died, 1860)

nationality
English

contribution to science
first to recognize symptoms resulting from deficiency of adrenal cortical function

BIO-DATA CARD

ALCMAEON OF CROTONA
(c. 500 B.C.)

nationality
Greek

contribution to science
first to document animal dissections performed for scientific purposes

BIO-DATA CARD

ARISTOTLE
(born, 384 B.C.; died, 322 B.C.)

nationality
Greek

contribution to science
first to document a study of sea creatures in their natural habitat for scientific purposes

BIO-DATA CARD

WILLIAM MADDOCK BAYLISS
(born, 1860; died, 1924)

nationality
English

contribution to science
with E. H. Starling discovered the first hormone: secretin

BIO-DATA CARD

WILLIAM BEAUMONT
(born, 1785; died, 1853)

nationality
American

contribution to science
performed the most classic study of digestion on an animal trapper who had been shot in the stomach

BIO-DATA CARD

MARTINUS WILLEM BEIJERINCK
(born, 1851; died, 1931)

nationality
Dutch

contribution to science
coined the term "virus" for the microscopic germ that caused tobacco mosaic disease

BIO-DATA CARD

CLAUDE BERNARD
(born, 1813; died, 1878)

nationality
French

contribution to science
demonstrated the functions of the pancreas and liver and is considered the "father of experimental medicine"

BIO-DATA CARD

SIR WILLIAM BOWMAN
(born, 1816; died, 1892)

nationality
English

contribution to science
discovered the function of the kidney and its microscopic "filtering unit," the nephron

BIO-DATA CARD

ROBERT BOYLE

(born, 1627; died, 1691)

nationality
English

contribution to science
showed that air was necessary for life

BIO-DATA CARD

CHARLES BROWN-SÉQUARD

(born, 1817; died, 1894)

nationality
French

contribution to science
elucidated the roles of hormones in the development of secondary sex characteristics

BIO-DATA CARD

WALTER BRADFORD CANNON

(born, 1871; died, 1945)

nationality
American

contribution to science
coined the term "homeostasis" to describe an organism's ability to maintain internal equilibrium

BIO-DATA CARD

NIKOLAUS COPERNICUS

(born, 1473; died, 1543)

nationality
Polish

contribution to science
aroused bitter controversy with his "sun-centered" view of the solar system that spread to other fields of science

BIO-DATA CARD

RAYMOND ARTHUR DART

(born, 1893; died, 1988)

nationality
English

contribution to science
discovered the first true prehominid, Australopithecus, in 1924

BIO-DATA CARD

CHARLES ROBERT DARWIN

(born, 1809; died, 1882)

nationality
English

contribution to science
discovered the theory of evolution, now the predominant theory guiding the study of biology

BIO-DATA CARD

RENÉ DESCARTES

(born, 1596; died, 1650)

nationality
French

contribution to science
saw the human body as a machine whose function could be explained by the same laws that governed the physical universe

BIO-DATA CARD

MARIE EUGÉNE F. T. DUBOIS

(born, 1858; died, 1940)

nationality
Dutch

contribution to science
discovered in 1891 the first "human-like" species fossilized in the jungles of Indonesia

BIO-DATA CARD

SIR JOHN CAREW ECCLES
(born, 1903)

nationality
Australian

contribution to science
discovered the mechanism underlying the transmission of nerve impulses with A. L. Hodgkin and A. F. Huxley

BIO-DATA CARD

PAUL EHRLICH
(born, 1854; died, 1915)

nationality
German

contribution to science
developed the first techniques in chemotherapy using synthetic drugs to kill infectious organisms

BIO-DATA CARD

WILLEM EINTHOVEN
(born, 1860; died, 1927)

nationality
Dutch

contribution to science
used an electrocardiogram to show that an irregular heartbeat was an "electrical" irregularity of the heart muscles

BIO-DATA CARD

ERASISTRATUS
(c. 304 B.C.; c. 250 B.C.)

nationality
Greek

contribution to science
accurately described the function of heart valves and the general route of the blood but got the direction wrong

BIO-DATA CARD

GUSTAV THEODOR FECHNER
(born, 1801; died, 1887)

nationality
German

contribution to science
developed the mathematical Weber-Fechner law expressing the relationship between stimulus strength and response

BIO-DATA CARD

PIERRE JEAN MARIE FLOURENS
(born, 1794; died, 1867)

nationality
French

contribution to science
found the location of the brain region responsible for regulating respiratory rate in the brainstem or medulla oblongata

BIO-DATA CARD

AUGUST FOREL
(born, 1848; died, 1931)

nationality
Swiss

contribution to science
studied the degeneration of nerve tissue to discover the pathways of nerve bundles

BIO-DATA CARD

OTTO FUNKE
(born, 1828; died, 1879)

nationality
German

contribution to science
his work on organic compounds led to the discovery of hemoglobin

INSTRUCTIONS TO TEACHERS
Xerox and cut out the Bio-Data Cards below and keep them in a handy file. Instruct students to choose one card and neatly glue it to the front of a 5" × 8" index card. They can use the school or public library to find out more about the scientist they have chosen. On the back of the index card they can draw a cartoon, write a poem or short paragraph that illustrates an important event in the life of this famous personality.

BIO-DATA CARD

GALEN
(born, 129; died, 200)

nationality
Greek

contribution to science
medical theories dominated Western medicine for over 1,500 years throughout the Dark and Middle Ages

BIO-DATA CARD

FRANZ JOSEPH GALL
(born, 1758; died, 1828)

nationality
German

contribution to science
developed with J. Spurzheim the later discarded study of phrenology that led to productive neuroanatomical research

BIO-DATA CARD

LUIGI GALVANI
(born, 1737; died, 1798)

nationality
Italian

contribution to science
discovered that touching a charged piece of metal to a frog's leg dissected free of the animal caused the leg to twitch and flex

BIO-DATA CARD

CAMILLO GOLGI
(born, 1843; died, 1926)

nationality
Italian

contribution to science
described networks of neurons fused at dendrites, supporting the later discarded reticular theory of the nervous system

BIO-DATA CARD

ROBERT JAMES GRAVES
(born, 1796; died, 1853)

nationality
Irish

contribution to science
described symptoms resulting from the overactivity of the thyroid: a condition called goiter

BIO-DATA CARD

ERNST HEINRICH HAEKEL
(born, 1834; died, 1919)

nationality
German

contribution to science
showed that a developing embryo passes through stages that oddly resemble early evolutionary transitions

BIO-DATA CARD

ALBRECHT von HALLER
(born, 1708; died, 1777)

nationality
Swiss

contribution to science
suggested that the nervous system was the site of sensibility but dependent upon the actions of "the soul"

BIO-DATA CARD

WILLIAM HARVEY
(born, 1578; died, 1657)

nationality
English

contribution to science
demonstrated how the heart and blood vessels circulate blood throughout the body

BIO-DATA CARD

HERMANN L. F. von HELMHOLTZ
(born, 1821; died, 1894)

nationality
German

contribution to science
invented the ophthalmoscope to examine the interior of the eye

BIO-DATA CARD

FRIEDRICH GUSTAV JACOB HENLE
(born, 1809; died, 1885)

nationality
German

contribution to science
discovered the tubelike structures of the kidney leading to the renal vein known today as Henle's loop

BIO-DATA CARD

HEROPHILUS OF CHALCEDON
(c. 330 B.C.; c. 260 B.C.)

nationality
Greek

contribution to science
made detailed records of dissections performed on living criminals condemned to death

BIO-DATA CARD

WILHELM A. O. HERTWIG
(born, 1849; died, 1922)

nationality
German

contribution to science
showed that fertilization involved the fusion of a single sperm and a single egg

BIO-DATA CARD

HIPPOCRATES
(born, 460 B.C.; died, 377 B.C.)

nationality
Greek

contribution to science
called the "founder of modern medicine" for his theories about health and the body

BIO-DATA CARD

WILLIAM HIS
(born, 1831; died, 1904)

nationality
Swiss

contribution to science
his embryological studies contributed to the understanding of the nervous system

BIO-DATA CARD

WILHELM HIS, Jr.
(born, 1863; died, 1934)

nationality
German

contribution to science
described the nerves innervating the right side of the heart that initiated cardiac contractions

BIO-DATA CARD

ALAN LLOYD HODGKIN
(born, 1914)

nationality
English

contribution to science
discovered the mechanism underlying the transmission of nerve impulses with Sir J. C. Eccles and A. F. Huxley

BIO-DATA CARD

ERNST FELIX HOPPE-SEYLER
(born, 1825; died, 1895)

nationality
German

contribution to science
discovered hemoglobin in addition to a variety of other organic compounds

BIO-DATA CARD

ANDREW FIELDING HUXLEY
(born, 1917)

nationality
English

contribution to science
discovered the mechanism underlying the transmission of nerve impulses with Sir J. C. Eccles and A. L. Hodgkin

BIO-DATA CARD

IBN AL-NAFIS
(born, 1205; died, 1288)

nationality
Egyptian

contribution to science
first to accurately describe the cardiopulmonary circulation of the blood between the heart and lungs

BIO-DATA CARD

WILLIAM JAMES
(born, 1842; died, 1910)

nationality
American

contribution to science
founded the functionalist school of psychology to discover how the mind evolved out of adaptive necessity

BIO-DATA CARD

EDWARD JENNER
(born, 1749; died, 1823)

nationality
English

contribution to science
succeeded in finding an effective vaccine against smallpox in 1796 but could not explain how his treatment worked

BIO-DATA CARD

DONALD CARL JOHANSON
(born, 1943)

nationality
American

contribution to science
in 1978 unearthed one of the most complete prehominid skeletons named "Lucy" dated at 3.5 billion years old

BIO-DATA CARD

ARTHUR KEITH
(born, 1866; died, 1955)

nationality
Scottish

contribution to science
with Wilhelm His, Jr. described the nerves innervating the right side of the heart that initiated cardiac contractions

BIO-DATA CARD

H. H. ROBERT KOCH
(born, 1843; died, 1910)

nationality
German

contribution to science
developed techniques for isolating and culturing bacteria to be used in studying diseases in laboratory animals

INSTRUCTIONS TO TEACHERS
Xerox and cut out the Bio-Data Cards below and keep them in a handy file. Instruct students to choose one card and neatly glue it to the front of a 5" × 8" index card. They can use the school or public library to find out more about the scientist they have chosen. On the back of the index card they can draw a cartoon, write a poem or short paragraph that illustrates an important event in the life of this famous personality.

BIO-DATA CARD

RUDOLPH ALBERT von KÖLLIKER
(born, 1817; died, 1905)

nationality
Swiss

contribution to science
made the first notable descriptions of
nerve cells under the microscope

BIO-DATA CARD

EMIL KRAEPELIN
(born, 1856; died, 1926)

nationality
German

contribution to science
divided the major forms of psychosis
into two categories: dementia praecox
and manic-depression

BIO-DATA CARD

RENÉ T. H. LAËNNEC
(born, 1781; died, 1826)

nationality
French

contribution to science
invented the stethoscope in 1816
permitting physicians to listen closely to
the rhythmic beating of the heart

BIO-DATA CARD

KARL LANDSTEINER
(born, 1868; died, 1943)

nationality
American

contribution to science
discovered the existence of blood
groups: A, B, and O

BIO-DATA CARD

ANTOINE LAVOSIER
(born, 1743; died, 1794)

nationality
French

contribution to science
made the connection between
combustion of oxygen in air and
respiration in the human body

BIO-DATA CARD

LOUIS SEYMOUR BAZETT LEAKEY
(born, 1903; died, 1972)

nationality
Kenyan

contribution to science
with his wife, Mary, discovered the
remains of early prehominid species in
Olduvai Gorge, East Africa

BIO-DATA CARD

MARY DOUGLAS LEAKEY
(born, 1913; died, 1996)

nationality
English

contribution to science
with her husband, Louis, discovered the
remains of early prehominid species in
Olduvai Gorge, East Africa

BIO-DATA CARD

ANTON VAN LEEUWENHOEK
(born, 1632; died, 1723)

nationality
Dutch

contribution to science
credited with the invention of the
microscope which he used to observe
and draw microorganisms

BIO-DATA CARD

CHO HAO LI
(born, 1913)

nationality
Chinese-American

contribution to science
isolated and synthesized
growth hormone

BIO-DATA CARD

JUSTUS VON LIEBIG
(born, 1803; died, 1873)

nationality
German

contribution to science
examined excreted products like urea
and carbon dioxide in relation to
ingested proteins and plant sugar

BIO-DATA CARD

CAROLUS LINNAEUS
(born, 1707; died, 1778)

nationality
Swedish

contribution to science
described the reproductive cells of plants
as analogous to the reproductive cells
of humans

BIO-DATA CARD

JOSEPH LISTER
(born, 1827; died, 1912)

nationality
English

contribution to science
performed the first
antiseptic operation in 1867

BIO-DATA CARD

MARCELLO MALPIGHI
(born, 1628; died, 1694)

nationality
Italian

contribution to science
discovered capillaries, the microscopic
channels between arteries and veins

BIO-DATA CARD

JOHN MAYOW
(born, 1841; died, 1879)

nationality
English

contribution to science
showed that air is necessary for life

BIO-DATA CARD

ELMER VERNER MCCOLLUM
(born, 1879; died, 1967)

nationality
American

contribution to science
discovered the importance of amino
acids as the building blocks of proteins

BIO-DATA CARD

GREGOR JOHANN MENDEL
(born, 1822; died, 1884)

nationality
Austrian

contribution to science
discovered the laws of inheritance and is
called the "father of modern genetics"

BIO-DATA CARD

JULIUS LOTHAR MEYER
(born, 1830; died, 1895)

nationality
German

contribution to science
contributed to the discovery of hemoglobin

BIO-DATA CARD

SIR ISAAC NEWTON
(born, 1642; died, 1727)

nationality
English

contribution to science
established the basic laws of optics that led to the invention of the microscope

---

BIO-DATA CARD

JEAN NOLLET
(born, 1700; died, 1770)

nationality
French

contribution to science
investigated and elucidated the phenomenon of osmosis

BIO-DATA CARD

GEORGE OLIVER
(born, 1841; died, 1915)

nationality
English

contribution to science
discovered the functions of the adrenal medulla in the production of the "flight or fight" hormone: adrenaline

---

BIO-DATA CARD

LOUIS PASTEUR
(born, 1822; died, 1895)

nationality
French

contribution to science
proposed an overall theory of germs and discovered pasteurization still used today to rid foods of bacteria

---

BIO-DATA CARD

IVAN PETROVICH PAVLOV
(born, 1849; died, 1936)

nationality
Russian

contribution to science
discovered the conditioned reflex that led to the behaviorist school of psychology

---

BIO-DATA CARD

WILHELM F. P. PFEFFER
(born, 1845; died, 1920)

nationality
German

contribution to science
elucidated the osmotic process by developing a device to measure osmotic pressure in 1877

BIO-DATA CARD

PLATO
(born, 427 B.C.; died, 347 B.C.)

nationality
Greek

contribution to science
relegated sensations to that part of the soul residing in the heart

BIO-DATA CARD

JOSEPH PRIESTLEY
(born, 1733; died, 1804)

nationality
English

contribution to science
isolated and identified oxygen in 1774

BIO-DATA CARD

WILLIAM PROUT
(born, 1785; died, 1850)

nationality
English

contribution to science
identified the active ingredient in gastric juice to be hydrochloric acid

BIO-DATA CARD

SANTIAGO RAMÓN Y CAJAL
(born, 1852; died, 1934)

nationality
Spanish

contribution to science
established the neuronal theory of the nervous system

BIO-DATA CARD

RENÉ DE RÉAUMUR
(born, 1683; died, 1757)

nationality
French

contribution to science
demonstrated the effects of gastric juices on food

BIO-DATA CARD

FRANCESCO REDI
(born, 1626; died, 1697)

nationality
Italian

contribution to science
first to prove that living things could not be spontaneously generated by decaying matter

BIO-DATA CARD

S. RIVA ROCCI
(born, 1863; died, 1936)

nationality
Italian

contribution to science
invented the sphygmomanometer, allowing physicians to take less invasive blood pressure measurements

BIO-DATA CARD

MATTHIAS JAKOB SCHLEIDEN
(born, 1804; died, 1881)

nationality
German

contribution to science
with Theodor Schwann derived the cell theory in 1838

BIO-DATA CARD

THEODOR SCHWANN
(born, 1810; died, 1882)

nationality
German

contribution to science
with Matthias Jakob Schleiden derived the cell theory in 1838

BIO-DATA CARD

EDWARD A. SHARPEY-SCHAFER

(born, 1850; died, 1935)

nationality
English

contribution to science
elucidated the roles of
sex hormones and adrenaline in
controlling body functions

BIO-DATA CARD

CHARLES ROBERT SHERRINGTON

(born, 1857; died, 1952)

nationality
English

contribution to science
demonstrated that when a muscle is
activated its "antagonist" is inhibited: the
law of reciprocal innervation

BIO-DATA CARD

B. F. SKINNER

(born, 1904; died, 1990)

nationality
American

contribution to science
popularized the behaviorist school of
psychology

BIO-DATA CARD

JOHN SNOW

(born, 1813; died, 1858)

nationality
English

contribution to science
proposed that the agent of transmission
causing the spread of cholera was in
contaminated water

BIO-DATA CARD

JOHANNES SPURZHEIM

(born, 1776; died, 1832)

nationality
German

contribution to science
developed with F. J. Gall the later
discarded study of phrenology that led to
productive neuroanatomical research

BIO-DATA CARD

ERNEST HENRY STARLING

(born, 1866; died, 1927)

nationality
English

contribution to science
coined the term "hormone" and with
W. M. Bayliss discovered
the first hormone: secretin

BIO-DATA CARD

ARNE W. K. TISELIUS

(born, 1902; died, 1971)

nationality
Swedish

contribution to science
used his newly invented electrophoresis
technique to isolate disease-fighting
antibodies

BIO-DATA CARD

ANDREAS VESALIUS

(born, 1514; died, 1564)

nationality
Belgian

contribution to science
in 1543 published the first book
that contradicted
the outdated anatomy of Galen

BIO-DATA CARD

LEONARDO DA VINCI
(born, 1452; died, 1519)

nationality
Italian

contribution to science
artist, inventor, and scientist
who began a new and thoroughly
scientific study of anatomy

BIO-DATA CARD

ALFRED RUSSEL WALLACE
(born, 1823; died, 1913)

nationality
Welch

contribution to science
co-discoverer of the theory of evolution
with Charles Robert Darwin

BIO-DATA CARD

JOHN BROADUS WATSON
(born, 1878; died, 1958)

nationality
American

contribution to science
founder of the behaviorist school of
psychology that analyzes performance
to explain the nature of behavior

BIO-DATA CARD

ERNST HEINRICH WEBER
(born, 1795; died, 1878)

nationality
German

contribution to science
deduced Weber's law relating the
magnitude of a response to the stimulus
that elicits that response

BIO-DATA CARD

WILHELM WUNDT
(born, 1832; died, 1920)

nationality
German

contribution to science
used the method of introspection to
study states of consciousness, sensation,
and emotion

BIO-DATA CARD

JOHN R. YOUNG
(born, 1782; died, 1804)

nationality
American

contribution to science
discovered that saliva and gastric juices
were released simultaneously with the
introduction of food into the mouth

BIO-DATA CARD

THOMAS YOUNG
(born, 1773; died, 1829)

nationality
English

contribution to science
developed the trichromatic theory of
light asserting that the retina is sensitive
to three primary colors: red, green, blue